THE TEARS OF
THE WHITE MAN

Compassion as Contempt

THE TEARS OF THE WHITE MAN
Compassion as Contempt

Pascal Bruckner

Translated with an Introduction
by
William R. Beer

THE FREE PRESS
A Division of Macmillan, Inc.
NEW YORK

Collier Macmillan Publishers
LONDON

Copyright © May 1983 by Editions du Seuil
Translation copyright © 1986 by The Free Press
A Division of Macmillan, Inc.

The Free Press
A Division of Macmillan, Inc.
866 Third Avenue, New York, N.Y. 10022

Collier Macmillan Canada, Inc.

Printed in the United States of America

printing number

1 2 3 4 5 6 7 8 9 10

Library of Congress Cataloging-in-Publication Data

Bruckner, Pascal.
    The tears of the white man.

    Translation of: Le sanglot de l'homme blanc.
    1. Developing countries—Colonial influence.
2. Developing countries—Social conditions.
3. Developing countries—Politics and government.
I. Title.
JV305.B7813   1986   909'.09724   86–14291
ISBN 0–02–904160–0

Contents

Introduction
Third-Worldism in France
and the United States

The Tears of the White Man is a critique of "Third-Worldism," a set of attitudes toward underdeveloped countries and the West that has flourished, mainly among left-wing intellectuals and journalists, over the last 20 years. It is based on a conviction that the countries of the Third World—countries as different as Costa Rica and Libya, and the Philippines and Cambodia—have long been victims of the West. They have had their resources stolen by imperialist colonialists or multinational corporations, their cultures destroyed by commercialism and exploitation, their pastoral sensitivity toward nature corrupted by industry and pollution.

But Bruckner's thesis is that it is the passionate Third-Worldist who is most often exploiting the poor nations. Starving people are carefully chosen or ignored, depending on whether they can be portrayed to suit specific political programs. Bruckner, himself active in a humanitarian relief organization, argues that the much-touted compassion of most Third-Worldists is really a form of contempt, because they use the suffering of others for their own ideological purposes. As soon as these miserable folk have served their purpose, or begin to act in ways that contradict Third-Worldist fantasies, they are promptly forgotten.

The idea of the Third World as a political bloc grew up after the Bandung Conference of Colored Peoples in 1955, a meeting that was heavily influenced by Communist China and its allies. A direct consequence of the Sino-Soviet split, the conference's central notion was that a third power bloc had to be formed, one that was distinct from the capitalist industrial world (the United States, Canada, Western Europe, Australia, New Zealand, and Japan) and the communist industrial world (the Soviet Union and its eastern European satellites). The states within this third agglomeration had two important things in common—they were poor and they were nonwhite. It was imagined that having these qualities in common would be enough to form a basis for a political movement—the so-called "nonaligned movement."

In practice, of course, the concept ran into trouble. The Third World includes millions of human beings of widely different races, cultures, levels of wealth, and industrial development. Some commonalities may be shared by some of these countries, but "nonalignment" is not one of them. In fact, the nonaligned movement has been notoriously active in making anti-American and pro-Soviet declarations at the United Nations and elsewhere.

The idea of a Third World has fired the imagination of Western intellectuals, however. The French economist Alfred Sauvy is credited with having popularized the term, which in French is intended to evoke powerful political images. *"Tiers monde,"* which includes the antiquated word for "third," makes a clear historical reference. It calls forth the picture of France on the eve of the Revolution, when the demand for political representation by the Third Estate, along with the First Estate (the clergy) and the Second Estate (the aristocracy), led to the overthrow of the entire established order. It may be that Sauvy saw himself as the modern-day equivalent of Abbé Sieyès, whose essay *What Is the Third Estate?* has that mobilizing effect on the forces of Revolution. Supposedly, the Third World was demanding power equivalent to that of the "First World" and the "Second World." But it is not at all parallel to the mixture of bourgeoisie, peasantry, and artisans who made up the Third Estate in pre-revolutionary France. The concept, even in its origins, is ideological and polemical.

It does serve useful political purposes, though. In the French-speaking world, for instance, Frantz Fanon's fantasies of violence as a means of self-purification were enthusiastically presented by Jean-Paul Sartre in his introduction to *The Wretched of the Earth.* Fanon's vision was of a white world at war with the nonwhite world, where the former was finished and the latter was emerging through violent self-emancipation. Sartre's introduction crystallized much French and European self-loathing. Sartre may have been one of the most famous *tiers-mondistes,* as they are called in French, but he was only one among many. Pierre Jalée's book about the rape of the Third World (*Le pillage du tiers monde*) and René Dumont's book lamenting European economic policy in Africa (*L'Afrique noire est mal partie*) are other notable examples of the position; Bruckner presents and dissects the school of thought they represent in the pages that follow.

Bruckner identifies three versions of Third-Worldism as it has flourished in Europe during the last two decades: solidarity with, pity for, and imitation of the Thirld World.

The first stance is one of fellowship—that "their fight is our fight"; that the forces of oppression are the same around the world. We in advanced industrial countries are oppressed, too. The same forces that exploit the Burmese peasant oppress the middle-class housewife in Paris, homosexuals in Berlin, and factory workers in Lagos. This position holds that, every time a Communist guerrilla shoots a soldier in El Salvador, I am a little freer; every time Lesbians demonstrate for the right to adopt children, the herdsmen of the Sudan are a little freer.

The pitying attitude holds that, because we are rich and they are poor, we are their oppressors. Being rich is tantamount to being guilty; being poor is proof of innocence. Further, our wealth is the cause of their poverty. Our consumer-oriented economies cause their suffering because our greed for microwave ovens and hair conditioners forces them to produce raw materials for our factories, rather than the products they need for themselves. Moreover, our tolerance and democracy are possible only because they are based on our wealth, which in turn is the cause of the suffering of the poor. The price of our well-being and liberty is their misery and oppression.

The third version of Third-Worldism holds that the people of the developing world have a wisdom that we have lost. Peasants and primitives are seen as somehow closer to nature and to one another then we are. The frippery and complexity of our modern societies contrast with the noble simplicity of their lives. To redeem ourselves as individuals, we must try to be like them; to redeem our societies, we must try to make them pre-modern, more organic. This involves pilgrimages—the word is Bruckner's and precisely appropriate—to somewhere in the Third World, where one picks up a little savvy, and perhaps a costume or artifact.

Third-Worldism has deep roots. One lies in Western culture's persistent belief in a Golden Age. Classical Latin literature is one of our main sources of the myth that there once was a time when the gods walked on Earth and all was harmony. The Judeo-Christian belief in the Garden of Eden is another version of the same idea: There was a time when Man was pure, innocent, and at one with himself, others, nature, and God.

The Marxist myth of "primitive communism" grows directly out of the same tradition. It holds that primitive man was—at some imaginary point in our prehistory—innocent of property relations, free of alienation. The "serpent" that crept into this Marxist paradise was private property, rather than original sin, but the message is the same.

Another derivation of the fantasy was presented by Rousseau, who argued that mankind's state of purity and innocence is evident in contemporary primitive societies. The innocence of the Noble Savage is corrupted by what we now call "Western civilization."

Rousseauism and the belief in a Golden Age feed the Third World theory with a simple argument: Modernity is evil; therefore, primitivity is good. The Third World is thus transformed into a vast empirical hunting ground, where intellectuals from advanced countries can search for confirmation of what they already know—that somewhere along the banks of the Amazon or in the wastes of Mali or in the snows of Bhutan they will find a purity their own societies lack.

This much all Third-Worldism has in common, in Europe, as well as in the United States. Where the two versions diverge is in their historical origins and their roles in domestic politics.

Much of French and European Third-Worldism stems from guilt—guilt over the wars and conquests that established the colonial empires, the economic exploitation that was part of colonialism, and the bloody wars of "liberation" that were waged, in some cases, to achieve independence. Colonization, according to the image projected by anti-colonialist historians, was a brutal confrontation between naive, outgunned natives, and technologically superior, arrogant Europeans. Colonization inspired the pitying view of the natives as childlike, which justified the necessity for undertaking and maintaining colonialism. Decolonization also fed Third-Worldism, because it questioned not only the usefulness of fighting to hold onto the empires, but also European civilization in general.

These attitudes grew up on the Left, but only relatively recently. In France, the left wing has long been ambivalent about colonialism. During the period of overseas expansion, many Marxists were in favor of it. From the Marxian point of view, their logic was impeccable: Pre-capitalist societies were being colonized, and as they were being subjugated, their primitive and peasant peoples would be rapidly brought into the capitalist system and enter the class struggle as proletarians. This analysis was not only theoretically sound, it was strategically astute. Many French socialists believed the newly proletarianized masses of the colonies would enter the lists on their side in the worldwide struggle against the bourgeoisie. There was little leftist opposition to the colonialists' violation of the national sovereignty of these peoples, because orthodox Marxist theory holds that, in any case, nationalism is merely a tool of the bourgeoisie to divide and rule the exploited masses by whipping them into a patriotic hysteria.

Much of the French Left proved to be no more enthusiastic about decolonization after World War II than it had been opposed to colonialism when it had been imposed. When the Vietminh fired the first shots of the Indochina War, the French Communist Party declared its opposition to Vietnamese "liberation." The Party was equally hostile to the Front de Libération Nationale, at least in the beginning stages of the Algerian War of Independence when it was not at all clear that they would win. Subsequently, in both Indochina and Algeria, the Communists, in true Leninist fashion, adapted their analysis to which way the wind was blowing. Their ambivalence about the "liberation" movements was a mirror image of the leftist endorsement of colonialism 70 years before. (Besides, the more colonies a potentially Communist France controlled, the better.)

Throughout most of its history, then, the French Left has not been Third-Worldist; it has not had to be, because it has long had a domestic constituency that not only supported it electorally but acted in accord with Marxist notions of class conflict. It is no accident, as Marxists are fond of saying, that Marx derived his sociological analyses of capitalism primarily from France, one of the most class-ridden societies in history. The Left in France, until quite recently, could inspire the passions of its followers with the rhetoric of class warfare; it did not need bogus Third-Worldist analyses that seek oppressed peoples abroad, because there were plenty of Frenchmen who felt they were oppressed.

As class conflict in France has tapered off, Third-Worldism

has gained strength as the trump card of leftist intellectuals. In the words of Professor Nicholas Wahl of New York University's Institute of French Studies, the rise of Third-Worldism in the French Left represented a "deflection of the revolutionary project." Moreover, the revelations of Stalin's crimes, the aggressive threat posed by the USSR since the Second World War, and the fading of the Soviet model as a society to emulate, all combined to reduce the appeal of the classical Communist revolutionary formula.

Third-Worldism, then, is a sign of the intellectual sterility of the Left, which must seek abroad for people to liberate because class struggle and Marxian revolution are becoming increasingly irrelevant at home. The course of Third-Worldism in the United States has been quite different, and in its peculiarly American guise, remains politically influential. It also takes on some different forms.

Still, in America, as in France, the downtrodden countries of the world are glorified, while the West is denigrated. Third-Worldists never criticize Soviet colonialism in Central Asia, Chinese Communist colonialism in Tibet, or Vietnamese colonialism in Cambodia. Third-Worldism is directed almost exclusively against capitalist democracies. Noam Chomsky, for example, one of the best-known American Third-Worldists, blames the United States for the numerous "bloodbaths" that have occurred since World War II. Even when massacres and repression are the work of leftist totalitarians, Chomsky holds the United States responsible, because its lack of acceptance drives leftist totalitarians to their actions (cf. Chomsky, *Towards a New Cold War*, Pantheon, 1982, esp. pp. 22–29). William Shawcross, too, performs the intellectual acrobatics needed to achieve this posture. In *Sideshow* (Simon and Schuster, 1979), his famous book on Cambodia, Shawcross attempts to blame the United States for the holocaust perpetrated by the Khmers Rouges. He alleges that the Khmers Rouges arose from the "inferno" that was created by American policy. "Statesmen must be judged by the consequences of their actions. Whatever Nixon and Kissinger intended for Cambodia, their efforts created catastrophe. . . . Cambodia was not a mistake; it was a crime" (p. 396). Simply put, Shawcross's argument says that Communists commit genocide and America is responsible. Chomsky and Shawcross are only two among many who unfailingly conclude that American policy must be held accountable for the "excesses" of Third World revolutionaries.

In the United States, Third-Worldism could not spring from the same guilt-inspiring colonial experience as it did in Europe, because the United States has never had a colonial empire. Third-Worldism in the United States does shape the thinking of some regarding the outside world, but these thoughts do not have the same expiatory impulse they have in European countries.

If the United States has among its allies countries that suppress dissent, brutalize the poor, and persist in undemocratic rule, this is to be deplored; however, few Americans can be induced to see such tyrants as American creations. For instance, the United States provided military and logistical support to the Shah of Iran. However, Iran was not carved out of an American colony, and the Shah's nastiness was a purely Iranian phenomenon. On the other hand, when an Idi Amin routinely disembowels Ugandans, English consciousness must be affected by the fact that both Uganda and Idi Amin are creations of the British Empire. Similarly, the Portuguese must be aware that the bloodthirsty Macias Nguema and Equatorial Guinea are excrescences of Portuguese colonialism. The American conscience must be touched by violations of human rights, yet few Americans are convinced that the United States has been directly involved in creating political monsters, the way European colonialism was. Although the Left does its best to argue that America is directly responsible for injustices in the Third World, most thinking Americans are aware that the U.S.'s responsibility is limited, and its guilt justifiably attenuated.

Though America never had an external colonial empire and did not conquer Africa or Asia, it did conquer the American West and built the country on this continent. Therefore, rather than an external Third-Worldism, America has a kind of internal Third-Worldism. And it is primarily a syndrome that makes use of "internal colonies" more than external ones, and leads to a search for oppressed folk at home.

Paradoxically, this syndrome has had more influence on the American Left than European Third-Worldism has had on the Left in France. This is partly because the United States is a former colony, and it is possible to ask Americans to identify with "liberation" movements on the grounds that America is a nation that was founded by a revolution. The American Left has been more susceptible to this Third-Worldist argument because it has no investment in American expansion overseas. Thus, it could be self-righteously against colonialism and imperialism at no risk to its political fortunes.

The American Left has also tended to be more Third-Worldist than the French Left because class hatred in our society has been conspicuously lacking, even during times of great economic hardship. The Great Depression created the largest mass of unemployed and poor workers in American history. Yet both socialists and communists had only modest success obtaining a following at that time. This "defeat" was more serious than may seem at first glance. The "working class" simply did not act the way Marxian analysis said it would. Instead of becoming revolutionary, the majority of the American people showed themselves to be not only democratic and reformist but, during the 1940s, ardently patriotic. Ever since the steadfast refusal of American workers to heed the trumpets of class hatred and be led by self-appointed liberators, the radical Left has been searching for other objects of its compassion.

The concept of a Third World at home inspired some to search for links between the "wretched of the earth" and minority groups to be mobilized in America. For instance, Stokely Carmichael and Charles Hamilton's influential book, *Black Power* (Vintage, 1967) strategically portrays the struggles of black people in the United States as part of a worldwide movement by people of color: " . . . Black Power means that black people see themselves as part of a new force, sometimes called the 'Third World'; that we see our struggle as closely related to liberation struggles around the world" (p. xi). The authors argue that black Americans form a colony within the United States, that they are "colonial subjects in relation to the white society" (p. 5). For them, colonialism is the same as "institutional racism."

In *Racial Oppression in America* (Vintage, 1972), Robert Blauner expands the notion of the domestic Third World to include not only blacks, but also Mexican-Americans, American Indians, Chinese-Americans and Japanese-Americans. He argues that all these groups have been subjected to "forced, involuntary entry," see their culture destroyed or changed as a result of being in the United States, are subject to control by government bureaucracies ("outsiders who look down on them"), and are subject to racism. Serious analysis shows that the argument is deeply flawed, if only in that the economic problems of American Indians and some Mexican-Americans stand in stark contrast to the astounding success of Chinese- and Japanese-Americans. Black Americans were brought here involuntarily, while Mexican-Americans mainly migrated here by choice, as did Chinese- and Japanese-Americans. If these groups collectively represent the domestic Third World, they are a category that is so heterogeneous as to be highly suspect.

Blauner and Carmichael and Hamilton framed their positions to show that allegedly oppressed groups at home were part of the same struggle being waged against America and the West abroad. Though intellectually spurious, these positions enjoyed a certain popularity for a while, and with traumatic results. Carmichael gave a condensed version of his argument in his celebrated "Black Power" speech in 1965. As a result, white Americans who until then had lent substantial financial, legal, and personal support to the civil-rights struggle, were purged from the movement. Whites were part of the colonizing force that oppressed blacks; whites, by definition, could not be seen as part of the internal Third World, and had to be expelled.

Unceremonious, bitter, and probably racist, the purge of white Americans expelled white radicals along with white liberals. What remained of the radical Left among blacks was the Black Panther Party, which soon disintegrated from its own personal struggles, lack of serious political analysis, and the attacks from police that it so eagerly sought. Most black Americans never seriously accepted the leadership the radical Left offered.

Around the same time, a new Noble Savage appeared—Youth. Several fateful developments converged in the mid-1960s to produce the appearance of youth—particularly college youth—on the political and social scene: the post-World War II baby boom, economic changes that seemed to make a college education necessary, and overall prosperity that enabled more families to do without the work revenues of children and send them to college instead. Against this background occurred the escalation of the Vietnam War, increases in the draft, and a system of draft deferments that ensured that colleges—naturally critical and questioning places— would be populated by disproportionate numbers of articulate youngsters opposed to the established order of things.

These primarily white, well-to-do young people, safely ensconced on their campuses away from the draft and from much of reality, did not act the way many thought they should. Many students, particularly the self-appointed leaders of the radical Left, behaved in what appeared to be promiscuous, anarchic, and violent ways. Most Americans, especially those whose sons were actual or potential draftees, were enraged by such conduct. But many on the Left, aided by journalists eager to sell copy and dramatize events, perceived the youth in quite a different way.

According to this perception, the youth were constructing a "counterculture" (as Theodore Roszak called it in *The Making of a Counterculture,* Anchor, 1969) that was the mirror image of mainstream American culture. The latter was portrayed as militaristic, murderous, intolerant, repressive, and "plastic." The counterculture was portrayed as pacifist, gentle, tolerant, permissive, and "natural." "Flower children" provided a photographic image that could be neatly juxtaposed with that of short-haired males in military uniforms or three-piece suits. The youth were pure, uncorrupted, and had been called upon to right the wrongs inflicted upon the country and the world by adults. One of the clearest expressions of this idea is contained in Charles Reich's *The Greening of America* (Bantam, 1970), a book whose immense popularity can be compared only to its astonishing superficiality. Reich argued that the youth were carrying out a peaceful revolution that will save us all. Rousseauism had come home. The Noble Savage was not in some far-off land, on a reservation, or in black ghettos; he was in our living rooms and college dormitories!

The Third-Worldist Left identified these primitive youths as comprising yet another group oppressed by America. The organizations of the New Left (such as Students for a Democratic Society) and the Old Left masquerading as the New Left (such as the Communist DuBois Clubs and the Trotskyite Young Socialist Alliance) did their best to assume the leadership of youth. SDS, in particular, provided an analysis that centered around the concept of "student syndicalism." One of the more grotesque but temporarily popular expressions of this train of thought was an essay in *The Realist* called "The Student as Nigger." This essay purported to show how students were oppressed and exploited in the same way that blacks were, and that "Authority" looked at them in the same way—as childlike, irresponsible, drug-ridden, promiscuous, disobedient, and devious.

Another "internal colony" emerged during the heyday of the anti-war movement and the student Left: interest in it has lasted much longer. The 1960s saw American women in previously unknown numbers acceding to university education, with the social power and personal freedom this move implied. Upper-middle class American women were caught in a contradiction between the vast new areas opening up to them, and the roles deemed appropriate to womanhood in an earlier age. Outdated expectations coupled with new potentialities—this was the dilemma facing female youth. What emerged to dissolve the tension was what can be called the latest wave of American feminism.

Feminism was not the *cause* of increased social and political power for the American woman (though, understandably, that is what many of its spokeswomen claim), it was the *consequence* of her emancipation. Its beneficiaries and partisans have, from the very beginning, been overwhelmingly white, well-to-do, and highly educated. Still, feminist rhetoric has tried to mobilize all women as if they were a coherent group.

As in the case of blacks and youth, a kind of internal Third-Worldism has asserted itself in the feminist movement. Women became the Noble Savages of the 1970s, and the now-familiar images were projected upon them—they are the oppressed, males are the guilty oppressors, women are untainted by masculine aggression and destructiveness, the world would be better off if women ran it, etc. John Lennon wrote a widely popular song expressing this position. It included the line, "Woman is the nigger of the world!"—a rather obvious transference of negritude from youth, where it had reposed a decade before, to women.

It goes almost without saying that neither young people nor women really were the way internal Third-Worldists portrayed them. They were simply so much intellectual ammunition for those who had no real understanding or concern for them. For proof, consider how little left-wing ink is spilled for young people today, now that they cannot be portrayed as angry, alienated, and rebellious. And consider the deliberate confusion between "women's issues" and the radical feminist agenda, as if they were really one and the same.

What I have tried to show in this essay is that, in America, the role of Third-Worldism has been somewhat different than it has been in France. Overall, it stems from the same cultural roots but, because of the peculiarities of American history, it has taken two forms. One is external Third-Worldism, which exploits the suffering masses of the underdeveloped world to score points against America and her allies. This form is different from the Third-Worldism indicted by Bruckner only in that it does not spring from post-colonial guilt and self-loathing. The other form has sought to make Noble Savages out of groups within the United States. Both forms purport to express sympathy for the oppressed, but in reality both are contemptuous of the oppressed, making much of their problems as long as they fit a certain mold of analysis, identifying their interests with those of the Left, and abandoning them as soon as they are no longer useful.

In his prologue, Bruckner admits that his criticism of Third-Worldism is above all a criticism of himself. I have a similar motivation for wanting to introduce this book to American readers. Many of the ideas Bruckner criticizes are ideas that my contemporaries and I once shared. I do not personally agree with all of Bruckner's analyses. But he is part of a generation of Europeans who suffered from Third-Worldism and its illusions. I am from a similar generation of American intellectuals, and I hope that the publication of this book will be part of the healing process.

WILLIAM R. BEER
February 1986

THE TEARS OF
THE WHITE MAN
Compassion as Contempt

Prologue
Orlac's Hands

Once upon a time, there was a famous pianist named Stephen Orlac. He thrilled music lovers with his talent, and was on his way to world renown. Tragically, at thirty years of age, his brilliant musical career ended when he was seriously wounded in a train accident between Montgeron and Paris. He had to have new hands sewn onto his arms by a surgeon named Dr. Cerral. From that moment on, he was a changed man. He gave up performing on the piano, and began acting strangely, committing a series of crimes in spite of himself. He even threatened his beautiful wife Hélène, even though everyone knew that, until then, he had felt an overwhelming passion for her. In the few moments he was lucid, he made a long and painful inquiry, and found out that Dr. Cerral had given him the hands of a murderer who had been guillotined shortly before. This man's hands, still obeying their former owner, were making Orlac commit horrible deeds against his will. In the end, Stephen Orlac's bloody hands were exorcised, he was found innocent, and returned to his music.[1]

Innocence corrupted by science, good misled by evil—both themes of this turn-of-the-century pot-boiler, a mixture of melodrama and social fantasy, are still prominent today. Interestingly, they predominate not in literature, but in politics, particularly in relations between the Northern and Southern hemispheres. In almost identical language, the callow Third World is described as having been robbed of its natural goodness by a diabolical and corrupting West.

In fact, every Westerner is presumed guilty until proven innocent. We Europeans have been raised to detest ourselves, certain that, within our world, there is a certain essential evil that must be relentlessly atoned for. This evil is known by two terms—colonialism and imperialism. And it can be summed up in a few figures—tens of millions of Indians wiped out by the conquistadores, two hundred million Africans deported or dead in the slave trade, and the millions of Asians, Arabs, and Africans killed during colonial wars and wars of liberation.

Crushed under the weight of this shameful memory, we have been led to believe that the very Western civilization our fathers thought was the greatest on earth is, in fact, the worst. We who were born after the second World War have been convinced that we belong to the dregs of humanity, to a loathsome gang that for centuries has been smothering almost the entire globe under the pretext of spiritual enlightenment. Our continent talked of humanity at the same time as it massacred people everywhere on the planet; it was founded upon pillage and the destruction of human life, and it deserves only to be trampled underfoot itself.

The West stands accused by the whole world, and many Westerners join in this indictment. Our guilt is asserted with indignation and hatred. No speech about the Third World can begin or end without the theme that the white man is evil. We sons and grandsons of the barbarians who pillaged the world are supposed to carry on with our self-denunciation. "Each of us is guilty before all others, forever and everywhere, and I more than anyone else"—Dostoevski's words are our innermost belief. The blood that has been spilled has spattered us, and it seems that nothing can redeem the oppressions committed, no compensation can right the balance upset by the sin of colonialism. All our claims to glory, the centuries of work, calculation, refinement, and achievement that have crowned a particular type of human wisdom, have been swept away and reduced to nothingness. The knowledge that this flourishing of art and technology carries with it an equal dose of self-abasement has discouraged us from accepting it or continuing with it.

The devaluation of the European message has become the common denominator of the leftist intelligentsia since World War II, just as hatred of the bourgeoisie in Europe after 1917 was a veritable intellectual passport when no writing was acceptable without its ritual invocation of the messianic proletariat and its standard disgust for the propertied class. But the independence of the former colonies now provides us with a chance at redemption. We can enlist on the side of peoples engaged in the struggle, and wherever and whenever we can, help the Southern hemisphere to overturn the golden calf of the West. The birth of the Third World as a political force has thus engendered a new species of activism—that of militant self-denunciation.

How self-hatred became a central dogma of our culture is one of the many enigmas of European history. It is indeed odd that in a century of militant atheism and agnostic thinkers who sharpened their weapons in the cause of fighting against the Church and its teachings have reconciled us all to the idea that is the very basis of Christianity itself—that of original sin. In thought and in morality, there has been a wholesale overthrow of accepted values—disobedience to authority, debunking of taboos and idols, and the simultaneous death of God and the Father so masterfully proclaimed by Jean-Paul Sartre. At the same time, there has been a growing sense of shame, as if the same societies that had gotten rid of the whole idea of sin simultaneously opened the gateway to collective guilt. This is the price that must be paid for being a European, the consequence of our brief triumph over the rest of the world. Modern politics may have given up its Christian motives, but its emotional foundations are still Christian. Our political world is turgid with religiosity, drunk on martyrs, and fascinated by suffering, and even the most secular speeches are usually only inept rehashings of priestly homilies.

It is not really a paradox that such a taste for suffering, for the image of the oppressed, should coexist with enduring hatred of the Church. A guilty conscience always weighs heaviest when it is denied, particularly because guilt is not openly admitted by all. Marxists of various stripes, for instance, deny its existence, as if it were some sort of leftover religious residue. But the emotion emerges in their rote incantations that go along with and support rigorously objective analyses and statistics. The assumption of one's own blame is the crutch that shores up faulty reasoning, the finishing touch that tops off a stumbling argument. Fuzzy analyses get a stamp of approval in advance as long as they begin and end with an underlying invective of guilt. There is implicit emotional baggage in a value system that pervades language unbeknown to the listener, and that means something quite different from what is openly expressed. If there is any flabbiness of definition or hobbled logic, an authoritative argument that overcomes any hesitation and wins support can be called up—"In any case, the West is guilty!"

Clearly, guilt is primarily a rhetorical device, the only sparkle in an otherwise wooden language. Whoever uses it is sure to have the last word and hold his own against any argument. Guilt is what is left when you have run out of everything else.

In this study, therefore, I want to focus on guilty conscience to study the history of the idea of the Third World in Europe and America since 1960, a date that roughly coincides with the Bandung Conference of 1955 and the end of the war in Algeria in 1962. Twenty years is enough time for the memory of great trauma and pain to start to fade. Moreover, since there must occasionally be a re-reading of recent history, I think the time has come to set up a balance sheet of what in France has been called "Third Worldism." What is particularly interesting is that the desire for repentance shown by a minority of intellectuals, militants, and schoolteachers expressing this current of opinion lives side by side with the placid indifference, if not the hostility, of most people toward so-called underdeveloped countries. I will attempt to show that this is not really a paradox, and that they are simply two sides of the same coin.

I aim to uncover the devious chicanery of the virtue professed by self-appointed partisans of the Third World, their self-admiring sophistry, their selfish alibis, and their dishonest bombast. But I want to make clear that I do not wish to wage yet another campaign of denunciation. I do not intend to point my finger at the confusion and mistakes of my elders from the lofty position of hindsight that youth affords. I do not aim, as others have, to settle accounts with previous generations, whose only mistake is to have come before mine. We have learned from their teachings, as well as their mistakes, and we must look to them still for the sources of arguments to refute them.

I want to be free of a vision of the world that may once have been fruitful but is clearly useless now. But this does not necessarily mean putting it on trial, passing sentence, and viciously trampling it underfoot. All the writings I quote below are dated, which means that the people who wrote them should be held accountable only for what they wrote at that time. And none of them deals exclusively with the thesis that I am presenting here. Many of them have changed since that time, and it would be dishonest

not to point this out. This is all the more true because I am study-
ing the distortions of a sense of guilt that ran amok and turned
on its own presuppositions, and I myself was part and parcel of
its excesses. My criticism here is above all a criticism of myself.

It is interesting how the jargon or babble of a minority can
become the truth for many people. The acceptance and success of
the Third World line are very revealing. When a whole generation
has the same illusions, it is less an instance of blindness or confusion than a cultural fact. Of course, out of the mass of writings
on this subject over the last 20 years, I had to be selective, and I
have omitted many writings that deserve examination as much as
others. The Third World has produced a veritable tidal wave of
literature; fortunately, all the writings inspired by anti-European
acrimony are all alike. Thus, it is inevitable that they overlap and
repeat themselves. Some sing a song of shame to the sound of a
minuet, while others dance a more leaden tune on our heads,
thumping out their chorus with hobnailed boots to get the message across. Sophisticated or crude, little-known or famous, the
members of this company all deliver the same clichés and gather
like elephants at the same watering hole in the evening. In this
muddle, the same ideas keep turning up, so much so that once you
have read one you have read them all.

Three main types can be sorted out of the attitudes of these
Westerners toward the Southern hemisphere: (1) solidarity, the
"we are all in it together" stance; (2) compassion, the "put ourselves in their place" position; and (3) imitation, the "we are just
like them" attitude. These three categories seem best-adapted to
covering atypical or unusual attitudes as well, without concealing
the dangers of arbitrariness implicit in such a classification. Between the apathy of majority opinion and the masochism of Third
World apologists, I have tried to find another course, which I describe at the end of this book. It is a course chosen to find a way
out for Europeans without denying their history. The man of the
Third World is approached as the stranger who is our fellow man.
This approach, which in the final analysis tries to enlighten us
about our own conduct, is somewhat of a gamble. I am fully granting, at the outset of the game, that it is a delicate task.

1

Solidarity; or, The Bad Guys Against the Good Guys

[Western visitors to Moscow in the 1930s] are unquestionably one of the wonders of the age, and I shall treasures till I die as a blessed memory the spectacle of them travelling with radiant optimism through a famished countryside, wandering in happy bands about squalid, over-crowded towns, listening with unshakeable faith to the fatuous patter of carefully trained and indoctrinated guides, repeating like schoolchildren a multiplication table, the bogus statistics and mindless slogans endlessly intoned to them. There, I would think, an earnest office-holder in some local branch of the League of Nations Union, there a godly Quaker who once had tea with Gandhi, there an inveigher against the Means Test and the Blasphemy Laws, there a staunch upholder of free speech and human rights, there an indomitable preventer of cruelty to animals; there scarred and worthy veterans of a hundred battles for truth, freedom and justice—all, all chanting the praises of Stalin and his Dictatorship of the Proletariat. It was as though a vegetarian society had come out with a passionate plea for cannibalism, or Hitler had been nominated posthumously for the Nobel Peace Prize.

> *Chronicles of Wasted Time,*
> Malcolm Muggeridge

"They are very gentle, and know nothing of evil"
—Christopher Columbus

In the autumn of 1492, at the end of an exhausting voyage, Christopher Columbus reached San Salvador in the Bahamas, Cuba, and then Haiti. He was convinced that he had found heaven on earth. He had read in Pierre d'Ailly's *Imago Mundi* that the Garden of Eden had to be in a warm climate on the other side of the Equator, and so was enraptured by everything he saw from the moment he arrived. "They were all very well-built, very beautiful, with attractive faces."[1] "They go naked as the day they were born, the women as well as the men" (op. cit., 158). "We Christians said they were remarkably beautiful, the men as well as the women" (op. cit., 143). "This beauty was moral as well as physical. . . . They are the most pleasant and peaceful people in the world" (op. cit., 146). "I think that there are no better people and no better land in all the world."

Two of the Indians' traits are constantly emphasized by the navigator from Genoa—their generosity and their fearfulness. From the very first contacts, the Spanish exchanged trinkets for gold with them, and Christopher Columbus constantly praised the generosity of natives who gave everything for nothing.

"The Admiral said he could not believe that a man could have ever beheld people so good of heart, so generous and timid, because they all gave away everything they had to us Christians, and ran to give us whatever they had as soon as they saw us" (op. cit., 159). "In exchange for anything you give them, no matter how trifling, they immediately give you all their possessions" (op. cit., 127). "They do not covet other people's property. . . . Whatever you ask for that belongs to them, they never refuse. On the contrary, they ask you to help yourself, and show so much love that you give them your heart" (op. cit., 48).

Their fearfulness resulted from their kindness. "The Admiral swears that they are so timid and cowardly that with ten men he could defeat ten thousand" (op. cit., 125).

They were helpless because they were innocent, and the condescension of the white men toward them was the other side of a boundless admiration. In one single move, within several weeks, Columbus invented the myth of the Noble Savage and all that it implies. After that, he could make the following definitive judgment of the Indians: "They are very gentle, and know nothing of evil. They know nothing of killing one another" (op. cit., 100).

The quasi-divinity of the natives came from the fact that, without knowing it, they were confirming the Holy Scriptures. But this extraordinary state of affairs could not last. They were given the formidable privilege of being perfect, but because of this were in danger of being designated savages if they failed in their mission.

The dream could not endure, as it turned out. By the time Columbus returned a year later, everything had changed. Gold fever gnawed at the sailors from Spain and the first settlers left behind had been massacred for trying to rape the wives of the natives. These natives were not as sweet and angelic as had been thought.

A single incident—when some Indians went to take things that they wanted from the Christian explorers—was enough to make Columbus forget his earlier hymns of praise, to declare that they were all thieves and brutes, and to inflict cruel punishment upon them. "During your voyage to Cibao, if an Indian steals anything at all, you must punish him by cutting off his nose and his hands, because these are the parts of the body that they cannot hide" (op. cit., 106).

Burdened by increasing difficulties, Columbus turned gradually from a positive perception of the peaceful nature of the Indians to an overly hostile judgment. The same people who, in 1492, "loved their neighbors as themselves," and thus showed a natural tendency toward Christianity, were transformed two years later into ferocious beasts who deserved enslavement. The last letter from Columbus to the Spanish kings (dated July 7, 1503 from Jamaica) is revealing: "I am alone in my suffering and sickness, and each day await my death, surrounded by a million cruel and hostile savages. I am so far from the sacraments of the Holy Church that my soul would be lost if it departed my body in this place" (op. cit., 215).

At no time were the Indians given the right to express their own will. The Noble Savage was condemned from the very beginning, because he had been declared perfect. His superiority in the ideal had to change to inferiority in light of the facts. Beneath the surface of the native's over-obliging exterior lurked a cur; natural gentleness concealed vindictiveness and dishonesty. The discovery of the New World confirmed belief in the Bible, the Golden Age, the Hesperides, but then immediately undermined it. These pure and happy creatures were forthwith suspected of harboring abominable evil within them. Not only did their infamy follow immediately after the belief in their purity; the two are inextricable. Pastoral peace gives birth to condemnation and calumny.

Leaving aside the complexity of Columbus' writing and the many implications of his explorations, one thing is clear.[2] The exaltation, followed by a complete about-face, of the navigator from Genoa, was almost identically duplicated in other terms in Europe at the beginning of the 1960s, following decolonization. In fact, the independence of subordinate countries was for many leftists like the discovery of a new continent, and was to evoke the same intellectual reactions, the same intensity of feeling, that experiencing America evoked in the imagination of the men of the Renaissance. The Carib Indian was a blank slate upon which the conquistadores drew a picture of the Christian revelation. This was the hopeful emblem of the Third World guerrilla who appeared in revolutionary mythology 460 years later.

In both cases, there was the notion of a historical beginning— a human topsoil that became fertile ground for the most lunatic fantasies. Colonized societies had histories, of course, but the fact that they were free from the European yoke conferred instant childhood upon them. The appearance of this huge world in the universe of possibilities called everything into question. A great expectation was aroused among men, and the downtrodden of the Southern hemisphere were going to dominate modern history. The outlines of our own history all the joy of our new beginnings, could be discovered in this Eldorado. The civilization of those who had been the wretched of the earth emerged from the nightmare of colonialism, was burdened with all the unfulfilled hopes of the industrial world, and "added a new color to the rainbow."[3] Enslaved people had been freed. Until now they had passively accepted the scourges of hunger, poverty, humiliation, and ignorance as part of their lives, but their uprising was a "wellspring" and, thus, they reconciled themselves with countless other human societies. "A new philosophy of the Earth"[4] was taking the place of the dreary uniformity imposed by the white man, and led to what the Swedish economist Gunnar Myrdal called the "Great Reawakening," a historical fact of incalculable importance.

With this raw material, left-wing intellectuals disappointed by a lack of political prospects in Europe and particularly by the adoption of the strategy of peaceful coexistence proclaimed a messianic vision that the revelation of Stalin's horrors had not affected. The Bandung Conference of 1955, in which 29 African and Asian countries laid the foundations of a new international cooperative order, seemed certain to signal the beginning of a world that was wider and more generous. The elevation of poor nations to the status of proletarians gave new life to a revolutionary principle that had been betrayed by the "people's democracies." It allowed the Communist plan to begin anew, in a way that the founding fathers had conceived it. The Third World acquired the freshness of a pure virgin and the first steps of these infant regimes had the beauty of an enchanting childhood. Unhealthy shanty towns, burgeoning ghettos, and crowds of sick and hungry people—the accursed legacy of the colonial era—suddenly became so many fabulous lands in which the makings of the New Man were being fashioned.

What was more, poverty itself was valued, because the oppressed presaged their own redemption.[5] Only suffering has a future, because it is about to produce its own alleviation. Every evil is a blessing in disguise because it eventually opens the way to revolution. In total contradiction to Marxist philosophy, the simple fact of being poor was supposed to make particular peoples the carriers of progress. What was important for those who fancied themselves partisans of the Third World was not one particular injustice or another, because these were little more than horrifying anecdotes. What was important was the general principle that all the injustices revealed. This overarching principle was, of course, the basis of the system that prevailed in Western democracies—capitalism, and its highest stage, imperialism.

By attributing all the evils of the world to profit and money, the interests of all the oppressed could be seen as identical. The exploited were a homogeneous mass fighting against a handful of pot-bellied robbers with American accents. French peasants could declare that they were the brothers of their counterparts in Upper Volta, and the humble of Europe could join hands with the poor people of India and China, because each movement was simply a particular response to the same injustice. Because a single law was seen as dividing the world into two parts, the transformation of postwar colonialism into the Third-World worship of the 1960s demonstrated how self-hatred was metamorphosed into adoration of the redeeming tropics.

> *"America is a mad dog"*
> —Sartre

A confused certainty, one expressed in more or less subtle fashion depending on the political stripe inspires Third-Worldists—and on this matter, the main "worker" parties in France, the Socialist Party and the Communist Party, were the most moderate. What is certain is the infamy of the West, a single and absolute truth as unchanging as the law of gravity. Just as the lion is carnivorous—a fact that goes beyond the limits of human understanding—the Western world is a predator. Thus, a chasm between which there is only a choice of acceptance or rejection separates the realms of total good and total evil.[6] And so, by taking the part of peoples that Europe held underfoot until recently, the horrifying period of our domination can be glossed over or wiped away.

No one was better-suited to arousing and legitimizing the feeling of a debt that could not be repaid than Sartre, as he did in his preface to *The Wretched of the Earth*.[7] According to Sartre, we are personal accomplices to the crimes committed in our name, because it is in our power to stop them. We must take upon ourselves this unfamiliar but inherited guilt, and abase ourselves in order to be able to bear it. "Have the courage to read Fanon," Sartre said, "because it will make you feel shame, and shame, as Marx said, is a revolutionary emotion" (op. cit., 14).

Because of this, many "progressive" Europeans became living torches of self-punishment, ready to immolate themselves to redeem the debts incurred by their fathers. Miraculously, hostility to "Father," far from being a fault that would burden his offspring, as the Freudian vision would have it, was one and the same as justice.[8] This explains why the support of progressive Europeans went only to those regimes that openly proclaimed their disgust for white civilization.[9] It would never have occurred to any of them, at the time, to sing the praises of the Senegal of Senghor, the Ivory Coast of Houphouët-Boigny, or the democracy of Indira Gandhi, or to celebrate the carefree joy of the Papuans and the sweet life of the Polynesians. Rather, it was essential to pillory the industrial nations and all they stood for—parliamentary democracy, the rights of man, culture, and Christianity.

It must be understood how, in this emotionally overheated context, America could be the focus of so much hostility in the post-World War II period, and particularly during the 12 years of the Vietnam conflict. She provided the ideal guilty party. She was guilty on many counts, particularly because of the help she had given us. Neither France, nor Italy, nor Germany could forgive America for having liberated them from the Nazi and fascist yokes.

Western Europe knew that, without the help of the Marines, they would purely and simply have been wiped off the map. But some forms of generosity are insulting. Because salvation came from the outside—except for some weak internal resistance whose effect was more symbolic than military (De Gaulle's genius was to purge France of the dishonor of collaboration)—America showed very clearly the life force that had once been alive in Europe. The little American cousin had surpassed her European elders in vigor, power, and creativity. It is hard to forgive assistance when it shows up such weakness. And so, the liberator of 1944 became the enemy of mankind. From then on, every occasion was sought to get back at the USA, at least symbolically. The Cold War, McCarthyism, and then the Korean War were to constitute the first occasions for an outpouring of bitterness.

For a degenerate Europe that had watched rather than participated in history, however, there was a particularly sweet revenge to be taken on a New World that was still trying to teach it something when the first units of the American expeditionary forces landed in Saigon in 1965. The old whore, poor and needy, scolded the young prostitute for her wrongdoing, in order to expunge her own earlier misdeeds. On the morrow of the Algerian War and its bloody excesses, what a pleasure it was for the French to unload the colonial burden on Uncle Sam, who, as it happened, had shown a remarkable hypocrisy. Nobody in Paris had forgotten that the Eisenhower administration had refused to help the defeated French army at Dien Bien Phu on May 7, 1954. Upon our transatlantic cousin, who pillaged Central America, re-established dictatorship in Santo Domingo, showered fire and napalm on Vietcong guerrillas, organized the blocade of Cuba, and overthrew the socialist regime of Allende, we could vomit forth accusations of what we ourselves once were—the inheritors of a colonial culture—and we could be repulsed by an image that horrified us. Faced with rejection from the four corners of the world, in the face of European traditions of culture and refinement America the Evil was showing all the symptoms by which the guilt of the West was known—she was rich to the point of satiety; imperialistic, domineering, insolent, and polluting; alienating her youth; exploiting her minorities; glorifying her foundation on genocide; and prospering only because of massacre and murder. She was a nation that had replaced the good things in life with the pursuit of profit, and moral values with the cult of the almighty dollar. In a word, she was the very apotheosis of rapacity and violence.

The brutal policies of the Johnson, Nixon, and Ford administrations toward Vietnam, and the shocking extremes to which they allowed themselves to go, soon raised anti-American phobia to a fever pitch rarely reached among European youth. It was like a prairie fire that smoldered and spread to the four corners of Europe—a colossal, informal, unorganized network, all the more powerful because it had a common denominator.

The myths of anti-Americanism began to teem like worms on the body of the United States, from which they drew their nourishment. Every intellectual fervently hoarded his handful of anti-Yankee dogmas, knowing that they constituted his greatest resource. Quickly forgotten were the sins of the American Army or Air Force and America's support for a cruel puppet government, widely differing actions that would have required highly critical judgment to understand the essence of America's national character. The hatred was essentially aimed at the fact that America was what she was. America's actions were seen as following from her perverted nature, and came to be simply consequences or illustrations of it. The polemical escalation went on and the controversy degenerated into a kind of metaphysical confrontation: America did not commit misdeeds, she herself resulted from a fundamental injustice. She was execrated not as this or that, but purely and simply for existing. Everywhere, at all times, it was necessary to denounce "the planetary empire of North American hegemonic capital,"[10] the underlying pathology of barbarism.

The "American challenge" changed into the "American evil,"[11] one whose dimensions had the virulence of a plague. The famous cry uttered by Sartre in 1953, "Beware! America is a mad dog!" (Libération, 22 June 1953), seemed to come true in December 1972, when Nixon's B-52s carpet-bombed Hanoi and Haiphong. Then we could adopt as our own Eldridge Cleaver's phrase, "I will spill my blood and put my life on the line and try to kill the pigs in power in Babylon."[12]

An expression invented by a famous American anti-war linguist to describe his country made a stir at this time: the Bloodbath Archipelago, as opposed to Solzhenitsyn's Gulag Archipelago.[13] The United States unleashed unlimited resources for killing because of a profound internal moral putrefaction.[14] There was no "American way of life," only an American way of death. This insane civilization was rapidly self-destructing before our eyes, and René Dumont perceived a general failure throughout its inhuman supercities when he declared in 1973 that "New York had already become almost unlivable,"[15] and was destined for a speedy ruin because of the combined effects of unemployment, garbage, and crime.

Parasitical, murderous, and sick, America was the ideal scapegoat. Every bombardment, torture, and cruelty performed by her boys fed our resentment, which no gesture of appeasement could have disarmed. We stood to lose too much to even think of forgiving her.[16] The existence of a total, absolute, perfect enemy bestowed on us a free hand for hating with serenity, hating with legitimacy, and even hating with a high moral purpose.[17] In sum, in expansionist America, the Western world believed it had found its own disgraceful quintessence. Four hundred years of conquest, pillage, and massacre achieved their supreme expression and converged under the roof of the White House. All the loathing for a particular culture could be concentrated in a single place, in a single people, in a single system. Because the American Devil could serve as a fixed abscess, evil ceased to be free-floating, and the Old World, soiled by age-old faults and born on the back of its transatlantic relative, could finally regain some measure of the purity it had lost during the long centuries that followed the Renaissance.

Suddenly, the internalized hatred of the European was directed at another party, one that was a symbol of absolute crime. But this party had to be quite similar, had to have all the traits that we hated in ourselves. The memory of colonial collapse was still strong, and an old historical people had ceased to be dominant and had acquired a huge inferiority complex as a result. America

presented the surreal vision of a great Western power that was
again undertaking imperial adventure when the other colonial
powers had called it quits.

The Old World was angry and fearful that America might succeed where she had failed, and set up a Manichean distinction. At
the time, each of us felt remorseless venom, as if it were a com-
pelling national religion. The American was attacked because of
his tiny differences from the European, his fraternal enemy. He
was almost the same, but was slightly different from us and was
all the more resented for this difference.

It was hatred of a relative, of an intimate whose intolerable
closeness was disavowed.[18] America, the unnatural offspring, concentrated all the negative traits of her parents: automation, mech-
anization, materialism, and anxiety.[19] Perhaps she was Europe's
double, but in the sense in which the healthiest parents can sire
monsters. For an irrevocable verdict to be passed by the community of nations, this disgraceful progeny had to be cast in contradictory roles—that she be both relative and outcast, that her
similarity be accompanied by an unbridgeable gulf, that she be the
pustule throbbing at the heart of the West. It made no difference
that the United States was still playing the thankless role of policeman of the world. We could take shelter beneath her nuclear
umbrella at the same time that we scolded her for threatening
peace. We could profit from the cultural, economic, and financial
benefits of an alliance with her at the same time we denounced
her hold on Europe.

Through this fraudulence, Europe became a new province of
the Third World. For, at all costs, we had to purge our sense of
guilt by pouring it onto this empire that was a focus for all our
bile. Because France, Italy, and Germany had turned into political
midgets, all they needed was to slip into the guise of victims. The
dishonor of America guaranteed their own virtue, and returned
some measure of vigor to these depressed and diminished
societies.

The certainty that we were living in a decisive epoch balanced
on the brink of a cataclysmic revolution that would cleanse the
impure face of the universe reinforced the desire for punishments,
misfortunes, and vengeance to be visited on the imperialist scum.
Everything that could harm, weaken, and abase this figurehead
of the white world was acclaimed—from the rebellions in ghettos
and the Indian insurrections to the anti-war agitation of youth and

the disintegration of American Army morale. A frantic war dance commanded us to applaud the death of every GI, every news report of a Vietcong victory. Everywhere, and without letup, we encouraged the "political, military, economic, and moral" debacle described by Senator George McGovern in September 1971. And, finally, in the victory of General Giap's troops, we hailed the revenge of Sitting Bull against Buffalo Bill, of the Indian and the "nigger" against the bloodthirsty cowboy.

The Indochina war gave immense psychological satisfaction as an anti-Western on a global scale, one that carried the crusade against Western democracies to its zenith. The fall of Saigon in April 1975 consummated the defeat of the Yankee giant who had pushed to its farthest point "the propensity to support and organize the most barbarous and brutal systems of terror" (Chomsky, op. cit.). The military genius and courage of a little people combined with the forces of good to conquer the capital of South Vietnam, the symbol of all the rottenness of the imperialist system.[20] The Vietnamese were exemplary in the defeats they wrought, much more so than in the model of society they were proposing.[21] We struggled "to set up in Saigon a regime we no longer wanted to see in Prague," to borrow Edgar Morin's apt phrase, because the blow thereby inflicted on the American Goliath was much more important than the well-being of a tiny country at the end of the Asian continent. This humiliating rout was supposed to render impotent the power that poured forth the greatest measure of evil. The emperor now had no clothes and soon showed his embarrassment: America was detested for its role as world teacher of capitalism, and was now equally hated for her decline.[22] Clearly, her death was at hand. And in our revulsion toward the USA were mixed emotions of terror inspired by her wrongdoings and disdain for this vanquished empire, like the feelings aroused by the thief who has failed in his robbery, but who is still the object of our condemnation.

"You have been condemned to death, O Western world"
—Aragon[23]

Solidarity with oppressed peoples is above all a gigantic weapon aimed at the West. The logic of aggression is at work in Third World solidarity, and this has made it a continuation of the Cold

War by other means, with other countries replacing the "reformist" USSR as worldwide adversary of imperialism. There is an important feature characteristic of Third World-lovers: *They know.* They have made an inevitable choice in favor of the Southern hemisphere. They have not simply taken the side of justice and the oppressed; history is on their side. They pass judgment as diagnosing physicians rather than hate-blinded murderers. "Europe is finished. This is a truth that is not nice to say but which all of us know in our flesh and bones" (Sartre, preface to Fanon, op. cit. p. 10). "I felt as if I belonged to a species that was on its way to extinction," wrote Marie-France Mottin when she left France for Cuba (op. cit. p. 11).

In commitment to the Third World, what must be takes over from reality. The revolt against the Old World takes on a strange fatalism. What good is there in defending unstable democracies, when the march of history demands their disappearance? In short, the answer has been found. We know more than our fathers, and they are doubly contemptible because they are not just colonialists, but out of date. We are the end of history. Our way of looking at blacks, Indians, and Asians no longer is burdened by the ignorance, prejudice, and fears that characterized the white man from Cortez to Kipling. Inexorable destiny now commands us to vanish. This leads to a piercing irony, the analysis of even the most moderate moralizers: At the end of our day, it is too late to save our values, and the only thing left for us to do is to collaborate in our own downfall.[24] Now that the former colonial victim has been freed from his chains, he has a wisdom that approaches the mystical. With great seriousness, a whole generation of European and American intellectuals, fortified by Sartre's authority, subscribes to the prophecy of Frantz Fanon, who said that "the Third World now faces Europe like a colossus whose task must be to try to resolve the problems for which Europe has not been able to find solutions" (op. cit., p. 241).

Imperialism has transformed the planet into a gigantic world market, in which each part complements the other. The battle, therefore, must be waged everywhere. Others are fighting for us at the other end of the earth; here we must fight for them. There is a strict clockwork that governs all these struggles, and whatever helps the liberation of mankind in Vientiane, Peking, or Bamako reinforces liberty in Paris.[25] Every time the white man is kicked out, driven away, or eliminated, humanity regains a little of its independence.[26] Wherever the native is oppressed, our dignity is reduced and wherever he raises his head, we regain a reason for living.[27] Even in his smallest gestures, everyone must demonstrate in favor of the side he has chosen. Refusal to take sides is still the choice of the stronger, and is tantamount to complicity with evil.

This political viewpoint makes all morality temporary and even irrelevant in the face of the Promethean confrontation that is tearing the earth into two factions. Being non-European is enough to put one on the side of right. Being European or being supported by a European power is enough to make one suspect. The bloody messes in banana republics, and butchery of political opposition and the dictatorial lunacy by their petty chieftains are all brushed aside. Such trifles will not restrain the progress of these peoples toward socialism. What seems criminal in Cuba, Angola, and Guinea has the real purpose of washing away the far greater crime of colonialism.

Against every kind of moral reservation, then, there is a guilty conscience that can paralyze any thought of criticism. For this generation, which saw colonialism in its worst moments and for which it has a deep disgust, guilt lives on long after the circumstances that gave rise to it. And the severity of the judge is in inverse proportion to the distance of the country in question. The farther away the country is from European shores, the greater is its claim to total freedom from condemnation.

The slightest scuffle with the police in the streets of Paris, Berlin, or Milan proves the monstrous nature of the capitalist system. Every year, some magazine or pundit predicts the return of fascism in France, Germany, or Italy. In contrast, hangings by the dozen in some Near Eastern country, the almost systematic use of torture beyond the Mediterranean, and "reeducation camps" in socialist countries are looked upon either as negligible or as ideologically justified. South of the Equator, assassination is a humanitarian act and repression a historical necessity. The remorseless and self-righteous critic who endlessly denounces the deceptions of parliamentary democracy is suddenly rapt with admiration before the atrocities committed in the name of the Koran, the Vedas, the Great Helmsman, or negritude. Because perfect democracy does not exist anywhere, the imperfect democracies of the West can be damned and the worst forms of political power legitimated.

What was a partisan feeling in the Northern hemisphere became conformity to tyrannies elsewhere. There was no need to
subscribe to the disciplines or dogmas of these regimes. The fact
that they were far away gave them a seal of authority that would
have been suspect in Paris. This led many non-Marxist intellectuals, even many Christian activists, to fawn on these states and
the scholasticism they spout as doctrine. Because of the unforgettable mistakes committed by the West, they placed their greatest hopes on those who hated us and spat in our faces. Many could
have echoed the phrase of the poet Louis Aragon, who wrote in
1925, "We are the defeatists of Europe. . . . We are the ones who
always hold out our hands to the enemy. . . . "

Third Worldism validates this black-and-white vision, which
would have the sinfulness of one side stand forever as witness to
the grace and virtue of the other. The spiritual bankruptcy of certain liberation movements and the crudest slogans of their leaders
are exhibited as so many words from the Savior. At the same time,
intellectual rigor, logic, and education, which are the exclusive
property of wealthy countries, are rejected as diabolical imperialist ploys. Puny insurrections and the slightest of uprisings are
given enormous attention, far out of proportion to their real importance. The ignorance and sectarianism of tropical gangsters
are treated with reverence. Glory is given to the parade of splendid Asians who have been called upon to destroy European civilization. The most outrageous lunacies are praised to the skies by
enlightened intellectuals, who are only too happy to submit to a
primitive authority to abase themselves "before the splendor of a
healthy barbarism."[28] By this axiom, anyone who uplifts, praises,
or celebrates the West is suspected of the worst sort of evil. Modesty, humility, self-destructiveness, and whatever else might lead
Europeans to efface themselves and give up leadership are honored and saluted as wonderfully progressive. The golden rule of
this masochism is simple: Whatever comes from us is bad; whatever comes from them is perfect. Formerly colonized peoples are
prized as perfect through and through.

Love your enemies. Our atheistic times never followed this
Christian exhortation more faithfully than in the 1970s. Of course,
there was little difference—*we do not hallow the enemy in hopes
of a future reconciliation but rather seek in him our own destruction.* Since the Westerner was not a man except at the expense
of the rest of the human race, mankind will not become human

again except at the expense of the West. This is why the outlaw has been a figure of frenzied adoration in the West for the last 30 years.[29]

How many of us, in our heart of hearts, have regretted that he was not born a worker, a woman, a Chinese, Indian, or Ghanaian, since these are the categories of people endowed with innocence in the European imagination? This is the typical mistake of Third World-lovers, as soon as they become convinced that solidarity with underdeveloped countries requires that they admire, rather than correct, the sufferings. In 1839, Lord Macaulay, Minister in Charge of Indian Affairs for His Majesty the King of England, declared, "Our native subjects have more to learn from us than we do from them" (cited in *Imperialism,* Phil Centin, NY, Walker & Co., 1971). His great-great grandsons, only too happy to make up for past mistakes, say exactly the opposite, again and again. The passionate belief in fantasies of the world dreamed by the formerly oppressed is the price for redeeming Europe's classic claim to define itself as the only measure of what was human. The white man, strangely enough, tries to describe himself in the same oversimplified and malicious terms once used by the colonizer to describe the colonized.[30] Carefully selected accounts end up showing only those episodes of Western history that demonstrate that he is loathsome. A sort of generalized and sweeping reductionism is practiced—one that cannot see subtleties. The more simplistic an explanation is, the more chic it is. The "headhunter complex"—the ability to reduce a society to a few salient features in order to dismiss it—is at work here, just as the Jivaro headhunter shrinks the head of his enemy to the size of an apple.

Flirting with the Tropics

Let us pass over the fact that, from the mid-1960s on, we tried to serve up to the Third World, "with condescension, the remnants of a progressive philosophy of history whose failures and crimes we acknowledged every day."[31] Let us also set aside the fact that, in those far-off times, everything that did not fit into the schema of imperialism-versus-revolution (such as, for example, the two wars in Kashmir, the Indo-Pakistani conflict, the civil war of the Shan warlords against the Burmese government, the confrontation between Eritrea and Ethiopia, and the genocide in Biafra) was discreetly relegated to the dungeon of silence. And let us leave out the fact that, among the famous, prophecy erased the boundary between will and power. I am suggesting something further—that Third-Worldism grew to be a kind of love affair because, in the hopes it projected on underdeveloped countries, an erotic urge was at work. We ardently searched for satisfaction from the object of our revolutionary desire.[32]

It was an amazing coincidence—at the other end of the earth a little nation spoke our language and carried out our fantasy in one stroke. What a wonderful echo. Our longing for human brotherhood was satisfied in this idealistic militancy: Humanity's division into blocs and races was supposed to be erased and replaced with a single type of person. All foreignness was thereby eliminated because, in listening to these new regimes, we were listening to one another and making use of them as far-off mouthpieces.[33] The shameless advertising of whatever was different should not be allowed to disguise the fact that Third-Worldism was, above all, in love with its own reflection. It gathered up all the most unusual traits of native cultures to put them together and squeeze them into a useful order of things. We thought we were getting clear of our own culture, but we were projecting our culture on others.

Of course, the old cult of the exotic had to be excoriated, because it was merely a rich veneer Europe had painted on the abject poverty of its victims. Loti, Malraux, Buck, Bromfield, Cendrars, and Morand had to be cast as part of the whorish crew of colonialist agents.[34] What the militants did not see, however, was that, under the cover of rigor and scientism, they were simply watching a little morality play when they saw workers at work, mass meetings, and "people's courts." The foreigner becomes picturesque when he is nothing but the illustration of a doctrine and part of a theorem, because then his foreignness no longer seems transcendent. This is why, from the very beginning of Third-Worldism, there have been useful idiots (useful for proving theories), and useless idiots, who had the misfortune not to fit into an analytical framework and, therefore, did not deserve any consideration at all.[35]

Thus, the cultures and traditions of each country were neglected in favor of their political line, which meant the extent to which they were like us. Hinduism, Confucianism, Hispanic civilization, and black African culture were boiled down to the terribly superficial imagery of some strikes, some commands from chieftains, reports of demonstrations, and economic developments. It was as if the entire essence of these peoples could be reduced to slogans and numbers. It was a crazy time, when the projection of fantasies led people to sort through the tiniest details, when the smallest statistic on pig-farming in Hunan, rice production in the Mekong Delta, or the sugar harvest in Cuba gave Left-wing Frenchmen shivers of pleasure that approached the orgasmic. But the future worthlessness of these places shone through in our lack of any real curiosity about them. In their hostility to cultures that they thought of as mere remnants of the past, as mental handicaps to be overcome by the triumphant revolution, Third World-lovers give first place to socio-economic variables. To make massive Marxian analyses work, religions and customs had to be thought of as negligible, and left to be picked over by ethnologists, who were always suspected of being in collusion with the forces of the past.

We had fantasies of rape, seduction, ravishment—the foreigner was no longer a threat but, instead, became the unknown savior to whom we could safely confide our dreams. We were like those Victorian girls who had suffered the seclusion dictated by their fathers, and who pined for the seducer who would intrude on their humdrum existence and bring new beginnings into their lives. But in transferring our hopes that, until then, had been invested in the Proletariat, to the wretched of the Southern hemisphere, we made these people hostages of our own political systems.[36] In making the Third World our new spiritual leader, we superimposed a prefabricated schema on it. An impersonal logic was supposed to be at work in societies all the way from Dakar to Dar Es Salaam, from Paris to La Paz—one that considered a single idea of time and a single historical actor, whether he was black, Indian, Arab, or Oriental. Aberrant chronologies were lumped together as unforeseen accidents, and this underestimated the weight of traditional structures such as tribalism in Africa or the caste system in India. Third-Worldism amounted to our graciously granting permission to Africans, South Americans, Chinese, and Indonesians the opportunity to run in the gigantic planetary sweepstakes called the coming of world socialist revolution.[37] The exploited peoples were denied the right to make their own place in history; there was no place for them in the drama unless they submitted to the role fashioned for them. We tried out our dogmas on them, just the way arms merchants try out their wares in overseas wars.

The Excitement of Ideas

What was the Third World at this time? A knife without a handle or a blade, an elusive object. The philosopher Lichtenberg would call it a pure idea. The wretched of the earth were doubly disembodied: Living thousands of kilometers from our borders, they were as far from our lives as we were from theirs. Our distance from the actual battlegrounds, in a Europe shorn of its former colonies, encouraged us to experience far-off events vicariously. We had no other power over far-off foreigners than by projection. Not long ago, France had imposed her ways of speaking, eating, and drinking on the world, and she commanded things by hook or by crook for hundreds of millions of people. But now things are happening somewhere else. Theoreticians vainly formulate the concept of "imperialism without colonies,"[38] or "the pillage of the Third World,"[39] but the fact remains that, without exception, no European country is intervening directly in these lands. Only yesterday, Frenchness was universal; today the homeland of Descartes has been reduced to its original borders. From now on the African, the Asian, and the Indian are only footnotes.

How is it possible to think about "the Other" when I have no relation to him but through books and other media? The answer is to make him into the personification of an idea.[40] A tiny number of militants actually went to live with the guerrillas and paid the price of their convictions in jail and in sickness. But almost everybody else was ignorant of the countries they talked about; that explains both the emptiness and the radicalism of prattle about the Third World. The less effect the words had, the more loudly they were shouted.

Distance made things malleable, and far-off people were a foundation for a faith that no facts could question. "Their struggle is our struggle," we said of the Palestinian guerrillas, the Vietcong, Venezuelan revolutionaries, and strikers in the shipyards of Nantes. "Their struggle is our struggle" meant that all the locales, peoples, and battles all over the world are interchangeable, none is worth more than the other. Concrete facts were thus swallowed up in an abstraction. Everything became simple, formulaic, and we could steep ourselves in Latin American revolution as easily as in the rampages of the Red Guards. We jumped from one latitude and climate to another, playing with slogans and ringing declarations. The world was a coatrack upon which we could hang our fantasies. We searched for a more intense and, therefore, more innocent version of ourselves in Angolan soldiers, Bengali Naxalites, and Bolivian guerrillas. Aggressive and childish speechmaking was supposed to fill the void left by the departure of the colonizers and European troops. The solidarity of European intellectuals developed like a monstrous growth as the real power of Europe retreated to within its original frontiers. These intellectuals were like Rousseau, who wrote in his *Confessions,* "Ignoring the real human race entirely, I imagined perfect beings, with heavenly virtue and beauty, so sure in their friendship, so tender and faithful, that I could never find anyone like them in the real world."[41]

Because we never were lucky enough to be where the action was, we vented our frustrations by rites of imitation, by using sympathetic magic. Beards and berets like Che Guevara's, Mao jackets, a cigar like Castro's, and, today, an Afghan turban—these were the ultimate declarations of solidarity for many on the Left. On the sidewalks of Berkeley, the boulevards of the Latin Quarter, or the streets of Berlin, wearing such outfits was an attempt to make mere loitering look like the Long March.[42] (If I pretend to be the Other, his victories become my victories.[43]) We remained faithful to the Third World warlords by modeling our appearance after theirs, by trying to act like them. We shook the foundations of the hydra by waving placards carrying pictures of Ho Chi Minh, Arafat, Carmichael, Malcolm X, and Mao. A new kind of fetishism took the place of brotherly imitation, a fetishism whose aim was not so much to find a revolutionary way for France, as to imitate the different rebellious movements of the outside world.

To paraphrase a famous line of Marx, every event during this period repeated itself—the first time as action in the Southern hemisphere, the second time as theater in the Northern. We shopped among the guerrillas as if we were in a fashionable boutique, to satisfy our need for dress-up and camouflage. But the abundant repetition of certainties never really went beyond an imitation of their clothing.

The Joys of Self-imposed Blindness

In the eighteenth century, notes Jean-Baptiste Duroselle, the rise of the Ottoman Empire evoked among Europeans two diametrically opposed reactions.[44] The first called for a crusade against the infidel Turk; the second saw the Ottoman Empire as a sort of model state Europeans should think about and even imitate. The Turkish spirit of tolerance and natural modesty was praised and contrasted with our own fanaticism and arrogance. The perfect harmony of the individual and society in the Turkish domain was praised and Christian monarchs and princes were called upon to ally themselves with Turkish moral and military might.

In the same way, in the aftermath of decolonization, there have been two ways of rejecting the West. The first denounces the West as the bastion and crucible of capitalism, but says it will be pardoned if it gives up its wicked ways and chooses salvation. The other is more radical; it rejects European civilization in its entirety and condemns it to follow the norms and customs of other cultures that are portrayed as superior.

As colonized peoples were liberated, their values were warmly endorsed. In Chapter 3, we will discuss this frenzied fad for the exotic that accompanied the rise of ethnology and the decline of religiosity. In this Third World worship, the universalism of the Left very often went hand in hand with recognition and praise of the cultural traits of the peoples being liberated,[45] who were thought to provide the solutions and models that could revive degenerate European culture. What was quickly forgotten was that the respect for cultural differences had long been a colonialist argument in favor of a policy toward the natives, as Durkheim argued, or for indirect administration that gave much leeway to local practices, as argued by the Dutch in Java, Faidherbe in Senegal, Galliéni in Madagascar, and, of course, the English throughout the Empire. Also quickly forgotten was that the right of people to cultural diversity had been demanded not only by anti-colonialists in their exhortations to Europe to withdraw, but also by the colonialists themselves to justify a policy of nonassimilation.[46] Our policy in Algeria was the most tragic example of this. It exactly corresponds to a whole segment of leftist thought that, in the name of the universality of the socialist message, denies natives the right to self-determination. For example, Georges

Marchais justified the Russian invasion of Afghanistan by pointing to the feudal customs of that country.[47]

The theme of cultural difference is in reality a convenient pretext that, in itself, has no truth. It is used in turn by different ideologies and sensibilities, and shows how certain values are ambivalent enough to be invoked in support of very different attitudes. It is useful only as an instrument, and by its very ambiguity can be used for opposing aims, with the purpose of giving the last word to political manipulations or appeals to emotions. But when cultural differences are mentioned, even intelligent people lose their perspective, and go into a kind of trance, like whirling dervishes. For them, these differences are a sign not so much of the basic brotherhood of man, but of the pure and simple denial of what is European. The fact that some rebellion or riot erupts against the West is enough to give it absolute value.[48]

Latin America was the spot in the belly of the imperialist beast where the fire was lit; Vietnam was the beast's graveyard. But China was a whole counter-model to the hellish ways of the West. China was supposed to be where the rebirth was taking place. The blending of deep-rooted nationalism, anti-imperialist rhetoric and Mao Tse-tung's version of socialism combined to make China a new branch on the Marxist tree. More sophisticated ingredients were added to the basic anti-American recipe. Like the Noble Savage of the sixteenth century, the Maoist edition of the Chinaman was born in the salons and university amphitheaters in the middle of the 1960s. His appearance was like that of a new savior. The Messiah had returned to earth in the person of Mao, and every day brought fresh proof and signs of the divinity of the Red Idol.[49] Between 1966 and 1975, sycophants of Red China thought they had discovered heaven itself at the other end of the Asian continent.

How could you tell it was paradise? By the fact that everything there is the opposite of what it is here below. Since Europe represented an accumulation of human imperfections, China could only be an accumulation of human marvels. With the presumption of universal evil on the part of a single country and system, all doubt was resolved: The shining beacon of Peking divided the universe into darkness and light. The far-off Other could then be magnified according to the Christian schema of original sin (the West) and redemption (China).

This was a time of pious pilgrimages when, under the pretext of recounting what they saw, zealots puffed up the country they visited with their own enthusiasm. They were the useful idiots who were less interested in describing things than in confirming beliefs, so as not to disappoint the fashionable Left. "In the appearance of the first Chinese he sets eyes on, the traveler can feel a state of exaltation that is more impressive than happiness itself, because it is a perfect state of fertile, active creation."[50] "In China, throughout a whole day of work, you will never hear anyone complain or disobey or talk back." Because what you see in the man in the street is not politeness but "a deep brotherhood, an almost passionate seriousness, the selflessness of socialist man."[51] Obviously, these mesmerizing beliefs made it impossible to see anything other than our own spellbinding in the Other. At that very moment, hundreds of thousands, if not millions, of Chinese were being killed, massacred or deported on the orders of the Great Leader, as the Chinese Communist Party revealed several years later. The shock of this discovery would have been comical if the European intelligentsia had not drowned out the cries of China's martyrs with its shouts of praise, thereby making itself an accomplice to the crimes committed. It made no difference, since those who followed a phony dogma could paint their cartoon-like version of China at a time when the Middle Kingdom was being put to the sword and the torch. They drew a picture of a perfect nation with no crime, no poverty, no madness, no sickness,[52] and even no dirt.[54] It was a place where the blind could see, the deaf could hear, and, of course, the mute could speak, as if it were the steps of Lourdes.[55]

China became the poultice for the wounds of a world in convulsions. Once and for all, China put an end to unnatural distinctions that led to oppression by the powerful. In Peking, as in Tirana,[56] the New Man was supposed to have sprung forth—the Total Man who was the resolution of all contradictions,[57] free of the selfishness and mistrust of those who live in the West.[58]

China was the invention of total otherness, of absolute newness. The usual obstacles of the human condition miraculously disappeared there, and the impossible became possible. Thanks to the application of Mao Tse-tung's thought, a peasant could become a surgeon, a worker an atomic physicist, an illiterate could write poetry, and the masses themselves showed enough genius to deny that competence, work, and study were of bourgeois origin.[59]

When he came back from the USSR, Paul Nizan confided to Sartre that the best people there were still afraid of dying! This astounding statement was a harmless revelation compared to the oceans of stupidity and dishonesty spouted by armchair Maoists during the 1970s. Not since the days of victorious Stalinism had intellectual bankruptcy been so strong among those who wanted to deceive us into believing the same illusions about the Red sunrise that filled their own hearts. And whoever doubted that the Great Helmsman was leading a billion earthlings to heaven could only be in the service of the CIA.[60]

The sons of heaven in the Maoist pantheon had two contradictory qualities. They represented the best of mankind—they were saints of the human race, the supreme state of devotion. But they also were the manifestation of a difference so fundamental that they were not subject to our judgments and criteria. These two opinions constantly intersected in the panegyrics the brave French mandarins gave about "the promised land." For instance, if someone found that sexuality in China was repressed, it was supposed to be a mistaken perception, because the Chinese are asexual.[61] Did the reeducation camps look like the Gulag of Stalin? There is really no comparison;[62] freedom is a Western idea that the Chinese have never shared.[63] You can never understand China if you persist in looking at her with European eyes.[64] You see, the Chinese mind is a mystery that is inaccessible to our crude senses.[65] The Chinese are not like other people; their minds work differently. The proof is that they can do without the costly safety measures that we have in our factories in the West.[66] Does China seem austere to you? This is because you have been corrupted by your European taste for luxury, because China is a happy place, and the Chinese sing from dawn to dusk.[67] Besides, it's really very simple—the Chinese are angels,[68] and they have in them "such a sum of virtues that it makes your head spin."[69]

Far from representing a realistic alternative for our own societies, the Maoists' utopia was simply an extension of their childish urges. The disdain for mere facts was necessary for this enthusiasm, since what people saw in China was simply what they had imagined in Paris, Rome, or Berlin. They presented themselves as hard-headed materialists, but the worshippers of Peking

were benighted by the most vulgar sort of idealism. They swallowed the lies of Maoist propaganda with relish because, for them,
slogans had long since taken over from reality.[70] This is why, as
a former devotee reveals in a striking self-criticism, it was not
even necessary to understand the thought of Mao to support it.[71]
Abstract, bloodless belief had no need of the test of reality to ad-
vertise itself. China itself was the last thing the "pink guards"
(as Claude Roy aptly calls the Maoists) cared about. Their pseudo-
fraternity scarcely concealed a blatant dislike of the Chinese people themselves. The search for a perfect social order based on the
principal of all-or-nothing led them to submit not to nothingness
but to something even worse.

The Iranian revolution represented the second type of this
addiction to exaggeration, in a minor key. It broke out at a time
when the enthusiasm of many Third World-worshippers had been
cooled by numerous disappointments. The major leftist newspapers—Le Monde, Libération, Le Nouvel Observateur, Le Monde
Diplomatique—were very wary of it. They had long seen the dangers of an explosion, and were laudably perceptive of its religious
dimension. These things had a noticeably dampening effect on the
zeal of the faithful, and from the very beginning, reduced their
credibility.

Still, from the first days of the Iranian uprising, there was a
little contingent of believers who were enthused by the most questionable demands of Khomeini's partisans. They hailed insurgent
Iran as the Persian version of Nasserism and of the great Arab
nationalist revolutions, particularly that of Algeria, by linking the
deep feeling of the "Community of the Faithful" with the political
importance of a nationalist rebirth. Above, all, though, the Iranian
revolution represented for them a negation of the purest kind—
it was not just a revolt against imperialism or capitalism, but
against the entire West as a cultural entity. They admired Iran
because it opened a third way, and because it showed neither of
the two signs that, for us, signify revolutionary struggle—class
struggle and the presence of a guiding party, or avant-guarde.

Finally, though, there was a revolution that did not obey any
socialist or Marxist criteria. The Iranian phenomenon was so foreign to Western values that it was hailed as the new rising tide
that would effortlessly sweep away the rotten fortifications of the
Northern hemisphere. The old man who marched with head held
high and hands empty against a corrupt monarch and the strong-

est army in central Asia represented the victory of good over evil, the infusion of the spiritual into the political world. The timeless vitality of Islam showed itself unexpectedly there, so after that, some people attributed the overthrow of the Shah to sacred values. The word went out and spread quickly. The rioting vandals of Teheran, Tabriz, and Isfahan were honored as a "symbolic challenge to the whole Western value system," as Baudrillard called them.[72] Others portrayed Islam as "the great healer of wounds and disappointments that carried out a rejection of what was useless, the forced and the falsified."[73] "In Iran, Islam embodied an identity murdered by invasion, oppression, and falsification," the latter word, of course, denoting whatever was Western under the regime of the Shah. Blessing were heaped on "the ability of a spiritual morality to overturn what appeared to be the strongest state in central Asia, and the refreshing renewal that it inflicted on the part of strategic hegemonies and the falsehood of modernity."

Islam's nature was judged on its hostility to us and was welcomed for it, as if the criteria for a movement's authenticity consisted of its being anti-Europe.[74] Because they hate us, they must be right. In fact, being anti-European is the only merit the Khomeini regime can be granted and, because it had this highly prized characteristic, more than one observer in France applauded the taking of hostages in the American embassy in November 1979. What a wonderful coincidence that the revelation of truth coincided with anti-imperialist struggle! And even if the prophet from Qum did turn into a dangerous visionary, the terrorism of his troops could be perfumed and forgiven in the name of the just struggle against the wealthy, American imperialism, and its Jewish helpmate, Zionism.[75]

In Iran, God took a stand against America and charged Khomeini with making this known. Even though things were not turning out as expected, the verbal diarrhea of justification was flowing. The more outrages and massacres the Imam's torture squads carried out in the name of Allah, the Merciful, the more commentators in newspapers and magazines tried to persuade us of the tolerance and humanity of that Islamic religion, while minimizing, passing over, or pardoning the liquidation of whole national or religious minorities.[76] The fanaticism and chauvinism of the mullahs were applauded because we were their target.[77] The peoples whom the Iranian nihilists in power terrorized, impris-

oned, or tortured were considered expendable, with good reason—
it was Iranians and not we who were paying the price for this
extremism. Thus, we could discern in Shiite Islam an enormous
subversive force that was capable of rocking the industrial world
on its foundations. The "friends" of the Iranian revolution were,
in fact, the enemies of the Iranian people, just as China's friends
had been her enemies in the past.

The Narcissism of the Left

What looked like an opening to the outside world was really a
terminus. Another boundary line had been drawn between the European intelligentsia and the rest of the planet beneath the deceptive and misleading promise of communion that it had trum-
peted loud and long. Between 1960 and 1980, it appeared that the
Left in the West had acquired a voracious curiosity about the rest
of the world and took joy in all the corners of the earth. However,
this really amounted to nothing but a fascination with itself. Just
like a father who projects failed hopes on his son, the Left was
fascinated with a false pluralism, a false idea of the Other that
covered up its own intellectual poverty. There really was a Third
World, but it was just a reflection of the one we had devised. A
devilish game of mirrors and reflections led the Western ego to
puff itself up and raise its voice every time it pretended to express
humility. Third-Worldism was thus a political counterpart to the
emotional disconnectedness that for so long had been condemned
by moralists—a love in love with itself, a self-satisfied love incapable of attaching itself to a specific object.

Like the dandy Raymond Roussel, who sailed around the
world without ever leaving his cabin, the Third World-lover col-
lects riots, rebellions, and revolutions, but the price of this orgy
of accumulation is a lack of real experience. The actual differences
in customs and people involved are much too much a part of the
real world, which the Third World-lover wants nothing to do with.
Real "Otherness" asserts that one's relationship is with a social
reality infinitely distant from one's own, without the relationship
narrowing the distance, or vice-versa.[78] Rather than follow this,
the exotic Left gained nothing from the Third World it did not
already have. This politics of the ideal demonstrated an intellectual laziness whose only aim was to preserve the socialist utopia

in its most childish fantasies.[79] Such was the sort of intellectual gymnastics to which the Left devoted itself for almost 20 years—affirming the existence of foreign nations, but at the same time denying their independence of action; imagining a Third World exists, but denying it the privilege of its own history; and, once again, confirming its victory over the Other.

Because it possessed the key to everything, the Left could simultaneously satisfy its desire for clarity and manipulate the oppressed like marionettes. The Third World nations had only one useful purpose, being hostages, and it functioned as those summoned to be unwilling guarantors of a promise they had not made. We used them as a means to an end, and were not at all aware of their uniqueness and differences from one another. By baptizing the Algerian FLN as "the only organized force of the French Left," and the Palestinian fedayeen as "the vanguard of the world Revolution," we appropriated movements that, in the words of Jean Daniel, "had never promised us anything,"[80] and had not undertaken their rebellions for our pleasure. Since the Third World-worshippers wanted these liberation fronts linked to themselves by an unspoken tie, they spoke about themselves as if they were the future of the worldwide class struggle. The Southern hemisphere was already a vast source of raw materials for multinational corporations; for part of the Left, it also became a gold mine of illusions, the incarnate enthusiasm of a new dawn for mankind.

A Don Juan syndrome—when a man casually drops one woman as soon as another seems more exciting—was at work. This kind of syndrome starts out with a sincere desire for universal brotherhood. This leads to enthusiasm for revolutions in other lands; but these are disappointing. Hopes are switched to other areas; but these are dashed. Faith is then rekindled, followed by more romances, and yet more betrayals.

A comic opera of infatuations and breakups made Third World solidarity one romantic disappointment after another. Each country proved exceptional in some way, but it was only a transient version of the chosen one that, time after time, betrayed our confidence. African country or Caribbean island, poor or overpopulated, black or yellow, they all had one thing in common—the duty that our love imposed on them. A few years and a few massacres usually were enough to destroy our illusions, which led to their reincarnation somewhere else. What was adored in one country soon fled, only to appear in another, and then pass to a third. Does

this mean that those wondering fans of the Revolution were fickle? They were not even that, because being fickle means becoming tired of a person who does not change. However, they have
always been faithful to the unfaithful creature who betrayed their
affection. In each place they thought they saw a new version of
their beloved. But quickly, too quickly, they sensed that the spirit,
the ideal to which they swore all their vows, had secretly deserted
an imperfect regime and stolen into some other one.

> To see the creature who has hitherto been perfect, divine, lose un
> der your very gaze the divinity which has informed her, grow com
> monplace, turn from flame to ashes, from a radiant vitality to a
> relic, is anything but a pleasure for any man, and has been nothing
> less than a racking spectacle to my sight.[81]

Such intellectuals were always in love but never satisfied, and
were obliged to seek infinite variations in search of the right partner, ravishing the earth in a frenzied race. They were fickle only
because they had no one to be faithful to, and their cosmopolitanism was joyless, barely concealing a nostalgic nationalism. Their
affairs were pushed to the ends of the earth until, finally, there
was not one virgin country left to woo. Vietnam has been plunged
into the iron fist of bureaucracy, Cuba is a base for Soviet imperialism, and China is revealing the atrocities of its cultural revolution. The world no longer has a single ray of light to shed on
our benighted senses. Nowadays, underdeveloped countries are
portrayed in terms as dismal as they were brilliant just a short
time ago.[82]

Non-European continents have entered into a melancholy decline. We are suspended between loyalty to old orthodoxies and
new beliefs. All the emotional investments of the past are losing
value. In the past, the fact that a person was foreign was enough
to ensure his being praised, flattered, and intellectually lionized—
as long as, of course, his country was in style at the time. Snobbery, fashion, and faddism had to be taken into account; these
things are healthy after all, and they clear the air. Not long ago,
people swore by Peking, Hanoi, and Havana. But even while Kabul
is still in demand, the overall market value of Third World stock
is definitely dropping.[83]

It had been too good to last. Proliferating, pullulating solidarities wrought their own ruin. The abundance of support groups,
appeals to the emotions, indifference to facts that were manipu

lated according to the demands of the faithful, and the tendency to parade outrages to strike a sympathetic chord all had the final effect of turning Third World solidarity into overinflated puffery. Rhetoric that multiplied illusion by illusion ended up with nothing but illusions. The conscience inspired by solidarity ended up dying of indigestion after overeating. The ability to make distinctions, the miraculous capacity for moderation, were missing. And the marriage made in heaven turned out to be an abominable mistake for which both partners refused to take responsibility. We had solemnly committed ourselves to a task of universal brotherhood, but this was to avoid the pain that real contact with a foreign culture would have provoked.[84] It was doomed from the start, and all the high-flown propaganda could not cover up the vicious narcissism that was the basis of our concern. The idol-worshippers declared their idol to be supreme, and whispered to it: "Don't do anything. You are perfect." We infantilized the Chinese, the Cubans, the Vietnamese. We treated the Indians as inferiors and diminished the South Americans by attributing our own motivations to them. We refused to grant them the most basic freedom—the freedom to make mistakes, to be guilty in their turn.

The Days of Atonement

The long litany of bitterness, disappointment, and betrayal that has confounded the creed of Third-Worldism is well-known: the Chinese-American rapprochement at the height of the Vietnam War; diplomatic relations between Peking and Santiago after Pinochet's coup d'état; the Ethiopian revolution and its waves of liquidations; the intervention of the Cubans in Angola and against the Eritrean guerillas they had previously supported; the genocide in Cambodia; the flight of the boat people from the shores of Indochina; Muslim fanaticism in Iran; and the civil war in Lebanon. All these events punctured once and for all the illusion of worldwide reconciliation. The romantic Left has paid a high price for its disregard of details. Its taste for absolute ideas was cruelly mocked and manipulated by the regimes and states that bent its rhetoric for their own purposes. In its enthusiasm, it had so systematically shaped people and things to its own convenience that it took a long time to realize it had made a tragic error. But it became clear that the Left put much more stock in the purity of the people of the Third World than they did themselves. Bitter and disappointed, the former allies became carping critics, and transformed the lake of genius into a sewer, detailing with cynical fascination all the failures of their dream. And because resentment is all the more fitting when a promise has been broken, the display of all the failures of the Third World became an occasion of obscene jubilation. Those who had made up far-off utopias turned and suddenly became mournful catalogers of the hell that the tropics had become.

This was the agony of a solidarity that had been a trap from the very beginning. Scarcely 20 years passed between its high point and its decline. A child who, at age 10, had watched the first demonstrations for Algerian independence, entered his prime without the fervent belief he had had as a college student that Algeria was laying the foundations of a brilliant future. Many intellectuals were disenchanted after the war in Algeria, finding their expectations and hopes thwarted by the realities of the newly independent country. This should have put a damper on future messianic beliefs. As it had done to the FLN through the agency of chiefs of staff and foreign countries, the West continued to settle scores with itself by reducing others to the level of tools in its own civil warfare.

This led to the brutal about-face of the leftists when their exotic playthings disappointed them. Their excessive sympathy carried within it the indifference that inevitably followed at the end of the 1970s. Revolution or oblivion—this was the stark choice set before the downtrodden, an all-consuming act beside which nothing else was important. Our intoxication, therefore, became maudlin. We had guzzled the wine of brotherhood until we were drunk, and then awoke with a terrible hangover. We had gone to bed at night with a beautiful woman, and at dawn awoke beside a hideous hag who exhaled a repulsive breath into our faces. Thus, solidarity was two-faced—it was faithful until it came time to be unfaithful. It wanted to be insatiable, always leading to yet more passion and closeness. It was a dizzying spin that ended because of its own frenzy.

Following the initial mindless declarations of brotherhood came the disappointing listing of crimes. After adding up his conquests, Don Juan added up his failures. A romantic disillusionment followed from the failure to find a single cause of justice and the need to apply a different kind of analysis to each country. There was no longer an inner harmony or marriage between the great struggles going on. What was false in Europe was true in Latin America. Reagan, the oppressor of Nicaragua and El Salvador, can be seen as an ally against the Russians in Poland. The mechanical phrase-making of the propagandists has given way to the remorse of former lovers. They see the ghosts of the countries their excitement had successively idealized, and they are embarrassed by their mindless love affairs. Their disenchantment has turned to anger and, rather than blame themselves, they blame the countries they once adored by turning their backs on them. They have blamed the objects of their affection for their own sins. Although it is their own fault, they put the blame on the shoddy goods they bought. They see themselves as victims of a plot, whose trust has been abused.[85]

Clearly, the Third World is like a woman blamed the way Eve was in the Bible. Full of illusions, Westerners imagined that they had pierced the wall of hatred and contempt erected during the colonial era. But that was an illusion, because self-preoccupation was its integral weakness. Every day a new god was worshipped, new values were declared as certainties, but they changed immediately. The worst sort of moral relativism—one that negated historical thinking, as well as the timeless accomplishments of mankind—was endorsed. The great causes that once filled the boulevards of European capitals with hundreds of thousands of young people now inspired nothing but a shrug of the shoulders. As soon as the Third World refused to be oversimplified, we turned away from it, frightened by the complexity we saw there. Yesterday's sinner swears that he will not be taken in again, and viciously tramples underfoot the false symbols of fellowship.

This is what caused the terrible silence of the Left toward the butchery in Cambodia, the exile of the boat people, and repression in China, which were denounced only by individuals or private organizations.[86] What is astounding is the contrast between the clamor of yesterday and the supineness of today. There are no more demonstrations, no more marches, no more analyses—nothing. Our erstwhile fraternal nations have been wiped off the map.[87] Aside from the continuing warfare between the Israelis and the Palestinians that was renewed by the Lebanese War in the summer of 1982,[88] every country in the Southern hemisphere is a matter of supreme indifference. What could concern us less? China leaves us cold, Cambodia frozen, India stony, and as for Albania, it is as if it had never existed at all.

We are not so much disengaged from the countries them-

selves as from the socialist ideology of which they were supposed
to be the most vigorous offspring. Because we merely looked at
our own reflections when we turned the mirror toward China, Angola, and Vietnam, we are really only damning our own reflection
when we attack these countries today. Our neurotic devaluation
of anything Western has changed into a systematic phobia against
anything that is not. The upheavals of the world, the continuation
of flagrant injustices, the continuing impoverishment of destitute
countries, the wanton slaughters committed by many governments—all this leaves us cold, impassive.

Our lasting bitterness is in direct proportion to the depth of
our disappointment; the glamorous and feverish tones of the years
of enthusiasm have given way to the lukewarm murmuring of "the
orphan years." Now that we have cooled, we have the wisdom of
old age, which is really clear thinking that can no longer do anything. We have come to terms with the follies of our youth, even
though some of us still have a feeling of affection for these shameful episodes. Depressed intellectuals now swear that they will
never again be deceived into supporting "crazy niggers," "yellow
devils," cigar-smoking dictators, or emperors in Mao jackets.
After discovering a distressing capacity for cruelty among their
own countrymen, they have to recognize the same propensity
among those they once praised to the skies.

So now there are no more obligations, no more duties to be
fulfilled to these far-off capitals where life is degenerating into
misery, anarchy, and repression. The Chinese, the Indians, and
the Lebanese are still my brothers in the sense that we cordially
share approval of the chasm that separates us. Our friendship is
above all the mutual recognition of the distance between us—
everybody in his place, and no more intermingling. Third World
worship, for all its outrageousness, gave men an opportunity to
meet one another, even if they might quarrel. It made friendships
precarious, because they were based on misunderstanding, but it
made them possible. It made people say "we" even if it did not
make this "we" into a magnification of "I." This is why, the more
serious it became, the more it isolated countries from one another,
separating races, temperaments, and cultures that thought they
were thereby overcoming their solitude. But in spite of its universal message, it proved incapable of making a link with the outside world. Friendship was subordinated to strategy, and the
guerrilla was only a fellow traveler. As soon as a fork in the road
was reached, friends were dropped.

Yesterday's true believer, who suffered from farsightedness in that things looked better the farther away they were, has now joined the myopic masses. For him, as for the great majority of the French, Spanish, Germans, and Italians, the order of the day is that of the followers of Raymond Cartier, who believe we should help the Correze before the Zambezi. Of course, the true believer no longer seeks to foist this truth on the Other, because now he cannot tolerate the existence of the Other as such. He has set up a barrier between himself and "them" that is stronger than one built by greed or imperialism—it is one of indifference. Now, awareness of the Third World wallows in a morbid fascination of continents that are falling apart. And a negative sympathy—one that derives from suffering and pity—grows. We lower ourselves through contact with the pain of the Southern hemisphere. We have passed from sloganeering to commiseration.[89]

2

Pity; or, The Gushing of the Ghoulish West

A young woman is irritated because she has leaky shoes. If I say to her, "What difference does it make? Think of the millions of people who are dying of hunger in China," she replies, "They are in China. It's my shoe that has holes in it." But here is another woman who is weeping about the horrors of the famine in China. If I say to her, "What difference does it make to you? You aren't hungry!" she will look at me with hatred and say, "My own comfort means nothing."

Simone de Beauvoir, *Pyrrhus et Cinéas*
(1944),
Gallimard, collection "Ideas," p. 236–237.

Perhaps it is time to recognize in hypocrisy not just an ugly fault of human nature, but the deep contradiction of a world that is attached both to prophets and philosophers.

Emmanuel Lévinas, *Totalité et Infini,*
The Hague, Martinus Nijhoff, 1971.

Two thousand years of Original Sin have ended up making you guilty accomplices.

Henri Corbin, quoted by Darius Shayegan.

The Celluloid Famine

The Eye of Cain

Not long ago, the following scene took place: Families are sitting down to dinner and watching the news on television. Their plates full, they start to eat. The anchorman appears, and begins a discussion of a serious problem—world hunger. The camera pans to the uttermost depths of the world. From the intrigue of international politics, it moves abruptly to poor countries who bare their breasts and display their running sores.

The Horsemen of the Apocalypse arrive in our homes in the form of crying children with bloated bellies who stare at us with a look that pierces our hearts. Or perhaps as a West African peasant plowing a few acres of millet and peanuts with a kind of timeless poverty that only seems to get worse. Or as a strikingly beautiful but horribly thin mother and her baby dying of starvation beside a highway in Cambodia. Or as a little girl wandering naked across some landscape; nearby are the corpses of her parents, who have died in the night and whom no one will bury. Or as a mutilated body lying on a sidewalk in San Salvador or on a roadside in Guatemala; or a corpse rotting in a ditch in Chile, or tortured remains washed up on a riverbank in Argentina. Or as rows of men with hands behind their heads, lined up against a wall in front of soldiers with automatic weapons aimed at their hostages.

The camera moves and shows poverty-stricken cities in Africa, the Caribbean, the Middle East, or Asia, where sickly children grow up amid the pestilential stench of swamps, surviving on the flesh of rats they catch or garbage they find. It is a nonstop display of weak, undernourished people, of crumbling hovels sinking into the village muck that bore them, of lumps of humanity surrounded by garbage, whose horizon is a sewer and whose food is carrion. The eyes of these living corpses accuse us—their stares are a verdict that orders us, secure and sated,[1] to respond.

These starvelings are an irritant; their repulsive condition will ruin our dinner. Why do they put such horrible programs on television at a time when Frenchmen are eating? Suddenly, we are made responsible for a responsibility that is beyond our consent and, so, are put in an impossible position. We can no longer argue that we were blissfully ignorant, because now we know.

These images clearly describe the failures of our age. Their horror leaves no place for hope. Rather than broadening human possibilities, the dying hundreds of thousands in the Southern hemisphere defy the plans of others with their endless agony, deflating the values we hold dearest, ridiculing the greatest scientific and artistic achievements of the international community. We feel that our moral faith in mankind will not recover from this wound. And, because every day the media give the human race the knowledge of its own misfortunes, an apolcalyptic vision of the universe begins to spread. By setting forth daily the balance sheet of suffering around the globe, radio and television networks give our planet a terrible image—that it is unquestionably the worst of all possible worlds.

The Great Leveling

Suddenly, the picture on the television screen changes. A flood of news drowns out the famine in West Africa, the skeletons in Uganda, the slaughter houses of Phnom Penh. The diners resume eating, comforted by the trivial problems of the state budget, suburban juvenile delinquency, and the rehabilitation of prisoners.

A cycle is at work here. Imperceptibly, the horror diminishes, our nerves are dulled, and the intensity of our emotions is calmed with the babbling of the tube. The technology of the media has brought trouble to the center of our serenity; but it dilutes it, just as it aroused it. By bringing other peoples into our homes, it offers the illusory reflection of a common humanity with our neighbor. The reflection accuses us, but we are not harmed by threats made by a specter. The television screen makes a display when it purports to communicate, and in this way the rest of the world penetrates our lives without doing any damage.

The intermingling of our private lives and the destiny of the world always ends up diminishing the latter. And the functioning of the media requires this, so it would be wrong to blame the television watcher for a fickleness that is only partly his fault. Good newsmaking is not just covering a story, it is straining for something new every day. What is newsworthy is defined not just by what is presented, but also by its freshness. Thus, facts compete to drive one another out. A conference on disarmament cannot simply follow a report of famine in Asia—it overwhelms and supplants it. What follows something becomes the thing that replaces it, and chronological continuity is lost. From the perspective of the media, every story is of equal value.

That some things are forgotten is a necessary counterpart to the attention we must pay to the succession of news. Of course, there is outrage against the media when they present a horrifying scene. Showing emaciated bodies when Europeans are eating dinner verges on bad taste. It is a hole pierced unexpectedly in the deadening drone, an act that invades a world already saturated. But even such a trenchant piece cannot escape the impotence inherent in the media. The evil effect of television, newspapers, and radio is that they juxtapose facts in such a way as to neutralize them. Advertising spots, government decrees, distant wars, massacred minorities, royal marriages, the birth of quintuplets—the topics overlap each other. The most abominable acts are swallowed into the same torpor as the silliest clichés. One display of horror in one time slot is not going to break through the solid facade of our surroundings, and the anxious embellishment of others' sufferings ends up melting into journalistic somnolence.

As careful observers, we are always distracted from one image by the next, but no trait distinguishes one from the other. The high-opera litanies of apology and the repeated monotony of their prayers dramatizes the status quo. The media bring far-off catastrophes into our lives, but with a trivializing force that swallows up even the most shocking events. Every night, the television-watcher discovers a new crusade that soon relegates the previous one to oblivion. After the scenes described above, it should have become impossible to live and eat as before. The vision of pain should have left some trace, a tiny scar. But the worst outrages breed acceptance after a while. New ones do not disturb our daily lives, and the most monstrous stories come to us with the stamp of yesterday's news. On the little screen, horror becomes digestible, and is no longer capable of surprising us. There is a conflict between the message and the media that broadcast it, and television itself is the best antidote to the mobilizing power of its images.

Insignificant Overstatement

Let us suppose that a particularly heartrending report stayed with us after its time on the screen, and that it was not swallowed up in the ocean of forgetfulness. What happens then is what leftists call "consciousness raising."[2] A curtain falls away from our minds; a veil of ignorance is torn aside. We have been moved. Will we act on this emotion? What can we do?

How can the anonymous television-watcher, lost in the suburban masses or a small town, know what to do once he has turned off the set? Certainly, he has felt compassion at the sight of these miserable people. It is also certain that this compassion is tinged with fleeting shame. But what comes after this attack of guilt? To what extent can the TV-watcher feel concerned with problems that are 6,000 miles away, among people with whom he has nothing in common? With his feet in suburbia while he thinks about Addis Ababa, how can he persuade himself of the necessity for worldwide solidarity? It is a dream of vast dimensions. What relationship can the TV-watcher possibly have to those savage, hairy creatures who just paraded before his eyes—the Indians, Malians, and Guatemalans scorched by the sun, bound to the grudging soil, and subjected to the brutality of policemen or soldiers?

The result of all consciousness-raising campaigns is that one knows more and more about something without being able to do anything about it. The goal is the eradication of famine, an objective so vast that it is impossible to take a single step in the right direction. Writing a check seems ridiculous. This, in turn, requires journalists to try to shake loose our selfishness through hyperbole on two levels—that of the viewers and that of the images they see.

One message has to come through everything we see, with total clarity—that our own comfort is an abominable privilege. We are damned by aged children with matchstick legs in Calcutta or Karachi, and by the subhuman creatures in Dacca or Bamako. While we are stuffing ourselves, others are dying of hunger. Our stomachs are filled with food we have taken from them. "It seems that we daily steal the bread from the mouths of the poorest of the poor."[3]

Statistics pass judgment, too: 462 million people are underfed and 560 million are living in a state of abject poverty. Every day, 16,000 people around the world, mainly children, starve to death.[4] These deaths are our fault, "for the sole reason that we have not done everything we could to succor them."[5] "What is going on in the midst of our monstrous indifference? The greatest genocide in the history of the human race, which every year kills more people than Hitler or Stalin did in their concentration camps. . . . But taxes, government takeovers, the stock market, and the price of gasoline are much more important, because they directly concern us. What a disgrace!"[6] Jean Fabre tells us that "The world we live in is a gigantic concentration camp,"[7] where every day is a "permanent Buchenwald". The time of retribution is at hand, and it is not possible that such an outrage go unpunished. Under the rags of the hungry lurks a guerrilla who some day will make us pay for our shameful prosperity.[8]

It is impossible not to feel as if we are being measured by a superhuman standard, not to feel unworthy and defensive in the face of this great testimony of tragedy, whose rituals take place in the narrow confines of a television set or a newspaper column. We behold a Golgotha of suffering, and we are the direct accomplices of an economic system that pillages the resources of the poorest people of the earth.[9] Witnessing crimes like this, the television-watcher can hardly help thinking he is as guilty of mass murder as Goebbels.

To convince the skeptical, the media stop at nothing, and the excesses of exhibitionism are added to the accusation that we are worse than the Nazis. The camera shrinks at nothing, and no censorship can be imposed upon horror. Every image must shock by crossing a new frontier in outrage. We are invited to watch the extraordinary, that which has never been seen before, and then we see even more than that. Famines, floods, earthquakes—all get instant replay for the cameras. It is celluloid suffering; a continuous stream of images flows from those who produce pageants of others' deaths for a worldwide audience. It is a pornographic display, in that it gives us the right to see everything. And of all our impulses, the only one it stimulates is voyeurism—because the producers believe that, in order to get people's attention, the show has to be increasingly crude. The aim becomes that of showing mutilations, torture, and sicknesses that have never before been seen on the television screen.[10] It is not enough to show swollen-bellied children; they have to be displayed as skeletons. If this doesn't work, they are shown as a bundle of skin and bones. Blood, wounds, running sores, globs of pus, eviscerated bellies, spilled guts. . . . Only excess will shake up the public and concern them with these problems. If apathy persists, it is believed it is because the scenes have not been outrageous enough. There are no limits to the excessive display of grisly details.

This leads inevitably to the perversion of voyeurism. We get a taste for this game, and want more and more, and our threshold of tolerance gets higher and higher. We no longer seek to be shocked, just surprised; every time we want something more disgustingly juicy. The shock value of the news comes to be independent of the truth of what it says. The unusually scandalous is thought of as better than what is true. The only thing that counts is impact, not influence.[11] We no longer care if the pictures have anything to do with real people, we just want them to be more revolting, and the worst is the best.

The cataloguing of poverty is itself poor, and has to rehash the same figures constantly. We have been brought face to face with hell, but all excesses have a saturation point, and after months and years of this sort of experience, we inescapably are led in our disgust to lump together the people these images depict. Our shock has no consequence, no result; it appears and vanishes at the same moment. In this morass of disasters that are supposed to preclude business as usual, how can the viewing public avoid getting lost? The media succeed in making us indifferent to things over which we have no control, in making tolerable the intolerable. We go through opposite experiences at the same moment—we experience horror in the form of epidemics and mass murders at the same time that we experience satiation, because we cannot take any more and these images are unbearably repetitive. Value judgments aside, there are the two impressions that linger with the viewing public: a slight feeling of nausea and a feeling of shame and frustration.

At the beginning, these broadcasts are special, but they quickly become routine. Their violence becomes stale and their repetitiveness reduces the strength of their accusations. So overtaxed emotions lead straight to inertia. In a world where all countries seem like a nightmare painting from Hieronymus Bosch, in which men become more and more sophisticated in their murderous cruelty, our sense of guilt goes from depression to lassitude. The abnormal becomes banal, and our reason no longer tries to express itself, but "insanity rationalizes," in the apt phrase of Günter Grass.[12]

The result is a terrible paradox. *The more widespread hunger is, the greater is our indifference to its ravages.* Pathetic appeals to our conscience and manipulation by shock are reiterated by the tireless television. The phrase "You are all murderers" does not mobilize people, it makes them yawn. What remains is a guilty conscience that has no strength and no will. We have passed from being tragically ignorant of the Third World to being tragically inured to it. When it was not normally mentioned, famine was deeply touching whenever it was. What is remarkable today is that it is too well known, too much a part of the norm. Rather than a blackout there is a welter of studies, statistics, and calls to alarm on these burning topics. Our emotional appetites are beset from all sides, and rather than being misled by propaganda, we are being told far too much.[13] When catastrophe becomes an everyday thing, it ceases to be catastrophe.[14]

The Calcutta Syndrome[15]

The Best of Intentions

As soon as poverty is seen in real life—on a trip to the crowded tropical lands of Asia, rather than through the filter of television—everything changes. You leave home full of respect for these people, promising before you set out that you will avoid any emotion of dislike, any of the aftertaste of colonial arrogance that white tourists feel when they set foot in a far-off land. As soon as you arrive, you are seized by astonishment and fear. The streets are endless streams of pedestrians, a pulsating swarm of people passing ceaselessly to and fro, in which every face looks like every other. No one looks at you, each goes his own way, as if concerned only with his own fate, and you feel like a specimen from another world.

Buffeted by a flood of people with whom you have nothing in common, you come to understand the reaction of the Englishman a hundred years ago, who did not dare go out in the street in India for fear of being drowned. This human stream ebbs and flows but never dries up, and it reduces you to an infinitesimal spot.

After a while, you get used to it. You are less afraid of dying of suffocation, and your eyes begin to notice the variety of customs, the different kinds of faces, and the dilapidated buildings that drip condensation in the humid heat. You walk around the piles of garbage, and step across the open drains filled with slime, and over the countless children, old people, and adults lying on the ground, sleeping no matter what the time of day and in spite of the stench and noise and stifling heat. Resolved to facing this tireless flow of people, you begin walking. Right away, a one-armed man and a crowd of children surround you and beg you to give them something. It is terribly embarrassing, for they kiss your feet and point to heaven, doubtless promising you the greatest blessing in return for a kind gesture. You have been warned beforehand—if you give away one penny, you will never get rid of them. What obscene advice! There, before you, are people whose suffering is real, for whom this day may be the last. How can a person value his own well-being when so many people may not see tomorrow's sunrise? You cannot avoid seeing the shocking degradation of victims such as the legless little boy who rolls along on a little platform on wheels and propels himself by pushing against the ground with little irons he holds in each hand; the handless baby held up by a half-blind mother; the leper who holds out his ravaged limbs. You cannot refuse them.[16]

You know some parents deliberately mutilate their children so as to inspire more pity in the passersby, but isn't such despair itself proof that there is no hope? Of course, this cluster of beggars plays its role a little too glibly, babbling formulas in broken English, French, and Italian that sound like so many routine incantations. But what poverty-stricken person would not emphasize his distress to move people more deeply? Besides, this is no ploy or sham—you are in the presence of something intolerable, and the intolerable is destroying itself. So you give a couple of coins to one of them, some cigarettes to another, and you let a little shoeshine boy clean your spotless sandals. And then you go on your way, dazed by the scope of the thing, torn between disgust and terror. How can the rich people of these countries remain impassive in the face of such suffering of their fellow citizens? Your gift was only a drop in the bucket, but at least you have given these skeletons some sustenance. And you pat yourself on the back at the thought of the thanks these poor people will surely express if they see you again in the street. The knowledge of terrible social problems that affect the country has not kept you from giving in to compassion. And you recall the statement from Mother Theresa:

> Someone once asked me if it was better to provide hungry people with fish or fishing poles. The people who come to me are sick or dying. They are so weak that they cannot hold a fishing pole. They must be given the fish first; maybe the fishing pole will come later.[17]

Face to Face with the Unbearable

Your elation evaporates a few hundred yards farther, where you
see more beggars who are just as pitiful—some are waving their
amputated limbs, displaying their inventory of sores and ulcers;
some are girls of fifteen nursing sickly babies; some are half-
naked and whining boys. You suppress a feeling of irritation and
give again, and mentally run through the causes of this suffering—underdevelopment, overpopulation, the latest war, the lingering effects of imperialism, the unfavorable balance of trade,
the irresponsibility of the ruling classes.

The next day, you have scarcely left your hotel when once
again you become the center of a dance of supplication in which
the same people as yesterday have joined with some other brothers in misfortune. The sharp cries of the beggars, the scores of
hands pulling at you, force you to take notice. You protest, "But
I gave to you yesterday!" They all respond with big, delighted
smiles; even though they do not understand you, they are sure
you will give in. These poor devils have to eat every day, and the
rupee you gave away yesterday was spent long ago. You have put
on old blue jeans and a tee shirt so that you won't look like a
tourist, but it seems that the natives do not see the difference.
Your body is pleasantly plump, and every ounce of you is worth
its weight in firm, springy, well-fed meat. You can feel the smooth,
tender curves of your body. Overcome, you look in your pocket
and push away an old man who was about to kiss your feet. A
policeman armed with a long bamboo stick sees that you are beset
by these creatures and roughly drives them away. You are crushed.
He brutalized sick people, children and women, for the sake of
your comfort, you frivolous, spoiled brat. In just one moment,
you—an activist of the Left, a smug defender of human rights—
have become an accomplice to an act of oppression. You remon-
strate with the defender of law and order who is on your side; in
his mind, you should thank him for what he did.

You walk quickly away, deeply troubled. After that, you are
on the lookout for any kid, any crouching figure that might beg
from you. When you hear the rattles the lepers shake to attract
your attention, you flee as if from the devil. Your eyes cannot see
the milling multitude; the colors of the robes, the turbans, the
saris, the pajamas; the tailors who ply their trade on the sidewalk;
the peanut vendors; fruit-juice sellers; candy merchants; astrolo-

gers; and fortune tellers. In this beehive of activity, you see only destitution, guile, and survival. The whole country exudes the same hideous anguish. You make up your mind—you will go to the train station and buy a ticket out of this city as soon as possible.

You were going to wait for a while in the shade of the immense Victorian-style dome of the station, but as soon as you get inside, you feel as if you have entered the uttermost pit of hell. You have to catch your breath twice, because the stench here is the worst of all. The railway-station hall is a gigantic dormitory. Here, the suffering are not just little groups scattered in a crowd; they are laid out, row upon row, on the bare cement. There are far more of them than there are travelers. Creatures are lined up in rags made of bags and cloth, with arms that are eaten away by gangrene and repulsive pustules sticking out.

You walk uneasily past these prostrate figures, as if you were walking in a swamp, and make your way to a ticket window. Bodies are strewn about like damaged goods, as if waiting along with their emaciation, eczema, and lupus for street cleaners to sweep them up. It is impossible to tell if they are living or dead. Nobody pays them any attention. Occasionally, their eyelids open slowly, and their huge, deep, and empty eyes, surrounded by buzzing flies, stare at you. Around them lie others, convulsed by fever into twisted postures of collapse, too weak even to beg. Farther on, a group of children has collapsed on the ground, without the strength to sit up.

It is a kingdom of beggars, bags of bones, hair, tiny arms, and shriveled legs. It is an entire race of crushed, reviled, beaten down remnants, and this tide of flotsam begs you, calls to you, pulls at you, but so weakly that you push them aside with a simple movement of your foot. The waiting rooms are filled with people sprawled out on the ground, beaten down by fatigue, and obsessed by the desire to sleep so that they will not feel their hunger. Cockroaches run around on the dirt, unafraid of this human baggage that is breathing its last.[18] You stop, decide not to spend hours waiting in line, and retrace your steps slowly, even though you would like to run as fast as you can.

Outside, eager to get back to the comfort of your hotel, you take a taxi. But the cab gets stuck in some suburban traffic jam. The landscape around you is flat, relieved only by hillocks of filth covered with crowds of half-naked children sorting through them. Big vultures circle in the sky, stirring the stinking air with a rustling sound, and occasionally diving and fighting with the children over a piece of food. Bony cows with scabby skin browse among the garbage; behind them, two women carefully collect their thin dung, molding it by hand into fuel.

As soon as they see you, the children leave their smoking piles of trash and run to knock on the window of the taxi and ask for a *paisa*. The driver tells you not to give them anything. You do not know what to do, and quietly pray for the traffic jam to clear. A mass of little hands, resolved not to let go until you give them something, grasps at your collar. Your white shirt is now covered with black smudges. This little mob would not be so frightening if there were not a pair of watchful eyes in each of the emaciated faces. Their consciences devour you, dissect you, with a lingering stare of hostility and hatred.

Finally, the taxi moves. But the ugly scene worsens. Some children are still holding onto the windshield, the roof, the door handles. You have to get rid of these kids. The taxi accelerates, then brakes brutally. The children's grips are broken, and they are thrown to the pavement. You close your eyes in disgust at yourself. In a few minutes, you have committed all the misdeeds you once thought only the worst racists were capable of. When you open your eyes, you see the refugees from East Bengal camped by the thousands beside the main highway, in sewer pipes and on the ground, where they have been living for eight years without water or toilets, inundated by mud in the monsoon season and crushed by heat the rest of the time. Through the clouds of dust and trash, the whole city seems ruined, reduced to the degrading chaos from which it sprang, with none of the luster and dignity that antiquity is supposed to confer on even the poorest buildings.

You retreat to your hotel room and have a healthy slug of whiskey, "feeling a voucher of outrage."[19] You are all ready to talk forever about the appalling social situation in Bengal, to cry scandal, to swear that the proper authorities should . . . etc., etc., etc.

Back in France, while you were watering your plants or percolating a pot of coffee, the television showed children torn apart by mines, political dissidents tortured, refugees piled into junks and sunk and drowned along with their property, the victims of a storm or of pirates who sank their boats after stealing everything they had. You could believe it as a story, and only had to push a button for the nightmare scenes to stop. Here, though, misery pervades the very walls, the air you breathe, the horizon all around you, and forms the very substance of the city. The luxurious hotels and the well-guarded villas are isolated citadels surrounded by wretchedness and suffering. And at any moment, you expect the door of your room to open and let in a host of cripples, wretched starvelings, and maggot-ridden women to take over the space you unjustly occupy because you are rich.

Hot and Cold Emotions

The next day, your fears have subsided. A change begins to take place in you. You could go home to Europe, but you refuse to give up. There must be a way out. Perhaps you have been too emotional. Because you know that every day will involve a long, stubborn, unavoidable encounter with horror, you work out an ingenious way to protect yourself from the aggressive masses of humanity. You conjure up a bedside alter ego, another you whose job is to soothe your conscience and bind up your wounds. This double calmly provides you with a thousand justifications that contradict one another, but whose bad faith preserves your integrity:

1. All these people have to do is work; there is so much to be done in this country. They are lazy.
2. It would be an insult to their dignity to give them money. It would be a humiliating disservice to them.
3. Charity sacrifices the future for the present—it leads to a hopeless situation, and holds back the enactment of continuing reforms that would create a world of friendship between men.
4. My money would only be a drop in the ocean of poverty; besides, real charity is not fulfilled by a mere gift. If I gave to them, it would really only be to give myself a clear conscience on the cheap.
5. They have never known anything but starvation, and they are more used to it than we are. They should not become accustomed to luxury, because after I go away, their situation of want will be even worse.
6. We cannot take the place of their societies, and it would seriously damage their sense of national independence. If the local leaders do not do anything, it is because they have good reason.

7. Should I suffer, just because someone else is suffering?
   And, last, but not least:
8. All they have to do is make a revolution. In their place, that is
   what I would do.

Deep down, your fault is not that of being rich, but of having
all the exterior signs of comfort without having the feudal mentality it should entail. Your mistake is in not believing in the doctrine of predestination and natural inequality that is held by the
castes and upper classes in India.

From then on, armed with these certainties, you walk
through crowds of beggars as if they were an irritating mist, and
hold your nose so that you will not suffocate. But you are far from
being totally hardened. At least once a day, you give away money—
to a little girl whose big brown eyes and beautiful face have moved
you, to a leper whose humility and reticence make you favor him
over his clamoring and pushy fellows.

Your arbitrariness amazes you. You are irritated when you
give, and when you do not. You had promised yourself that you
would be firm, but a passing emotion makes you give away a few
rupees to one or the other. And then, when some more little brats
implore you, you chase them away. Why do you give to one rather
than the other? Because if you gave to all of them, you would
never stop. This continuous poverty is exhausting, and makes you
impatient at having to feel endless compassion. Pity needs to be
relieved.

These poor people with their empty stomachs, the little girls
who sell their bodies for a crust of bread, do not see it this way.
They make a mockery of your theories. They are so defeated that
the very idea of revolt is meaningless. They want immediate relief. They do not even ask for the right to live, only not to die just
now. Each one seems to protest—why should I be the one to die
of hunger? Because they are the ones sacrificed, they die in angry
astonishment. We feel hunger as something unpleasant, but for
those who suffer from it, it is a crime. Getting rid of everything
you have would only keep these wretches alive for a short moment. Only men with a burning selflessness could give up their
lives entirely to succor those who are suffering so. How can we
not admire those missionaries who have decided to live only for
others—which means not living at all? How can we not rejoice in
their giving of themselves, even as we regret that we cannot do

likewise? You are neither hero nor saint, and as Pascal would say, each of these orders has its unyielding demands.

There is no antagonism between those beggars and you; rather, there is a gulf so wide that it precludes any sort of human relation, even that of rebellion. All desire for rebellion left them long ago. They do not want to change by one iota the merciless social system of India. They are sinking wrecks just holding on for a while before they go under. This beggary is a system that degrades both the supplicant and the giver. If you do give, it will never be enough; but if you do not give, it is a demonstration of sordid miserliness.

The fact that we are alive while they are in agony makes us all guilty parties. Whatever is done, it will not be enough. The coin that is furtively slipped into an alms bowl does not satisfy a need, it creates two guilty people. You open yourself to condemnation at all times. If you refuse to take a rickshaw, you will be depriving a coolie of a meal. (Calcutta is one of the last cities on earth where transportation is provided by human beasts of burden.) Take the rickshaw, and the frail man whose life expectancy is no more than thirty years will exhaust himself in getting you where you want to go, bathed in sweat and gasping for breath for a few rupees. Whatever you do, you will have contributed to suffering, and whether you are involved or not, poverty traps you. When you multiply it by the number of people involved, it goes far beyond the boundaries of the fantastic and the incredible. No matter how you look at it, it is a permanent monument to the degradation of man by man.[20]

The disintegration of the person in these tropical climes is pushed to a point we can hardly imagine. There is always something worse. Beyond the lepers, the lunatics, the shriveled children are yet more fantastic degrees of degradation. There are skeletons dressed in strips of cloth who drag themselves along the ground and crippled monsters who, wriggling in the filth and rolling in the slime, gnaw at roots and eat what other people spit out. The more miserable they are, the more despicable. Can they really be human beings? Or are they just a sort of undifferentiated brown matter that comes out of the earth, oozing and begging, and then goes back to the earth without our noticing? Your reactions to the "dirty wogs" are exactly the same as those of your forefathers, whom you so berated. Bodies tortured by the most primitive forms of fear, suffering, and hunger end up leaving you cold. You start out ashamed of your privileges, then change into a typical colonialist of the old breed. The flashy leftist front you carefully kept up for years crumbles to the ground in 48 hours.[21]

Suffering Becomes Invisible

From then on, you put aside these abominations, and separate yourself from that world. The extended experience with horror that takes you to the outer reaches of a deranged universe leads to a psychological divide. The poor become invisible. Your left eye sees rags, amputated limbs, sores, and fleshless coolies; your right eye erases these images and sees pedicabs, temples, colors, and smiles. You are like the policeman in Edgar Allan Poe's "The Purloined Letter" who is looking for a letter that is right before his eyes but which he does not see. The visible becomes invisible to you, and you look without seeing. The macabre is so close that it is concealed by its own impact and becomes simply part of the landscape, and the nearness of these martyrs ensures that you will ignore them. Faced with such depths of suffering, you have only one choice—to go away or to distance yourself from it.[22]

Do you become a different person? No, but you know that, in this country, there is a whole category of people with whom you will have no contact. You can invoke "the people" as an abstract category, as the mother lode of revolution, but with these people, your ideas are useless. You used to be a communist, or a socialist, or simply a believer in democracy—and you still are—but these categories do not apply to the country where you are. Before you came here, you were told to live here in poverty. In what kind of poverty? That of the shopkeeper, the peasant, the untouchable? The differences in degrees of destitution are so vast here that to choose poverty is itself an option born of luxury. You ought to have plunged yourself into misery, lived in a slum, to embrace the nightmare wholeheartedly.[23]

You cannot feel fellowship with these people. To be honest, you feel more at ease with the most hateful Europeans or local bourgeois than with the poor natives. In private, or with other tourists, you can indulge in verbal diarrhea, but when you are face to face with a beggar, your rhetoric catches in your throat. You no longer have a choice between selfishness and generosity, but between the discomforts of refusing to give and of giving alms.

Whatever you do, you must rationalize. The disparity between their situation and yours is such that, no matter how well-meaning you are, you must ignore the calls for help, you must prevent them from registering on your ears or eyes. You must temporarily put aside your leftist sympathies, because the intellectual construction of this position has nothing to do with the present situation. Inequality existed long before you arrived, and it has predetermined your place and that of the natives. You can only be excluded from this world, inevitably. You can show compassion, help someone in need, avoid stepping on the dying, refrain from pushing aside the clusters of beggars that attach themselves to you, gently detach the skinny hands that grasp your clothing. But you cannot escape the self-deception, the indispensable sleight of hand that you need to adopt.

Of course, it's reassuring that you are not the only one to blame, but this does not absolve you. Garbage soils all it touches, obliging part of the human race to live in degradation and making the rest accustomed to living side by side with outrage without caring. It evokes horror and makes you immune to it at the same time. How can you be happy when there are people suffering all around you? By means of a schizophrenia that sidesteps evil. A screen is placed between what you see and what you think, and a filter keeps out unpleasant images.

The curtain has fallen for good, and even though it might open a little from time to time, because of the knocking of some fleeting expression of misery, that only confirms that it is closed. From then on, you pass through the wreckage, step over the human infections, pass by charnel houses and morgues without it affecting your mood or your appetite. Your assimilation into the ranks of the guilty and your random contributions to one beggar or the other become the very stuff of your passivity. There are some places on earth where there is no place for your humanity.

Face to Face with Our Own Past

Why don't we travel more? Why do so many of us refuse to go overseas, beyond the borders of Europe? Because of a fear of confirming what we vaguely suspect—that the hatred we may feel in North Africa, the Middle East, or Latin America, in the muck-filled and disease-ridden sewers the cities of these countries have become, is a hatred for our own concealed origins. In Europe, we are the spoiled children of development that caused fearful suffering in the people who contributed to it. We are the heirs of a history of sweat and blood, but today we see only its fruits—fruits that are sprouting from a hill of corpses.

Not long ago, the West too was a gigantic manure pile where miserable insects crawled while the tiny class of rich people arrogantly displayed their luxury. Hunger was a serious problem in Western Europe until 1955 and in Eastern Europe into the 1960s. Visiting an Eastern or North African city reminds us of something we have forgotten—that developing capitalism was like a steam roller. The vagabonds, serfs, lunatics, and migrants whose uprooting in the eighteenth century was described by Karl Marx in the first chapters of *Capital,* those dispossessed and torn loose from the family ethic and old rural loyalties, are the background against which our industrial societies are built. Our present comfort required atrocious exploitation and boundless oppression. *We are disgusted that we have come from such origins.*

In the exploding shantytowns of the Third World, we can read the calligraphy of our own history. Walking the streets of Dacca, Bombay, Jakarta, Manila, Marrakesh, or Bogota, we see before us the roots of our own civilization. We see a live performance of the novels of Hugo, Dickens, and Zola, with characters of flesh and blood for our terrified appreciation. All the literature of the nineteenth century, which was nothing but a long commentary on the degradation of millions resulting from the initial stages of industrial development, can be found in these cities in real life. The beggars driven from their villages, used and exploited lumpen proletarians breathing their last breath in some pestilential mine, working themselves to death for some pitiful wage, could be our own ancestors.

The glorious Western World was built on a nightmare, with a foundation of corpses. This is what the poor of the Third World whisper to us: Our own culture dons the exotic mask of dehumanization and accuses itself through them. It is the image of our own origins, and is the chasm into which we ourselves could fall if, through some misfortune, our wealth were to disappear. Never again, says the traveler to himself, because he needs to forget what he saw. And forgetting is his only way of preserving his innocence in a world saturated in reproach. This is the only way a person can become a journalist, businessman, political activist, orientalist, or globetrotting tourist—by becoming a professional in the art of selective vision.

From Accusation to Absolution

*"Your prosperity in today's world has
the same effect as a natural disaster"*
—Paul Claudel.[24]

It is well-known that today the inequality between industrial and developing nations is far greater than what existed during the most severe period of formal colonization. The countries of the Organization for Economic Cooperation and Development (OECD) benefited from the rapid economic growth of the 1950s and 1960s and achieved a level of wealth not known by most of their inhabitants ever before. Although they were interdependent, the relations between the countries of the two hemispheres were already out of balance before the two petroleum crises of the 1970s widened the gap geometrically.[25]

According to the extremely optimistic projections of one economist in 1971, it would take the Third World 270 years to catch up, even with a rate of growth higher than that of industrial countries.[26] Essentially, this means that the gulf is unbridgeable. It is precisely because the Western World has taken off from the same level as other countries that this gap troubles us. We have the feeling that we have not been faithful to the pact of poverty that dominated all great civilizations until the eighteenth century and that indicated there was not much difference between the France of Louis XIV, the England of William III, or the Prussia of Frederick the Great, and the India of Aurangzeb or the China of Kiang Hi. For the first time, something rudely disrupted the balance of scarcity. The West broke the rules of the game and gave all other societies an impossible but inescapable choice—be economically subjugated or enter into the spiral of industrialization.

Since the beginning of Europe's transformation, all the age-old civilizations have been deeply shaken and feel obliged to redefine themselves accordingly. The West freed the genie from the bottle, imposed its developing frenzy on everyone else, and called their way of life into question. Even more than technical reasoning, the West invented the most formidable idea of all—modernity. Modernity is a solvent force that is obedient to a logic not so much of imperialism as of challenge. Modernity issues a summons none can ignore. It is not linked to the possession of property so much as to endless experiment. It differentiates between developed and backward people, an incontrovertible categorization that is not a function of its content, because its content is always changing and the meaning it has for people changes from day to day. This leads to an abundance of strategies for dealing with it, including the ironic injunction that other cultures must fight the West with its own weapons.

The postwar generation in the West, no matter what the social class, was born to relative abundance, a source of both shame and pride. Their wealth was a miracle, but a scandalous one, because it left the Third World so far behind. This is how good luck strikes amid misfortune. Even if there is no clear connection between our wealth and their poverty, even if the economists are still in disagreement as to whether Europe's industrial takeoff was based on its own resources or on the pillage of the colonies, it is clear that the millions of impoverished people at our gates inspire a certain unease, even among the most hardened of us.[27] We belong to this small fraction of the human race who, for about a century, for its exclusive benefit and thanks to its technology, has enjoyed the untouched mineral and agricultural riches of the world. We feel all the more the victims of our wealth because it has come between us and others who are destitute.[28] All of us—bourgeoisie, salaried workers, unskilled laborers—are pampered and privileged in comparison with the downtrodden of the tropics.

What's more, the speed of communication and instantaneous worldwide broadcast of events via the media have given rise to a catastrophic vision of the world. Of course, there is no more anarchy, massacre, famine, or upheaval than there was in previous centuries, and our age has no monopoly on mass murder, but knowing about it and "living in a world that is more visible to itself in all its aspects than ever before"[29] deprives us of total ignorance. Because we have to live side by side with the suffering of others, our happiness today seems less certain, our surroundings less secure. Purges, plagues, arbitrary imprisonments, and hundreds of thousands of refugees reduce the scope of our own social problems to minuscule importance. The fact that there are almost three billion people in the Southern hemisphere multiplies the quantity of injustice to colossal proportions.

Our means of communication make contact easy, but produces shock and anxiety. The intermingling of the hemispheres makes comparison possible, and provides a measure of the gap between us. Third World poverty is scandalous only in light of our own comfort, and someone who is deprived cannot see himself as such except in relation to someone more fortunate. Just enjoying relatively better luck puts us in debt to those who are poorer.

The World of Infallible Logic

For the prophets of guilty conscience, the tireless sowers of discontent, this disquiet is not enough. They need to make us responsible for everything that goes wrong. Their trick is to confront us via the media with all the suffering of the human race, in the face of which the slightest gesture of generosity is an inadequate act of charity.

This accounts for their ceaseless and frantic recourse to their favorite weapon, statistics—a veritable secular weapon of sin, a perfect arithmetic club. We are beaten with figures so monstrous, quantities of suffering so enormous, that we hardly dare breathe. The panoramic road show of worldwide suffering has come knocking on our door. Everything is reduced to a sum of afflictions, in the face of which our existence seems obscene. Here are some examples:

In India, somebody dies of tuberculosis every minute.[30]

One Frenchman consumes as much energy as 46 Nigerians, 20 Indonesians, 10 Ecuadoreans, six Algerians and three Iranians.[31]

The inhabitants of the wealthy countries, thanks to their buying power, give almost as much grain to their animals as the amount eaten by all the inhabitants of the Third World put together (not including China).[32]

The landless peasants of the Third World have less disposable income than a cow in Normandy, a pig in Brittany, and a house cat in Paris, and, therefore, are less well-fed.[33]

Throughout the world, reason is stultified along with brotherhood and dignity. Narrowly perceived group interests are more important than the general interest, and thus sow the seeds of bloody confrontations and condemn a billion human beings to living on a yearly wage that is lower than what some spoiled brats in our country spend in a single weekend.[34]

The price of a night in a hotel room for American tourists in Cancun is equivalent to twice the annual wage of the average citizen of Bangladesh.[35]

In California feed lots, 100,000 steers being fattened eat 1½ million pounds of corn every day, which would be enough to feed 1.7 million East Africans, or almost the entire population of Zambia.[36]

When I eat a half-pound steak, I could feed 30 people with the protein that was used to feed the animal.[37]

If you take six hours to read this book, by the time you have turned the last page, 2,500 people will have died of hunger or of hunger-related disease somewhere in the world.[38]

What is our wealth, in short? "A sort of economic Nazism created by a master race of the wealthy, who reign over a mass of undernourished people."[39] After this, how can we fail to see ourselves as monsters devastated by shame?[40]

These are fallacious comparisons, of course, because they always fail to mention the different levels of industrialization that by themselves explain the huge differences in consumption between countries. When socioeconomic conditions are radically different, precise figures lose all validity and serve no purpose other than for slogans and reproaches. But there is no value in pointing out the uselessness of this quantitative overkill. Excess is the enemy of precision, and overstatement is deceptive. Overabundance of numbers becomes the rule, and indignant speeches answer with millions of starving people and contemptuous citations of the record books, where the number of hungry people is listed alongside the largest number of sausages, the longest kiss, the highest hairdo, and so on. These statistics pretend to be encyclopedias of suffering, packages of agony,[41] and the officious indicators of one sole message: We are all parasites and cannibals.[42]

Suffering humanity is placed on a scale and, on balance, the West is portrayed as worthless. Our way of life is put in numerical terms in order to ridicule it. The reasoning behind our scolding

Third World-lovers is that, the less we suffer, the more we must feel responsible. An elaborate, ramshackle, logical system that tries to establish a causal link, no matter how far-fetched, is set up between myself and this suffering. Highly technical explanations are worked out to demonstrate that, in the final analysis, it is still Europe that pulls the strings.[43] It is like the world of a detective story, the infallible deduction that unravels the problems of hunger like Sherlock Holmes:

> Who is guilty of these massacres that fill the morgues of the Third World every day? Is it mere fate? Are these men, women, and children the victims of uncontrollable and recurring natural disasters? No. For every victim, there is a murderer.[44]

Thenceforth, all of us, young and old, are at fault for what goes wrong on our unhappy planet.[45] We are participating in the destruction of the world[46]—from agricultural breakthroughs to woodcutting technology[47] to female circumcision.[48]

The West is the great and only guilty party to all the evils of the world. In sum, we are inhuman and criminal because we do not want others to exist,[49] and the causes of famine lie before us on the dinner table.[50] It makes no difference that this accusation cannot be proven. Guilt is an easy way of bridging distinctions and doing away with intermediaries, because it draws a pitiless red line between their poverty and our sated appetites. Remorse comes *before* wrongdoing, because our error is not in sinning but in existing. The mania of suspicion makes us guilty before the fact for the disintegration of Ghanaian society, for empty stores in Angola, for the rising prices in Central America, for clouds of locusts in black Africa, for hurricanes in the Caribbean, tribal warfare in New Guinea, and so on. Every study, every book on the Third World, whatever its subject, says the same thing. The guilt of the accused is confirmed, and more evidence is accumulated against him. They are like a storekeeper's books, where the long list of the evils of the Old World is neatly spelled out, while the merits of the Southern hemisphere stand out from the details of an implicit frame of reference that is never questioned. They are an exercise in malediction, which is supposed to make our horror grow as it convinces us all—salaried workers, professors, lawyers, laborers, truckdrivers—of our fundamental thievery. The reader himself is a convenient scoundrel. . . .

Obsessive repetition takes the place of a concern for precision, because we have to make our own breast-beating offering for the suffering of the world. Duty, that nameless and insatiable goddess, conducts a Kafkaesque trial against Europeans. This is the bad faith of bad consciences—unable to give solace for one scourge or another in any real way, we accuse ourselves of being the cause. The old relationship between colonizer and colonized is endlessly atoned for, and we search for aftereffects of imperialism everywhere. We can thus mortify our flesh with delight because we know how rotten we are.

The conclusion is that our very existence is an insult to the human race. We have only one duty—to wipe ourselves off the face of the earth.[51] The future of the West is self-destruction.

From Guerrillas to Baby Seals

That is the wellspring of this religion of compassionate sympathy, which strives to outdo itself with regard to everything that lives, suffers, and feels—from West African peasants to baby seals, to Amnesty International prisoners and fur-bearing animals that have been skinned to warm the shoulders of elegant ladies. The glorification of benevolent impulses is "an instinctive morality that has no head, but appears to be composed only of a heart and helping hands," as Nietzsche said. It is a glorification chanted day and night by the media, press, politicians, and literary and artistic personalities, and it wallows in the most bastardized form of Christianity.

This religion of affliction says that you have to suffer from life as if it were a sickness. As long as men are dying, children are hungry, or prisons are full, no one has the right to be happy.[52] It is a categorical imperative that imposes on us the duty to love man in the abstract, preferably when he is far away. Exactly as Jesus said that the poor are our masters, Third-Worldists make the suffering of the countries of the Southern hemisphere into a kind of virtuous model. These tropical lands are beloved because of their failings and their want, and hunger and evil are simultaneously fought, but subtly enhanced. This is the deep ambiguity from which the Catholic Church has never escaped, and it is the same one that contaminates all organizations providing assistance to the Third World. Even where suffering does not exist, it has to be created, and where it exists, it has to be accentuated. Everywhere, the worship of doom requires that we uphold the principal of universal human suffering. Of course, epidemics, wars, and millions of children with empty stomachs are intolerable, because my fellow man is my brother. But such pain is also necessary, because a world without misfortune is one that has taken the place of heaven.

In this way, people are put in the service of the poor, but also in the service of poverty, of sacrifice itself. There must be homeless people and orphans upon whom our liberalism can be practiced, to remind us constantly that "my Kingdom is not of this world," and to make all joy suspect.[53] As appeals for solidarity are made, the blows of misfortune are celebrated, because they are pretexts for humility. At a time when the Church, through its most qualified spokesmen, is questioning the ambivalence of Christian charity,[54] it is the laity—usually Marxists—who are reviving its most dubious reflexes. To take the most oppressed as a measure, as our good Samaritans do, is to imply that suffering and death are not just failures of an unjust worldwide economic system, but are also part "of the immemorial drama of our relation to the Creator."[55] It means that, far from being abominable and outrageous, the oppressed embellish and typify the human condition.

This bottomless pit of suffering[56] becomes the tribunal, the supreme court that admonishes the privileged and leisured members of the human race. The fact that people are wallowing in rags and mud strengthens the indictment of silk and ermine. The intolerable disorder of the world is constantly underlined, the eye of an avenging God is cast on it, and He watches over it and endlessly enumerates its weaknesses and faults. The West is satanized and the Third World becomes fixed in its role of the persecuted, the better to show that no compromise at all is possible between them, aside from the infinite repentance of the West.

With a remarkable talent for spotting every ethnic group, or others who have been subject to persecution in some way,[57] the world is searched for sadness, bad luck, and misfortune. An obscene joy lists the millions of alarms ringing in the world, and a sort of morbid delight is taken in the systematic ruin of the thousands of forms of life on the globe. Such liberals are like hemophiliacs in love with human suffering, ready to bleed for any cause; they are the professional mourners of modern history. They have no sooner dried their tears when a new subject for lamentation makes them start weeping anew.[58] Failures and distress are collected because they serve as a clear warning—*you have enjoyed yourselves too much,* you have wasted too much. You must prepare yourselves for abstinence,[59] chastity, and a return to the land. Hunger in the world is the punishment for our European sinfulness. Supermarkets, naked women, homosexuality,[60] paper money, Coca Cola—all these are the corruptors of the healthy young of the underdeveloped world.[61] The theme of atonement used to be one of the political Right, but it is now that of the Left. It is a miraculous reconciliation of the ashes of Marshal Pétain and Lenin's tomb under the patronage of a weeping Jesus Christ of Naples.

The Burden of the Professional Mourners

Supposedly, we do not have the right to rest "as long as a single child continues to suffer,"[62] because our moral monitors have ordained that we take on the whole human race as our responsibility. We must give up family ties, friendship, and nationality so as to honor only the universal figure of suffering Man.[63] Any struggle against oppression becomes my struggle.[64] It does not occur to our good apostles that there is no common denominator to these conflicts and that justice varies from one country to another, depending on its context.[65] I am supposed to extend myself everywhere, and in the same day I am supposed to mobilize for Nicaragua, the guerrillas in El Salvador, mutilated Moslem women, and vivisected cats, dogs, and mice, without forgetting the latest strike in a Parisian factory or some demand students have hurled at their professors.[66] Everything concerns me, and I must put myself into the midst of the welter of dying, suffering, agonized people, those in protest, the misunderstood, and the weak. All the world is my garden, and I must tend to it. I embrace the whole gamut of affliction around the globe, in one oceanic and inclusive emotion. I am the Christ bearing suffering humanity on his shoulders. I am a soldier of famine and a soldier of God. I indignantly refuse all thought of private pleasure. I will be on alert till the end of the world. I am a hero of unselfishness.

We cannot pretend to imitate Jesus. People exist for us only in situations where we encounter them. Of course, in all our actions the rest of the world is somehow involved and the extent of our responsibilities is related to the dimensions of our actions. But certain people need help from us right now, because they are our neighbors, and their expectations define our priorities of action. Even if every enterprise is ultimately tied to the rest of the human race, our solidarity is primarily local or national. What relation is there between a taxi drivers' strike in Marseille and a demonstration by peanut farmers in the Ivory Coast? What do roadblocks put up by wine growers in southern France have to do with the struggle of Arizona Indians against the U.S. federal government? The situations are not interchangeable. If you try to be everyone's neighbor, you will end up as nobody's neighbor. For me to proclaim my solidarity with the sufferings of the human race, to give up friends, relatives, and fatherland for some vague universal feeling of sympathy, is literally a mockery. It is impossible to escape one's time and country with a wave of the hand, and the attempt to assert world citizenship carries with it its own failure. An overblown conscience is an empty conscience.

Passive Pity

The cowboy humanitarians know all this. What they aim to do, because they cannot alleviate evil, is embellish the blame. They maintain guilt like technicians who polish and adjust the machines in their care. Their aim is to titillate our conscience, because they would like to see us bathe in remorse like so many French-fried potatoes in hot oil. They refine their invectives and preachments so as to plunge their audience into a despair that is passive, sterile, and unrelieved. There is a reason for this melancholy. There will always be enough sadness, somewhere in the world, for us to torture ourselves over, but this anxiety will never be more than a useless shudder. Compassion ceases if there is nothing but compassion, and revulsion turns to insensitivity. Our "soft pity" as Stefan Zweig calls is,[67] is stimulated, because guilt is a convenient substitute for action where action is impossible. Without the power to do anything, sensitivity becomes our main aim. The aim is not so much to do anything, as to be judged. Salvation lies in the verdict that declares us to be wrong, and this puts everything in its place in the world. What is fascinating about hunger is that it will not go away, and this gives us limitless freedom to berate ourselves for it.

This is why denunciation is the favorite stance of our punitive patriarchs. Everything revolves around the axis of anathema because its attraction is irresistible. It makes little difference if appeals to public opinion produce nothing in the way of action. We must besmirch ourselves with ashes, and the survival of the suffering peoples will follow. The power of a charity drive thus becomes measured by the degree of discomfort felt by those toward whom it is directed. It must evoke in the targeted listener the same reaction as a teaspoon of cod liver oil on a sensitive stomach.

Poor people exist so that the athletes of owing and the martyrs of malediction can work out with their broken hearts and lift aloft their cries of anguish like barbells. The poverty-lovers always need to speak of life and death, and this means that they need miserable people more than anything else, so that they can say that, down there, there is nothing, while up here, there is too much. This is why, wherever there is deprivation, it is called oppression; where there is discomfort, it is called misery.

History is the high-flown recitation of the inequality between the two hemispheres and its redemption. Ours is a light punishment, because we pay our dues for the poverty of the Third World through a guilty conscience; this absolves us from doing anything else. It is understood that we are the accused, who cannot avoid making other people suffer. We dress in sack cloth and parade around, bearing a burden that demands respect. This remorse is honorable, and uplifts us with a glorious feeling of the inevitable. We are guilty, and that means we are no longer responsible.[68]

Down with Meat!

Please do not misunderstand—the right to eat is the most basic of human rights, and hunger is an absolute evil that must be eliminated as soon as possible. Calling attention to the problems of famine in the world can be a good or a bad thing. It can be good if it is practical, precise, and calls for effective action in particular situations.[69] It is entirely futile if it is all-inclusive, and consist of appeals for the immediate eradication of the problem while knowing that this aim is impossible. This is mobilizing public opinion for nothing. Unfortunately, the second kind of campaign is most prevalent, whipping up a feeling of pity that is only rarely the starting point of effective action.

One operation against hunger, set in motion by the organizations *Terre des Hommes* and *Frères des Hommes* in a television broadcast in October 1981, exhorted us to reduce our consumption of meat.

Several types of vegetable protein are necessary for producing animal protein. By reducing our appetite for meat, therefore, we could supposedly allow the Third World, which is mainly an exporter of grain, to diversify its agriculture, thereby escaping the worst effects of the fluctuations of world-market prices. At the same time, this would make it possible to reduce the incidence of the so-called illnesses of civilization—coronary heart disease and high blood pressure—engendered by the high cholesterol content of meat. It was simple—so simple that one wondered why nobody had thought of it before!

Let us follow this valiant crusade step by step.

It began with a careful elaboration of our feelings—we take the food from others' mouths, as Michel Bosquet said, a proposition he also qualified:

> Of course, we are not individually or directly responsible. . . . The theft of the world's food stocks is organized by giant industries, brokerages that have a worldwide scope, oil companies and banks that have never asked us what we wanted. But we are profiting from this theft, and our eating habits show this.[70]

Thus, a pitiless conclusion, as if it were the conclusion of a mathematical theorem can be reached:

> Our poor eating habits result from the pillage of the Third World. Hunger in the Third World is the result of our poor eating habits.[71]

"Hungry Countries Feed Us" was the title of a broadcast on French national television on February 25, 1982.[72]

Fortunately, there is justice in the world, and it calls down on our metabolism the seven plagues of Egypt as punishment for our gluttony:

> . . . dental caries, cardiovascular disease, kidney stones, varicose veins, constipation, hemorrhoids, intestinal cancer . . . which lead to an enormous volume of medical and pharmaceutical consumption (ibid.).

We must correct these excesses, fight malnutrition in the Southern hemisphere, help the poor peasants and, while we are at it, denounce the barbaric practices of farmers, who

. . . imprison chickens four at a time in tiny boxes, and lock up hundreds of thousands of calves in cramped cages during the three months they are being fattened.[73]

These poor animals, too, are sacrificed to the evil god of profit. So all these struggles are part of the same fight. Who is the enemy? Agribusiness, of course, but we ourselves are, too. What is the instrument of our crime? Meat, that dietetic plague, is the guilty party! In *Le Monde*, October 18, 1981, Jacques Grall wrote:

When you realize that it takes six or seven vegetable proteins to make an animal protein, you realize also that, by reducing our consumption of meat, we can reduce the pressure on developing countries, whom we are asking to produce protein.

Later, he added:

It is not a question of declaring war on one crop or another, but of each family realizing that a rebalancing of our diets to include more raw vegetables and fiber, so as to help digestion. These are also ways of reducing the awesome power of worldwide food prices. Aside from programs and speeches, nutrition is politics.

These suggestions invite two remarks. The first is that the slogan "everything is political," from the 1970s, which included every aspect of private life, has now descended to the level of our bowels! Second, if we are to believe our informants, everything goes on as if we and we alone can help the Third World abolish famine, and they themselves are relegated to a passive role. Not only are we held responsible for the agricultural policies of the Brazilian or Thai governments, who have substituted the production of soy beans, manioc, or peanuts for that of rice, potatoes, or onions.[74] We are supposed to believe that the natives cannot solve these problems themselves, and that the solutions are in our hands.[75]

"The off-handed genuflection of the hurried worshipper"
—Gustave Flaubert

The sad fact is that all this information is false. Gilbert Etienne proved this in an article in *Le Monde*.[76] A television station and several major newspapers and magazines mobilized popular opinion on the basis of a fraud. In fact, the whole campaign was ridiculous. There is no need to make reference to the Third World in order to get people to eat less fat, sugar, and calories. The Ministry of Health, ladies' magazines, doctors, and *nouvelle cuisine* (with its penchant for small portions) have been telling us this for a long time. If it is a question of "supporting the peasants and states of the Third World in their demands for more equal terms of trade" we can only agree. If it is a question of reducing our waste of food and the cost of energy consumed in raising livestock in Europe, we can applaud wholeheartedly. But why try to convince people that, simply by reducing our consumption of meat, we can miraculously resolve the problems of underdeveloped countries? Jean Ziegler wrote:[77]

> Hunger is a totally absurd outrage. To eliminate it, all we have to do is change people's eating habits, particularly to reduce their consumption of meat. Westerners would be more healthy, and in the Third World millions of people would finally be able to live as human beings. There is no need at all to realign international blocs or to negotiate new world-trade agreements. A plain and simple consumer's choice would be enough.

Unfortunately for this miraculous solution, seven pages later in the same issue of *Le Monde diplomatique,* a series of articles reveals how a certain African leader systematically stole the funds intended for food aid.

> North-south relations are complicated. For the advocates of increased developmental aid, it would be enough, for example, to set aside a small part of our arms expenditures or end the waste of grain that is entailed by livestock raising, so as to put an end to famine and poverty. This ignores the fact that bilateral or multilateral aid follows a complex route that can generally be described as a transfer of money from the "poor people of the rich countries" to the "rich people of the poor countries."[78]

In other words, the money, gifts, and medicines that you can save on if you eat less meat will go directly to the pockets of the elites or businessmen of West Africa and will not pay to fill the empty stomachs of their own people. This was demonstrated in an article by Jean-Loup Amselle.[79] In their enthusiasm, our gentle vegetarian propagandists forgot one little detail: The Third World is not an empty, amorphous place, but a group of independent states with armies, police, and leaders who distribute food aid as they see fit. Here is the modest admission made by Charles Condamines at the end of his sermon:

> It would be naive, obviously, to believe that a reduction of our consumption of meat would automatically resolve the problem of hunger in the world. But it is true that our system of production and consumption of food creates greater and greater pressure on the use of available resources in the countries of the Third World. What we have to do is reduce that pressure.

But Condamines is seized with caution at the last minute, and slyly inserts a qualification:

> Of course, reality is more complicated than this.

Then he presents five technical details about the production of manioc, and shows how the interests of French and European livestock growers are in total opposition to those who grow grain. The reader shudders—Is this whole pretty argument about to fall apart? Is there no hope for a single front by victims in opposition to their oppressors? Condamines rallies the troops with a firm hand:

> But citing the complexity of things and the contradictory nature of the interests at work is an excuse for doing nothing. Joel de Rosnay said that eating is a form of "everyday voting." Some ways of eating are less oppressive than others.

The moral of the story is presented in the form of a triumphant peroration:

> If we get 100,000 people individually to commit themselves to this kind of solidarity with the hungry of the Third World, we will have achieved our goals. We will have conducted a mini-hunger strike. The health of the French will have been improved, and a great public debate will have begun and the peace of the world will be somewhat less endangered.[80]

What modesty, but what a revelation! All this clamor was to drum up support, to inflate the membership of *Terre des Hommes!* Something has to be done, and it is better to do anything than to do nothing at all![81] Even what Condamines had the gall to call a mini-hunger strike was really just an attempt to collect signatures for his organization.

Here we arrive at the depth of dishonesty, where the worst cynicism joins hands with the most starry-eyed naiveté. What is important, it seems, is to carry one's share of the Cross. Our sympathy is thus a condolence, a sharing of suffering, the act whereby we help our native brothers, by sharing a part of their destiny. This is sympathy through imitation, but only up to a point, because if I follow the advice of this organization, I will eat less but the Africans will still go hungry. Dieting for us and famine for them. These are rites of purification whose usefulness is hard to understand. What is really important, though, is to come to terms with the suffering of others, and even though we never experienced it, if we cannot know what it is like, we can still ape the conditions of poverty.[82] Of course, the hungry will not be fed right away, but this little ritual of atonement will have brought us closer to them. A little self-denial here, smaller helpings of food there, less butter on our bread, one lump of sugar instead of two in our coffee—all these recommendations are reminiscent of the indulgences handed out by priests in the sixteenth century. Our guilt becomes a commodity that can be quantified by the principle of less meat on the table and more grain. Exchange of absolution for eating rye bread, salvation guaranteed! Redemption can be bought with vegetables and fiber foods. Meat eaters are morally inferior, but vegetarians get unlimited credit. Blessed are those who eat bulgur wheat and sorghum, for theirs is the kingdom of heaven! They shall be given soup and meat out of the goodness of their hearts; besides, they shall be blessed with regular bowels! Meat is the root of all the evils of the West, and livestock suck the blood of the earth! But leeks, carrots, and celery will ensure the reconciliation of mankind!

In the old days, children were punished by being told they could not have dessert. Today, the Holy Church prescribes that the vile White Man will be deprived of meat every other meal. This provides us with two types of purge at the same time—of our passions and of our intestines!

Aside from the fact that it is based on distortions, this campaign is faulty on two counts. It reduces highly technical economic questions to questions of individual morality. Then, it releases us from blame by reducing that to a quantitative concept of eating more or less. Just as there are Sunday-morning Christians, these people are steak-loving Third World-lovers. They pay their debt to the Third World by abstaining from eating meat one meal out of three. Thanks to this sort of diet, you can be 100 percent moral while you are eating your soup. It involves a dishonest calculation, but no sacrifice on your part. It is a prudent disposition of sin, an asceticism that is good for us. The perfect health of my organs will go hand in hand with the full stomach of the little Chinamen. This fasting is a blessing. The Great Inquisitor is merciful in the end: We have been scolded, but it was the better to baby us. And in the calm that follows the scolding comes forgiveness. This is how humility and honorable penance become the agencies of deliverance from guilt. Campaigns against eating meat are primarily mechanisms for converting diffused shame into happy self-punishment.

Rhetorical Overkill

This might lead to the accusation that I am being evasive and fleeing the horror for frivolous analysis and hair-splitting, while the urgency of famine calls for action without delay. Not so. If words are to be effective, they must retain some meaning. When words deform reality, we enhance the deformity and reality vanishes. No political struggle can be waged on false premises. The cause of underdeveloped countries will not have any success in the West if it is based on phony diagnoses.

What is the point of complicating the problem with non-existent traits of the Third World, even with the best of intentions? As soon as the Southern hemisphere is brought up, the reality principle breathes its last, and is quickly replaced by incoherent ramblings that insult our intelligence, logic, historical facts, and common sense. Precision is superseded by artificial convictions and slogans prefabricated for any country or situation. The deterioration of hews into propaganda falsifies the noblest arguments, and a host of misunderstandings surrounds unthinking appeals to pathos. Very quickly, ridicule replaces shock, and phony solicitude toward the poor competes with total indifference.

Hunger is enough of a scandal all by itself. What is the point of declaring that we are to blame for it, then offering a vague dietetic palliative as absolution, following some sort of silly catechism? There are two ways of covering up a problem—either forgetting it, or washing it away in a flood of overstatement and confused morality. To deal with the question of hunger as if it were simply a question of moral attitudes is to falsify our choices with a perfumed philanthropy, a magical spell that effectively deadens the conscience. Our primary duty to the hungry of the Third World should be to analyze each situation in its particulars. We should weigh each word carefully, so that we can know the truth clearly and precisely. In moral terms, this means that we have to have scruples.

Defining the Third World

Routinization by Compassion

We all know that newsmaking follows the lure of trouble, and broadcasting means telling about what has gone wrong. The only thing that catches people's attention is dramatic and shocking news, in the form of mass murders or catastrophes. The trouble is that the media also pretend they are presenting what is really going on. They pretend they are showing the real world. This leads to distortion, because people see foreign lands always as if they were full of dissidents fleeing dictators, pariahs, and the sickly. In the public mind forms an image of a world in disintegration, where life can subsist only by some miracle. This deformation of reality is not a momentary lapse or an ideological perversion; it seems to be a precondition for reporting the news.

In the apparent truthfulness of journalism, where there seems to be no trickery or falsification, a subtle process is at work. Cruel and violent scenes shown almost nightly do not simply transmit real famines and obvious suffering. In the guise of facts, they objectify these things, and so a single moment in the life of a people is thought to be the sum of their life. The periodic sufferings of some tropical republic or the seasonal malnutrition of some region in Africa symbolize the constant and timeless anguish of continents beyond Europe.

What can be concluded from these images? They are honest and guileless, but above all they are stereotypes. In their desire to move us emotionally, the newsmakers produce poverty as the single truth of underdeveloped countries, and newscasting assumes the character of testimony.

The image we see, therefore, is both a copy and a model of reality. It reflects real events that are presented as the prototypes of all events. This is a double deception, because the camera denies that life "over there" is anything but a long cry of the oppressed. With regard to our far-off brothers, it means that happiness is a pathological symptom. Compassion is no longer one of the arms of charity, it has become a tool of geography. If, in spite of terrible difficulties, Indians, Thais, Koreans, Angolans, and West Africans feel joy, if those men and women are brought together by laughter and love exactly the way we are, if these people refuse to be defined by our compassionate view of them, it can only be a sign of corruption or of subversion by imperialist propaganda.[83] Man in the Third World is either a victim or a warrior, is caught in a logic of martyrdom or warfare, and has no right to exist except as a rebel or as one repressed. His reaction can only be one of depression or of outrage; there is no middle ground. A happy native is a contradiction in terms, a squared circle. It is much better to depict him as bent down in a valley of tears, and to mourn his loss of liberty by weeping over him. This law of compassion precludes any real relationship with him, and forbids free rein to feelings such as anger, admiration, mistrust, and fascination. It is so much easier to sympathize abstractly with unhappy people, because sympathy with happy people requires more nobility of the soul, because it makes us fight against the obstacle of jealousy within us:

> If man is capable of having compassion for the sufferings of others, only Angels share in others' joys. . . . [84]

The Southern hemisphere is presented in a true, but one-sided way; at the same time, it is raised to the level of a symbol, and this false projection is hailed as a "new" and "revolutionary" perspective. This is defining what the Third World should be, and the act of definition gives it the power of a moral principle, the quality of liberation. So the new crusaders, under the pretext of mobilizing the conscience of the Western World and showing the misdeeds we are guilty of, are pouring out stereotypes that are just as naive as the reports of Loti, Colette, and Paul Morand were in their day. The leftists portray the poor countries in shades just as stereotypically dark as the pamphlets of the colonial era were stereotypically rosy.

Whom are we supposed to believe? The spokesmen of multinational corporations that are quietly pillaging the Southern hemisphere? Or the querulous leftists who value man in the Third World only as poor, crushed, and wretched? Where is the prejudice greater? Is it in the curses heaped on the Southern hemisphere by the adherents of Raymond Cartier, or in the tearful image the so-called sympathizers present? It comes down to asking the far-off "other" what kind of subjugation he prefers—strangulation by neocolonialism or routinization through pity. This is a hopeless choice, and represents nothing but two aspects of the Western imagination.

The Third World as the Turd World

When underdeveloped countries are discussed, the most lurid descriptions are always the most highly prized. There is sadism in pity and an ostentatious pleasure is derived from the pain of others. Asians, Africans, and South Americans are seen in pathological perspective because we can only talk about them in numbers. *They are the masses; we are individuals.* No human quality can be seen in statistics, other than signs of the macabre. In all discussion of the Third World, there is, therefore, the temptation to overstate—statistics are juggled and figures are rounded upward.[85] This is alright, because people are not being discussed— downtrodden and swarming creatures are. To affect us, they have to be lumped together into masses, cut down by the millions. Reduced to the level of animals, the people of the tropics appear to us only as fragments among other fragments.[86]

Before the charnel houses of Cambodia, the massacres in Lebanon, the roads lined with skeletons in Biafra, and the Ogaden, horror negates itself and even the living already show the mute calm of corpses. They are the walking dead, hordes of people destined for putrefaction, whose extermination will make no more noise than the crushing of an insect against a window. Besides, because they are obliged to live off our gifts—what we have thrown away—they themselves assume the status of trash. Whatever method was used to explain poverty—unequal exchange rates, incompetence, the pillage of the periphery by the center[87]—our disdain for the Southern hemisphere is increased as soon as it is encapsulated and summed up in terms of its poverty. The people of these countries will forever be the targets of our generosity, and will not be revealed to us except by their abasement. Beyond the seas, there are only digestive tracts, and the only melody we hear from these far-off people is the heady music sung from Istanbul to Bombay, from Tangier to the Cape of Good Hope, from Panama to Rio—that of begging and pleas for charity. Arabs, Orientals, and Africans are nothing but an immense army of subhumans, the emanation of an abstract and reassuring idea: Indigenous people are indigent people. In other words, *pity becomes a form of hatred when it is the only basis for the image we have of the far-off "other."*

By broadcasting the image of these subhumans who are incapable of surviving without the crutch of our generosity, what is emphasized is their helplessness and our own exquisite solicitude. Nobody can talk about the Third World today without politely thanking the Red Cross, UNICEF, The UN High Commission on Refugees, lay charities, Catholic Charities, and so on, as if these organizations were a summary of the three underdeveloped continents.

To reduce a country to its material poverty, even if the poverty is very severe,[88] is to kill that country twice. Our estimation of a nation is tied in with our capacity to identify with it, to project ourselves in it. But, from everywhere, calls for help are made, and it appears that the task is endless. In this infinity, a definite image is formed—that of a Third World limping and sick, its hand outstretched.

Philanthropy, the appeal to love for our fellow man, has thus become a protective measure that can cover up the cruelest selfishness. One type of indifference is attacked by it, but a more terrible one is reinforced, because it has absorbed criticism without being affected by it. Our sympathy is accompanied by indifference; the sight of misery ceases to shake us, because too much effort at evoking pity ends up suffocating it. Now, horror becomes a sort of sedative, a magic potion that reduces all events to a common denominator. The aim was to provoke a guilty conscience, but this feeling is exactly what subsequently ensures our serenity. It would be dishonest to try to cover up the problems of the Southern hemisphere, but it is stupid to elaborate a systematic view of suffering that seeks to set up a common ground of misery on the despair of little darkies or pathetic wogs. This approach always raises the question in the public mind, "How can they live like that?" And the answer is obvious. They survive in a cesspool because they are part of it, and filth is their natural element, just the way mud is the cradle of pigs.

We Happy Few[89]

Tragedy and poverty have thus become exotic, so that when a European region is poor, it is mentally classified as part of the Third World. Naples, Andalusia, and Sicily have slipped into this category. This is necessary, for on the chaos of the Third World floats the life raft upon which we are rebuilding our identity. We establish ourselves by setting ourselves against their misfortune. Of course, it is criminal to let children in Africa and Asia die of hunger, because their lives are sacred; but their lives are sacred only because they are dying of hunger. They are victims of atonement who restore the harmony of our communities. The abuses that we denounce must be maintained so we can contrive to denounce them. And the more we attack Western democracies, the more they are secretly valued, because the verbal rejection of our wealth rests on the assumption that somewhere else there are impoverished cultures whose frugal lives will redeem our wastefulness, crowds in tatters who will make up for our sins.[90] Thus, our white priests slumming amid the poor believe they are shaming us by bringing us heartrending stories, but they give us cause for secretly rejoicing. Rather than making us ashamed of our serenity, the camera that travels amid the disasters of India and West Africa makes us need to reconfirm it. No matter what the dizzying dimensions of the world around us, the depth of our ignorance, the dangers of future catastrophes, and our individual weaknesses, we are certain that the West is a little island surrounded by oceans of indigence, and is all the more precious because of that. Faced with the lacerations of Africa, the crises of the Near East, and the calamities of Asia, we thank the good Lord that we are French. The horror of the Third World, which is confirmed as bestial in nature to us, becomes the shadowy foil we need to feel good about ourselves. Free men need martyrs like this. The movement that designates them as poor is precisely the same one that prevents us from seeing them as human. They are no longer like slaves of Ancient Rome, or Little Black Sambos, or Viets from French Indochina; they are the dregs of the Third World, and they are all the same. We lament their fate in order to detach ourselves from it a little, and the depths are described in order to make us feel more comfortable in our cozy lives. Blaming ourselves serves two ends; it makes life more pleasant and, in the end, does not touch us.

We dress in our finery and berate ourselves in a welter of guilt, enjoying our peace while we contemplate those poor souls ground down in the heat and the filth.[91] The shame they inspire makes the boredom of everyday life attractive again. The total disorder of the Southern hemisphere makes the Northern look like heaven on earth, which we must keep safe at all costs. The terrifying accounts of deterioration make the West look a lot better. Our happiness would not be so great if it were not for four billion nonwhite peasants beaten down by poverty, just beyond our borders, who make our own successes look both precarious and miraculous.[92]

3

Imitation; or, Getting
High on Paradise

*She was the sister of an English duke, and spent most of her time in
a cell in a Buddhist monastery in Bengal. She seemed not to find it
surprising that all the other inhabitants of the holy place were monks.
She told him that when she traveled, she always slept in the open on
the quay amid the coolies and the street sweepers. She said it was an
excellent way to purify the soul and that, in a few years, she hoped to
rise above all the petty aggravations of existence and attain Nirvana.*

Louis Bromfield, *A Night in Bombay*

*The West has produced ethnographers because it has been tortured by
a deep feeling of remorse, which impels it to compare its own image
with that of different societies, in hopes that they will show the same
shortcomings, or explain how it came to have them. . . . The ethnog-
rapher cannot be detached from his civilization and disassociate himself from its faults because his own existence is incomprehensible except as an endeavor at self-redemption; it is the very symbol of
expiation.*

Claude Lévi-Strauss, *Tristes Tropiques*

*In my case, the effort for these years to live in the dress of Arabs, and
to imitate their mental foundation, quitted me of my English self, and
let me look at the West and its conventions with new eyes: They destroyed it all for me. At the same time, I could not sincerely take on
the Arab skin: It was an affectation only. Easily was a man made an
infidel, but hardly might he be converted to another faith. I had dropped
one form and not taken on the other, and was become like Mohammed's
coffin in our legend, with a resultant feeling of intense loneliness in
life, and a contempt, not for other men, but for all they do.*

T.E. Lawrence, *The Seven Pillars of Wisdom*

83

Two men sat talking on the veranda of a bungalow in the Kyaut-kada district of Burma in 1926. One was an Indian Ph.D., the other an English lumber merchant. As usual, their conversation began with the state of the British Empire. The white man attacked colonials like himself in Asia, accused them of being racist and vulgar, and as his last word on the untimate nature of British colonialism, pronounced that it was interested only in making a profit, not in educating the natives. The Indian was shocked. How could he speak that way about the Empire? The English are the salt of the earth; they have brought culture into the backward Orient. The Englishman interrupted. We are only here to exploit you and to give your country over to gangs of Scottish freebooters. The Indian protested again. His friend was wrong. He was forgetting that Orientals were apathetic and superstitious. Without colonization, they would have remained in the Middle Ages. Wrong, cut in the lumber merchant, the Pax Brittanica was the alliance of banks with prisons, along with the introduction of venereal disease. The Indian interjected that it was the Indians who brought venereal diseases into the country. The conversation went on this way, and it was clear that there was no end to it.

The conversation was imaginary, and took place between two characters in a novel.[1] But this is not important. Whoever has traveled overseas will have had many conversations like it with strangers encountered on the way. The roles have been reversed from what they used to be. It is not a little ironical that, at the very moment when a large part of the world is striving to Westernize, Westerners are laboring furiously to denigrate their own heritage.

Ibn-Khaldun, the great Tunisian statesman, historian, and jurist, was the first man to present a sociological analysis of the fascination that power holds for those who have submitted to it. As he wrote in 1377:

> Those who are conquered always want to imitate the conqueror in his main characteristics—in his clothing, his crafts, and in all his distinctive traits and customs. This is because the mind always sees perfection in the person who occupies a superior rank and to whom one is subordinate. He is thought to be perfect because the respect in which he is held is deeply felt, perhaps because it is falsely supposed by the subordinate person that it is not the natural consequence of defeat but is the result of the perfection of the conqueror. If this false supposition is fixed in the mind, it becomes a firm belief.

The mind then adopts all the mannerisms of the conqueror and tries to be as similar as possible to him. This is imitation. . . . This attraction goes so far that a nation dominated by another neighbor will try very hard to become like it and imitate it.[2]

Ibn-Khaldun was describing, 600 years beforehand, the relationship of colonial culture to that of the colonizers. But what he said could be said in reverse. Europe's naive belief in its absolute superiority to all other cultures could be answered with the belief of many Westerners that their system is worthless. It is as if the only desirable conquests were those in which the native triumphs over the conqueror. The developed countries, having won, suspect that something they are eager to rediscover has been irrevocably lost. The arrogance of the imperialist world, which swept away all taboos and customs in order to establish its supremacy, has become the source of all its ills. What Georg Simmel called the tragedy of triumphant cultures has engendered a nostalgia for the past among Europeans and Americans. Harking back to the Greek influence on Rome, they no longer want anything other than to be conquered by the peoples they have subdued. They are expected to show virtue and demonstrate the qualities of the "Complete Man." Because he has demystified everything, in a wild and uncontrolled career, the Westerner mourns the lost paradise of faith that is in the Southern hemisphere.

The Third World has thus inspired two ideas of renewal. The first is universalist, and sees there the opportunity for a new start for the socialist idea. The second is differentialist, and proclaims that its different ways of life will provide the spiritual cradle where materialistic European culture should renew itself. When subjugated people restore their heritage, they will be able to offer their former masters the opportunity to rediscover their souls. After that, salvation consists not only in a futile exchange of influences, but in the recognition of the superiority of foreign thought, in the study of their doctrines, and in conversion to their dogmas. We must take on our former slaves as our models. It is no longer like Fanon's "black skin, white masks,"[3] but white skin and black masks, Balinese masks, Indian masks, Melanesian masks, etc. It is the duty and in the interest of the West to be made prisoner by its own barbarians. "The primordial phenomenon of the twentieth century is not the revolution of the proletariat, but the discovery of non-European man and his spiritual universe" (Mircea Eliade).

The Return to the Source[4]

In 1944, Somerset Maugham published a curious novel entitled *The Razor's Edge*. The hero is a young American, Larry, who is profoundly disgusted by the First World War in which he fought. He gives up the brilliant career for which his education prepared him. He breaks off his engagement to a beautiful and wealthy Chicago debutante, and goes to live for a while among the Bohemians in Montparnasse. He goes on to spend five years in India in the ashram of a yogi who teaches him the benefits of Oriental meditation. Finally at peace with himself, he returns home to help, console, and reassure his friends, who have all been ruined by the stock market crash of 1929.

The novel was immensely successful, but perhaps its most notable claim to fame was that it foresaw the hippy phenomenon almost twenty years ahead of its time. Regeneration through Eastern culture is an old attitude, which was already very widespread by the nineteenth century; among the Romantics, it became a veritable epidemic. It projected on the East the same kind of enthusiasm Europeans felt toward Greek and Latin antiquity at the beginning of the Renaissance. This taste for things Asian clearly came from the effects of the Industrial Revolution, which upset lifestyles, broke up ancestral customs, and tore people away from the countryside. It communicates the nostalgia of a world in motion for cultures that are static. Schlegel and Novalis, for example, urged their countrymen to study India closely, because this society alone was supposed to be able to overcome the mechanistic and leveling tendencies of Western culture. This view has persisted to this day, and has touched writers as different from each other as Goethe, Chateaubriand, Lamartine, Nerval, Vigny, Flaubert, Burton, René Guénon, Hermann Hesse, Keyserling, Michaux, René Daumal, Henry Miller, Allen Ginsberg, and Lanza del Vasto.[5] Heinrich Heine's apt description says these authors all show that "the West, disgusted with its weakened and cold spirituality, is searching for the warmth of the Oriental's heart."[6] The Orient, it seems, owes its integrity to the fact that it was left out of that accursed transformation called the technological revolution, which struck rich nations. This is why the true heart of humanity is beating there, in the living source where Europe must revive herself.[7]

But this "sentimentalized Buddhism," as Nietzsche called it, had never before achieved the proportions it did during the 1960s and 1970s. It was no longer a matter of intellectual style or private journey, but a mass enthusiasm that carried anxious young people to far-off and truly authentic climes. While America was at the height of her power and was dictating her will to the three continents, and the Star Spangled Banner waved over the most odious interventions, many thousands of young people took upon themselves the sins of the "free world" and made themselves poor among the poor. They went on the road to learn rather than teach, going to the Third World the way others at the time were going to work in factories, to share the life of the proletariat. At the very moment of the West's triumph, these desertions were evidence of its moral failure. This explosion of mysticism was the most serious crisis Europe and the West experienced since the Great Collapse of 1929. In the present context, we need only look at it from the perspective that concerns us here, that of pilgrimage to the Orient.[8]

Identification with an Asia in meditation was thus added to identification with Asia in revolution. Many people at that time embraced the dream of young nations, such as Vietnam and China, struggling for their sovereignty. Others wanted to cure the West of its faults, and to do this they studied philosophies that preached non-violence and self-denial, which our stupid arrogance had so disdained. It is important to note that there was not a little antagonism between the two camps, and this rivalry was an exact repetition of the one between the youthful Karl Marx and the Utopian socialists. For the radical leftist of the 1960s, the hippy could barely be credited with a diffuse awareness of the contradictions of imperialism. This was a fumbling precursor of the insights that the militant revolution was going to put to use. This is why the first wave of migrants came from Anglo-Saxon countries, which had traditionally not been deeply influenced by socialist ideology. It did not reach Europe until 10 years later, when the first failures of worldwide solidarity had turned many people off politics.

Marx had been angered to see French socialists such as Cabet, Considérant, and Enfantin desert the real scene of operations, the attack on the old walls of Europe, and go to live in Egypt and America. In the same way, the Third-Worldists jeered at the exodus of flower children who bowed down before repressive and backward religions. In return, the hippies made no secret of their hostility toward far-left movements and the ideology of

Black Power among black Americans, inspired by Stokeley Carmichael, who were prepared to seek independence by any means
necessary, including terrorism. And both sides accused each other
of being co-opted by Western civilization, which both rejected with
the same firmness. Like the guilty-conscience syndrome, however, the flight to the East contained a deep ambiguity that led
to its failure.

Redemption Through Exile

From the very beginning, the importance that had been attached
to the Orient had less to do with what it was than what Westerners no longer wanted themselves to be. They were not looking for
a real world, but the negation of their own. They were less attached to something true and material than to a plan for their own
salvation. They undertook a sort of geographic cure, as the tourist
brochures say; These places do not make you feel better unless
you come from somewhere else. In far-off lands, our own wandering Tamerlanes hoped to find deliverance in an Egypt full of
marvels, an India full of fantasies, a Tibet full of mystery.[9]
    The enchanting music of departure was itself enough to as-
sure them that they were doing the right thing, because distance
gives legitimacy to the fantasy of the perfection of far-off peoples.
If there really are happy people somewhere, they must be at the
other end of the earth. They have found the solution to the human
enigma, the key that opens all doors. This is why Hindus (or Ti-
betans, or Burmese, or Balinese) disply such a grave nobility that
shows us to be lacking, and beside which our affected fashions
seem so frivolous.
    Along comes an infallible and omniscient prophet in the per-
son of a yogi, a Buddhist monk, or a Hindu guru. Each has a ready-
made truth, a long-harbored secret that we do not understand but,
nevertheless, must be careful to imitate. The fact is that these
wandering Westerners, with their blond mops of hair and tired
faces all stamped from the same mold, had no understanding of
the continents they were exploring. They knew only that their
own societies were rotten. You need to have simple ideas to deny
your own culture, and theirs was: East is East, the birthplace of
our existence, as Kipling said, and in contrast the West can only
look like an accident.[10] Pilgrimages to Asia answer the need to

know that "the sacred" exists somewhere, the way the Pope is in Rome and the pyramids are in Cairo. The Orient is both a foreign land and a familiar countryside, to which we return as to our lost origins. An eternal vision is projected on these nations that has nothing to do with their real history. The joy of novelty is always joined by a little shiver of recognition.[11] This makes it possible to ascribe a moral character to the religious success of these countries, an absolute value that we like to imagine to be unchanging.

The Orient as a cultural model is, thus, the result of fiction rather than of a correct perception of reality. But this disparity does not reduce its effectiveness. On the contrary—seen from France, the ideal land seemed to offer so many doors to independence for young people in the 1960s and 1970s that they could not fail to behold in it some happiness and internal approval. But the road to Katmandu turned out to be a dead end, because the one who traveled it brought with him the answers to his own questions. The barefoot vagabond turned out to have the mud of his own country sticking to his soles.

The Impossible Connection

How is it possible to settle in Benares? The Westerner arrives in these countries not as a Frenchman, German, or American, but as a man. He does not arrive on a desert island, but into a society that is thousands of years old, with ancestors who left their mark and memories. He would like to appear as Good Will itself, but he is immediately classified as a white man, a somewhat bizarre descendant of the sahibs. He would like to show how he is different from other Europeans, but his pretensions to set himself apart look ridiculous. Simply because he looks like his forebears, this wandering sheep is put back in the fold at the very moment he is trying to flee it. Even the best of his intentions can do nothing to change people's memories.

He expects to find devout natives, but meets hucksters instead. What interests the Indians, Nepalese, and Thais is not his knowledge of the Vedas or his informed discourse on the "greater or lesser way" but, first and foremost, his money. With good reason—because even a poor Italian or Frenchman is much richer than the average person in the Third World. This inequality is disagreeable, because history flies back in the face of the pilgrim like a bad smell at the very moment he is trying to cover it up. And then, just when he tries to get rid of his old self, he realizes with stupefaction that the natives want nothing other than to imitate it. They are dressed in European pants and shirts, while he has put on the local fashion—Indian shirts, jodhpurs, dhotis, and Afghan vests. The Westerner expects the native to rain wise words, grave benedictions, and judicious pronouncements on him, but all they want to talk about is cars, money, machines, and gadgets. Horrors! They are more European than he is! Materialistic colonization has already corrupted them.[12] The natives are disappointing: Either they are greedy and want only to rob you, or they are too conformist and bore you.[13] They never exhibit the marvelous exoticism you had attributed to them.

The apprentice is in despair. He wanted to be absorbed into the Third World, but the Third World saw him as a tourist—no different from the charter-flight travelers for whom he has nothing but disdain. He left home in search of greater simplicity, but all he found was universal duplicity.[14] These countries are governed by authoritarian, violent regimes, burdened by desperate poverty, riven by inequality and injustice greater than anything he has ever seen, and patrolled by frightening armies and police forces. He expected to find a picture postcard, but instead found a state and its laws. In this world, he becomes keenly aware that he is given an identity he does not want and is in search of a recognition nobody will grant him. This leads to the first solution the hairy globetrotters fasten on, seeking one another out, seeking other pale faces. They set out to wipe the slate clean, but they end up among other fugitives like themselves. Running away turned out to be a cop-out, an alibi, an excuse. The sacred texts of the Orient had been mistaken for the Orient itself, and each country that makes it up was not conceived of as having a political constitution of its own.

So this led to the spontaneous recreation of white communities, little societies that flourished again the way they had during the heyday of the British raj, with natives on one hand and sahibs on the other.[15] They reestablished the pattern of "cantons" (the English residential quarters of the British raj), and reduced their contacts with the natives to the bare minimum. They met only the characters encountered by every tourist—hotelkeepers, employees, servants, customs agents, officials. Not to mention the personage that was indispensable to every traveler—the drug dealer!

Disappointment engenders isolation, and once the Oriental masses are left out, the European mentality can parade alone in an Orient that has been remodeled ad nauseam. The enchanting tropics thus take on the character of a prison. You are a captive there because you are a foreigner, and human relations take on a codified and rigid form, just like those under the Empire. This imprisonment takes place, paradoxically, in a limitless human ocean. As is well-known, some people turn to drugs, which are easily available in these countries, and this is a destructive path that is all the harder to avoid because it is in a foreign land.[16] Others pursue their dream of regeneration, in which the drugs are an adjunct, but not the sole purpose. Most mix the two. Then the guru intervenes to reconcile these young people with the "true India." Because these misfits need a man of the country who recognizes them for what they are—great initiates and future *sannyasins*—renouncers.

The Delights of the Cloister

With great business acumen, and a perfect understanding of the European mentality that has been refined by two centuries of British colonialism, some Indians understood what was going on when they saw hordes of ecstatic Californians alight on their soil in the 1960s and 1970s, ready to open wide their wallets for a little helping of wisdom. So they concocted the products sought by this alienated generation—a standardized spirituality and made-to-order ashrams. These ashrams, though thrown together, were more expensive then ashrams for Indians.

Today, this merchandising of the sacred is a veritable financial empire in India's economy.[17] It is not a question of distinguishing between the good prophets and the many charlatans. The deception is not the fault of the educated Indian or Tibetan who makes a profit from clowns who throw themselves into his arms, and who is only too happy to take some revenge on the rich and conceited white people. Every morning, Rajneesh, the famous pope of Poona, was accustomed to climbing into his sumptuous beige Rolls Royce and traveling the 100 yards between his house and the ashram, while his followers bowed down before him. What an irony, to see the anti-materialistic Europeans bowing down before a Rolls Royce! The deception was in the humility of the disciples themselves, in the blind confidence that guided them. They did not come to have a dialog, but to escape. Of course, the irony was also in the fact that, deep down, this humility revived the most lively colonialist reflexes. It was a double deception, because the whites chose a cut-rate wise man on whom they squandered their wealth in exchange for a phony religion.

This explains how adoration of Hinduism could go hand in hand with a disdain for the Indians. It should be no surprise that a colonial mentality and intellectual modesty could coexist. *The guru is the hostage the Europeans have taken against the people he belongs to.* They blindly follow the orders of this Indian, so that they will not see India, and avoid the self-questioning that would result from contact with Indians. The ashram becomes the Club Med of the mind, a way of catching a fragment of foreign spirituality without upsetting one's way of life in any way whatsoever. The apparel of Enlightenment permits some variations—local yokels, local teacher, local clothing, verses chanted in Sanskrit—along with the maintenance of privileges provided by the status of being white. In this way, it becomes possible to become Indian, Tibetan, or Buddhist without ceasing to be Western.

So here is the mysterious "swami," the greatest of the great, in search of whom the voyage was undertaken. He is the perfect sage at the zenith of excellence who pours forth beneficent and serene pronouncements like a quiet river. He is so beautiful, he is just the way he was imagined to be—venerable, smiling, bearded, full of goodness, but also full of a formidable energy that is astonishing. No doubt about it, he is the self-proclaimed living god in priestly piety and temporal power. He has seen things we shall never see, absorbed forces we shall never acquire. He has read all, understood all, and, because of this, we must believe his every word and follow him blindly, because in him are combined the authority of a father, the goodness of a patriarch, and the wisdom of a god.

The guru has to persuade his followers that everything can be learned, as if religious traditions were like recipes, as if spiritual messages were like mechanical principles.[18] What does he promise them, really? That M. Durand from Nanterre, Mr. Smith from Liverpool, and Herr Muller from Frankfurt will achieve the same revelation in a few weeks that so many others, who have labored through years of austerity and mortification, are still seeking.[19] The message itself is an eclectic mish-mash. The typical skill of the spiritual entrepreneur is to assemble together divergent and even contradictory families of thought and piety and to create a multiple and moving utopia that works on several levels, in which everyone can find what he is looking for. It synthesizes Western psychological techniques (primal scream, biotherapy, immersion, relaxation, rebirth, etc.) and Oriental techniques such as yoga and tai chi. It has a vast pantheon that includes Reich, Jesus, Buddha, Freud, Krishna, and Gandhi—a Rube Goldberg mix of religious mythologies, Rasputinist shamanism, Tibetan tantrics, and theosophy, all of which are mysteriously reconciled under the aegis of the swami. His strength is not just in juxtaposing contradictory religions, but in making them compatible, and offering his customers the pizzazz of a mixed bag of ecstasy.

The magnetic leader joins Orient and Occident, overcomes the opposition between science and religion. He is half-druggist and half-priest and combines all forms of mastery, the power of a sorcerer, and the knowledge of a specialist. He gives the novice just enough foreignness to dazzle him. He suggests the East rather than imposing it because, after all, exoticism has to stay within the bounds of good taste. Borders, police, technological madness are denounced, but in the end, a private enclosure is recreated, a family prostrated before its head. This crowd of Italians, Germans, and Englishmen in search of alternate needs, pushed along by a mentality violently hostile to Europe and its religions, suddenly loses all critical ability when confronted by a Buddhist lama, or a yogi, or a monk, and show the submissive reflexes of the most primitive form of Christianity. These rebels are ready to devote themselves, body and soul, to their master—to kiss his feet, pray before his statue, spread his thoughts, wash his underwear, sweep his room, paint his house, and weed his garden. All he has to do is bless them and bestow his enlightenment on them![20]

Everything in the ashram is totally regimented. This is the real diffuse religion at work there—the radical remedy for the sickness of life, the great treasure trove of consolation. From then on the little monk from a French or Italian suburb can believe that he has fulfilled the wild hope of having escaped all risk and danger of suffering. Of course, this means he has to make regular and prompt payments, or he will be sent away. Very quickly, his spiritual quest becomes a response to a demand for services, and his sponsorship is not only accepted, but required. There is no grumbling at the impositions of the "authority," the permanent control over his movements and speech. It is accepted that the "authority" knows all, and that, even in sleep and dreams, he maintains control over the psychic life of his petitioners. The totalitarian regime that establishes a hierarchy of functions and people makes impossible any reference to power that is not purely and simply one of devotion of each one to the teacher. Unlike a Western teacher, he does not simply dole out learning, he is the incarnation of a unique experience that guarantees the truth of his word. He is "the way" in human form. The faithful revolve around this marvelous beacon, competing for his attention with their zeal or mutual watchfulness. The "Saint of Saints," for his part, is inaccessible, and appears only once a day, protecting himself from too-frequent contacts by means of numerous bodyguards who shield his privacy. The great thing about the enclosure is that there is no need for anything other than what has already been written down. It is a total adaptation, because any misgivings or anxiety are suppressed to prevent the subject from feeling and experiencing his loss. The ashram once and for all projects evil on Western society (or that part of Indian society that is Westernized) and, in this way, presents itself as a total therapeutic community. The "Man of God" wields his power because of the great assiduousness with which he oversees the actions of his faithful, the manic attention given to respect for the rules he himself has promulgated. The guru had come to deliver the Orient, but this has produced nothing but a proliferation of sects.[21]

Because of the pretense that individuals will be revealed to themselves, the founders of the retreats are sick people, children afraid of the outside world, rather than wise men who have grown through meditation. The joy derived from devotion to the institution, and the ecclesiastical working of the sect that becomes an end in itself, make return to the outside world almost impossible. You cannot do without the ashram because the ashram has replaced the world from which it provides a sanctuary. What is disguised as initiation makes its members weak and fragile, establishes a relationship of moral dependence that is difficult to break off. In Himalayan valleys throbbing with an ancient magnetism, conditioning factories are mass-producing emotional cripples. After months of nonstop communication, obligatory intimacy, forced smiles, and maternal warmth, how can a person ever again be comfortable with the coolness of European relationships? When he falls from the nest, the baby bird is paralyzed. And to go back to the Master afterwards, he must subject himself to the most radical conditions, including total servitude. What is the matter with slavery if it gives you peace? One wonders whether the drop-outs of Asia are in search of an excess of discipline at the same time that the churches of the West are becoming more liberal.[22] These Nepalese or Indian retreats become clinics of our culture's failures, Disneylands of Western pathologies, where blond-haired hordes in search of "the light" come to subject themselves to irreparable damage.[23] Because the Orient has ceased to be anything other than an adornment of the treatment itself, the ashram could be transported anywhere, and could be in Texas as easily as at the foot of Everest; as easily in Los Angeles, as in Zinal. The Orient has ceased to be a geographic expression. The Orient has simply ceased to be Oriental.

The Would-be Look-alikes

The be-all and end-all of the pilgrim is to be as scrawny and fevered as the Indians. He follows the axiom that a living faith gives you sunken cheeks, so that when he has the fixed stare of the fakir and the emaciation of Jesus Christ, he feels he is ready for his great redemption. Whatever drugs they are addicted to, all these uprooted people have in common a taste for imitation that leads them to scrounge around for the Asian look, as if they were rummaging through a trunk full of costumes. This gives them scrupulous patience with which to dress up in the mannerisms and rags of the meditative man. Because they must play at who can be the most native, all the way down to how to stand, the European goes barefoot, dresses in a dhoti if he is a man and a sari if a woman and, inspired by the mendicant monks that live in the streets of the country, takes on a rough and rustic look. He copies their unkempt locks that look like uncarded wool, their grimy faces, their ash-covered bodies, says his companions are *baba* (Sanskrit for "sage") with a gesture, says *atcha* instead of "okay," strikes his forehead with his *shilom* before smoking, laps his tea from the saucer the way the locals do instead of drinking it from a cup. He plays with a jumble of pompous pronunciations, foreign

words, and obscure and elliptical expressions. For him, Sanskrit—
as Latin used to be in the Roman Catholic Church—is endowed
with mysterious powers simply because it is incomprehensible.[24]

All this is because appearances are more than superficial, and
truth is contained in externals. The intelligible world is the world
that can be perceived—clothing, facial expressions, and makeup
become the focus, the essence, while internal states are only the
covering. *The soul resides in the color of ones clothing, not in the
depth of one's belief.* The Absolute is touched through the weave
of a shirt or pajamas, which are experienced as ideas rather than
appearances. My costume is a sign of the Vedas or the Gita, it is
the symbol of a whole world behind the scenes, and proof that the
Orient has entered me.[25]

To feel like you are on the same level as Vishnu, your clothing
simply has to be appropriate. But such synthetic people, tinkering
with religion as apostles of counterculture, should not be under
any illusion. Under the contemplative coat of many colors, the
Westerner is still there. Because his pilgrimage is a sort of copy,
what he borrows from others is still proof of his superiority. He
is clearly just another sort of European, an insider who has experienced the "Big Thrill." The punk from Aubervilliers, the student from Berlin, and the potter from Liverpool have simply added
something to their nationality: mechanical recitation of mantras,
knowledge of yoga positions, familiarity with harmonious breathing techniques. They enjoy a double privilege, and affix their superiority to both cultures. They are "saved," and are part of an
elite who have taken the best Asia has to offer, while belonging
to the tiny fraction of the human race that knows "the truth."
The essence of their pious masquerade is in inverse proportion to
the interest they have for India, whether they are Devotees of the
Mother, Aurovillians, Hare Krishnas, or followers of other simplistic and synthetic religions, whether they are wandering, hairy
derelicts, angels, or jail birds. I am aping you, all the more willingly, they say to the East, because nothing that concerns you
interests me. I imitate you so that I will not be like you. These
crowds of creatures are both obscene and ridiculous as they wander—ageless, tasteless, and sexless; French, English, and German; pajama-clad monks who crisscross the subcontinent, tireless
cohorts of rancid and aging girls, and old hippies dressed in white
cotton—all under the same illusion in the cult of exotic piousness.

The wandering hippy recognizes no traditions, no laws, no

customs of the land, aside from its spirituality, and feels no tie to his country of origin except for the money orders sent to him by relatives. He is part of a double and negative social identity. He navigates between a far-off culture he has deserted to which he is no longer attached except by language, and a society that rejects and despises him. Even though he may end his life on a litter in a slum, ravaged by drugs[26] or poverty or self-punishment, he does not want to be confused with the local populace. He rejects Indian values because they are part of a world that has failed him, but he can no longer share the situation of tourists, foreign residents, volunteer workers, or diplomats. He may chatter around the *stupas* in the language of Saint-Ouen or Manchester, yet can enjoy the privilege of belonging to both camps but not participating in any, except the mysterious brotherhood of the road. He must constantly act out a separateness that threatens to go unnoticed unless he is constantly aware of it. His uprootedness is symbolic, because he has not passed from one side to the other; he is outside both civilizations. So these vagabonds who left home in a spirit of humility end up almost in spite of themselves in a colonial role, like their fathers or grandfathers. The effort at empathy and self-negation could only come about as a result of deeply-rooted inclinations, and the suntanned Kerouacs who came to think on the mysteries of the Absolute only became aware of the pathetic distance that sets them apart from an eternally alien Asia.[27]

They set out to redeem the Old World and cast off the selfishness of pampered peoples, but when they arrive, they end up affirming their existence and that alone. The great fraternity of outsiders culminates in the solitary revolution of an LSD trip. Faith, a simple matter of conviction, becomes lonely, and no longer brings people together. Each becomes an island who has established a contract with God. And since the self becomes the only point of reference they wish to take into account, all the belief systems of the world are heaped on top of one another like layers of pastry. The ruminating hermit, ready to believe all the merchants of illusion, fantastic cosmologies, and miraculous powers, locks himself up in his little ghetto of piety. The most ridiculous forms of mysticism exist side by side with the phoniest religious amalgams, and the inner life becomes a symbol of emptiness, where frauds, confusion, chic ideas, cut-rate occultism, and vulgar millenarianism all flourish together. It would be outrageous if it were not so ridiculous. What is left of Asia, this gigantic, swarming world? Caricatured rituals, plaster statues, tinkling sitars, sticks of incense, Afghan coats, cotton shirts—a whole supermarket display.

To be fair, the hippy movement had the great effect of making our generation sensitive to the benefits of travel and, in many ways, it is still a symbol of freedom and adventure. But, because it was a victim of its own excessive optimism and its belief in the permeability of cultures, it has taught us nothing about the East itself. All the great cultural ambassadors who have tried to build a bridge between East and West remain foreign to it. Whether they were agnostics, believers, or simply curious, they dove into a mass of humanity, only to end up suffering from the same foreignness that fascinated them. They paid for this effort with a lifetime of work and, often, with their health, until they became the offspring of a double culture, with all the tribulations and marvels that such an undertaking implies.[28]

The flower children of San Francisco, Paris, Rome, and Australia all shared the same indifference to the "otherness" of Asia. They wanted to be just like the Indians, more detached than the Buddhists, and they denied all cultural differences. This was their tragedy, because they did not have the distance necessary to communicate with people with whom they were living.[29] It is impossible to get rid of one's origins with a stroke of the pen. Infatuated with Nirvana, they thought they could leave Europe and become one with the Absolute. But Europe came back with a vengeance, and the Absolute was not where they expected it to be. These great travelers in search of "the Eternal" ended up face to face with themselves, closed forever within an impregnable fortress.

The Limits of Cultural Relativism[30]

"Wheresoever this flag flies, slaves will regain their freedom," declared Brazza to the African slaves he had just freed, as he bade them touch the folds of the French flag.[31] Even though French, Belgian, Dutch, and German domination over the peoples of Africa and Asia was accompanied by a naive belief that it bestowed freedom as well as progress and science, the actual process of colonization had to call into question this triumphant profession of faith. The more empires asserted themselves, the more they were exposed to hesitations. In the mother countries, many voices were raised in defense of the native civilizations that the earliest anthropologists and administrators had often described with admiration. In the occupied areas, a new class of intellectuals, thinkers, and jurists, often educated at French and English universities, were to throw back at Europe the values that had been taught there: respect for political sovereignty, democracy, and, of course, the self-determination of peoples. And the smug assurances upon which the industrial nations had founded their enterprises were shaken by the moral consequences of the massacre of World War I, the doubts about modernity (spelled out, each in its own fashion, by two very different books, Oswald Spengler's *The Decline of the West*, and Hermann Keyserling's *Journal of a Philosopher's Voyage*) and, above all, the irreparable damage done to the European idea by the convulsions of Hitlerism and Stalinism. The wars of independence and the process of decolonization succeeded in interrupting the self-assured slumber of the European. No one today would dare postulate the global superiority of the West, particularly when it is undergoing a crisis not so much of oil and trade, as of its very civilization.

It is possible, though, that this "new assault of the specific in contemporary history," to use Jacques Berque's expression,[32] may endenger other errors in its turn, in spite of its positive aspects. Certainly, the teachers of cultural relativism—by which we mean ethnologists and anthropologists, as opposed to Marxists, who are familiar with universal ideas—have inspired a religious and civil tolerance of which all persons of good will can be proud. But, beyond certain boundaries, this ideological flexibility confounds itself, and falls into a kind of skepticism that is hard to accept. These are the limitations we discern here, as we study the effect of ethnology on contemporary sensibilities.

Gauguin's Eldorado

We other Europeans are ailing. Our styles of life are far from the healthy state of nature, and our social relations lack charity and benevolence. . . . I often wish I were one of these so-called savages born in the islands of the South Seas, so that at least once I could savor human existence in its purity, without some artificial aftertaste.

Goethe, Conversation with Eckermann, 1828

The cultural heritage of mankind is fascinating for us Westerners because the most minor item of folklore, manners, or customs manifests that rare quality that has deserted us—authenticity. Because the gods have left our lands on winged feet, we must go off to find them again in the most distant places, under the most exotic skies. Of course, this idea originated in the eighteenth century, with Rousseau, Condillac, Condorcet, and Diderot.[33] It was absent during the nineteenth century, but nowadays it has undergone an unusual revival that has raised it almost to the level of a dogma. It was conceptualized by the linguistic anthropologist Sapir in 1925,[34] but popularized by the great Malinowski, who was so charmed by the way of life of the Trobriand islanders. To Malinowski, the discipline he practiced was a romantic flight to societies that had remained pure. For Tylor and Morgan, anthropology protected scientific civilization from the mistakes and crudities of savage people, but for Malinowski it played the role of a mission of preservation. Primitive practices, viewed with scorn by missionaries and ethnologists of the Empire at its height, were from then on cherished as so many treasures to be safeguarded. The idea of stamping them out gave way to a concern for their heritage that was the result of nostalgia inspired by fabulous discoveries. That the West was technically and economically more advanced meant nothing. Progress was a monstrosity, and an unjust one at that. "This might seem like a pessimistic view of progress, but many people feel it strongly, and in the aimless drive of modernization see a threat to all true spiritual and artistic values," wrote Malinowski in 1930 (*Africa*). "The modern world is a monstrous aberration," wrote René Guénon, at about the same time.[35] Earlier, Victor Segalen, describing the degeneration of the Maori people in *Les immémoriaux* (1907), had emphasized the inevitable degradation that contact with industrial civilization must entail for ancient ways of life. A half-century later, Claude Lévi-Strauss ashamedly spoke of "the monstrous and incomprehensible cataclysm that the development of Western civilization meant for such a huge and innocent portion of the human race" (*Tristes Tropiques*, op. cit., p. 375). More recently, Roger Garaudy concluded, in one of those sweeping epigrams of which he is so fond, "The development of the West is an accursed aberration" (*Pour un dialogue des civilisations*, Denoel, 1977).

    In sum, we, the masters and slaves of the technology to which we have lost our souls, are indebted to other cultures for the power of survival. On these tiny, backward societies the Golden Age is projected, and it is imagined that what once was believed to exist only in the past, is in existence there now. And, since the past is accessible by a simple move through space, it is in those societies that Heaven on earth is to be found, the Islands of good fortune, the "wellsprings of the human race in its infancy," in the words of Paul Gauguin. Whereas, in the nineteenth century the savage was nothing but a crude human sketch intended for protection by civilized peoples, at the beginning of the twentieth century, he became the original man, man without sin, and the West was called to renew itself through contact with him.[36] So it was that primitive societies were praised to the skies—they were called little communities with crystalline structures, where solidarity and reciprocity were daily practices, according to Lévi-Strauss. Pierre Clastres talked of the happy anarchy of the Guayaqui Indians of southeastern Paraguay, who lived with no central authority and no divisions. Marshall Sahlins talked of a society unified by the benevolent and nourishing presence of a forest, a jungle, or a river, that provided for the needs of all; Robert Jaulin of a society of spontaneous harmony and blissful contact; Malinowski of a profusion of the senses and of erotic happiness on the atolls of the South Pacific. These are the sorts of truly seductive utopias that inspire today's ethnology. We have the misfortune of living with debilitating values and preoccupations, while they have symbolism, happiness, and simplicity, all functioning together with the wonder of some social magic.[37] Without fail, in contrast to the frigid monsters of the Northern hemisphere, the great beauty of the primitive world is praised,[38] as is the revival of deceased identities and the rise of religion, fidelity to oneself, the ceaseless recapitulation of the cultural past, and this "living contact between a group and its foundations, a relationship that must be constantly maintained."[39]

The promises of renewal seem the more numerous since they are part of a long-practiced tradition. In the eighteenth century, the non-Western world symbolized a state of nature that contradicted the dogma of religion; today, it is the home of the sacred, the repository of a spiritualism that is missing in our part of the world. Whether used as a lever against the obscurantism of the Old Régime or a tool for awakening some lost truth, exotic cultures in both cases have served as a mirror in which the West looks at its own deficiencies and seeks to correct its faults. From this point of reflection, everything becomes authentic simply because it is old (meaning close to its original state). What is out of date is overvalued and stagnation is encouraged, as in the tourist brochures where archaic ways are always more "true" than what is modern.[40] The whole idea of outdated practices is rejected, because it is clear that "if some practice is perpetuated, it is because it has acquired a new meaning, a new function" (Malinowski). Besides, even this is a phony issue, because it is well known that "primitive societies represent the future of our own" (Jean Malaurie[41]), and that "the necessary revolution toward the past, which for the moment is only a dream, has everything to gain and learn from the Indians, and nothing to teach them" (R. Renaud).[42]

It should be obvious that the worship of differentness presupposes what it will consist of, and that Western intellectuals are falling back into ethnocentrism at the very moment they think they have left it behind. There is no impartiality in the search for living examples, because we ourselves set forth the values we propose to find among peoples at the other ends of the earth. The passionate defense of primitive societies is really nothing but a way of judging them and ourselves, by means of the prejudices of our own frames of reference. Whereas, in the old days, people complained of their barbarity, today they gush about their wonderful symmetry, but the approach is really the same, because the starting point is still the Western way of life. "The archaic [is defended] as a pure, anti-Western value because of the *Western* search for an ideal that is outside our experience."[43]

Praising negritude, the free love of Melanesians, the non-violence of Indians, the virginal innocence of the Araras and Bororos, and the spontaneity of the Balinese really means looking at them from the perspective of our needs and problems, to set them up as ideal counter-examples of the world we live in.[44] Why not celebrate cannibalism, then, or head-hunting, or the bloody worship of the Aztecs, since they are just as "authentic" as the pure world of the South Pacific? We glorify the natural man of the tropics because we already know what we are going to find—a treasure-trove of wisdom, depths of sincerity and otherworldliness, a celebration of the body, a diversion from our worries.[45] It seems to me, though, that all culture contact must lead us to recognize the impossibility of expecting the outcome beforehand. To think of the "other" as "a part of myself who lives within me and reveals to me what is missing,"[46] is to degrade the act of discovery to a simple return to a land that was lost. If I am what other societies are not, I am nothing but a sum of outside influences, a huge warehouse open to everything, where all behaviors, rituals, and gestures of the human race can be stacked up any which way.

The hatred of differentness that was typical of our expansionist era has been replaced by a fad for primitive man, upon whom is projected all the generosity and purity we fail to see in ourselves. The brown, naked, natural man, armed with bow and guided by infallible instinct, is only our fantasy-brother, born of our own nostalgia. Thus, in the last few years, it has been possible to construct our own anarchic savage, whose every act is aimed at preventing the growth of the state and social classes[47] (Pierre Clastres); a savage of exquisite manners, who rejects all the things that oppress us—taboos, taxes, envy, tolls, unpleasantness, competition, trickery, reinforced concrete, and flush toilets; a liberated savage, who is a tireless devotee of his sexual drives (Deleuze-Guattari); a sensual savage, who provides the splendid spectacle of unrepressed sexuality, for whom sodomy is guilt-free (Jacques Lizot)[48]; a primitive man right out of the eighteenth century, who knows his Rousseau by heart (the Nambikwaras presented by Lévi-Strauss); a savage who is generous with his wealth, free-spending, so far from our petty-bourgeois avarice (Bataille); a "cool" savage, refusing to be overloaded and working only four hours a day (Sahlins). In sum, he is always primitive man as a showpiece, a fantasy, a rhetorical figure, a mixture of gay wisdom and the joy of leisure, all for the greater delectation of the Left Bank or Manhattan.

It is reverse racism, but racism all the same. The easy ecstasy of being someone else leads to the crudest sort of reductionism. What is blessed in the "other" is nothing but the opposite of our own society; it is the hidden solution to our own anxieties, the expression of what haunts us.[49] Primitives are pure ideas, just as the Bolivian guerrilla or the Palestinian gunman were nothing but ideas for the Third-Worldist of the Left. They are a veritable miracle drug, to be taken regularly to immunize against the state, capitalism, pollution, frigidity, or whatever else happens to bother you.[50] Prehistoric man is a source of ecstasy because he does not want to become a capitalist, establish a state, or get rich, and we dream about him because we project on him the characteristics that are the opposite of what we are.

Once again, in looking afar and reviving our romantic sensibility, we are really looking at ourselves. The only societies that seem worthy are those that contradict our values, and our attempts to escape the grasp of our cultural milieu are a shameful way of asserting our superiority. So, under the pretext of glorifying the dawn of mankind, the cradle of our beginnings, the true man, we are led arbitrarily to choose the most perfect.

What society shall we love the most, for the range of choices is daunting. What far-off tribe of the Mato Grosso or Borneo should we choose as the paragon of symmetry and virtue? Our ethnological Don Juan has an overabundance of possible partners. He may proclaim that he is "searching for his inspiration among the humblest and most despised peoples," that "nothing that is human should be foreign to any man."[51] But he will immediately be lost in a multiplicity of myths and an endless stockpile of all the customs men have invented to cope with the hardship of being human. In the four corners of the planet, a hundred peoples fashion a hundred-thousand local gods. We are excited over these parochial divinities scattered among different villages and tribes, we marvel at little groups of people walled off in their particularism. And we are told that they are models of superior humanity.

It is well-known that the West has demystified everything. That is its crime and its sin.[52] But as soon as other systems of wisdom are placed in contrast to Western irreverence, they all compete with one another, and none has the right to be foremost, because all are "authentic," and our society can learn to ape any of them because it is unknown to all of them. To bow down before the absolute superiority of one way of life or another is like making the world into a big menu from which the West can choose. If all foreign peoples are alleged to have the unusual, the unique capacity for being full of the authentic, how can we differentiate between them? What one person praises in Islam, another does with Hinduism, and a third with Buddhism of the Lesser Way, while others praise the unforgettable joys of the Dayaks of Borneo, the Toradjas of the Celebes, the Eskimos, or the Lapps, or the Australian aborigines. And each one has arguments that are irrefutable, convincing, and enthusiastic.

Why follow a Druid rather than a Bonze or a Mullah? Each presents solutions for the whole world that are only individual choices, suited to them alone, even though they may be justified in this. This leads to the same sort of gratuitousness that applies in questions of attractiveness. Why does one man prefer blondes to brunettes, buxom ladies to slim ones, hairy ones to smooth ones? Each praises his own turf, asserting that it is the best, the chosen, and each asserts that he has a miraculous belief system that will move mountains, even as he villifies his competitors. Squabbles erupt between exotic dogmas, and fistfights break out in the name of the Koran or the Vedas. And, to top it all off, in the name of authenticity, we dare to lecture the natives who have betrayed their own culture.[53]

Very soon, the witness to these quarrels can see that all these prescriptions are the same, because none is worth more than any other, depending on the whim of one proponent or the other. In an attempt to overturn the simplistic distinction between superior and inferior societies, they are all lumped together. Relativism glorifies what is authentic, but at the same time raises doubts about whether authenticity really exists, because it presents too many examples that all make the same claim. There are too many points of interest, too many divinities. In sum, we suffer from too much sacredness, rather than too little. Our desire is whetted and dulled at the same time: The ultra-exclusive club of pure cultures turns out to be a huge auditorium crammed with crowds of all kinds of people. And the fervent worship of differentness turns into the approval of everything, of anything at all.

To Each His Own Barbarity

In 1947, the Executive Office of the American Anthropological Association submitted a draft declaration to the United Nations Commission on Human Rights. Noting the great number of societies that had come into contact with the modern world, and concerned with the promulgation of a declaration of human rights that could apply to all peoples and not just those of Western Europe and America, the signers, after mentioning the disastrous consequences of colonialism for the human race, made the following proposal:

1. The individual realizes his personality through his culture, hence, respect for individual differences entails a respect for cultural differences.
2. Respect for differences between cultures is validated by the scientific fact that no technique of qualitatively evaluating cultures has been discovered.

This principle leads us to a further one, namely, that the aims that guide the life of every people are self-evident in their significance to that people. It is the principle that emphasizes the universals in human conduct, rather than the absolutes that the culture of Western Europe and America stresses. It recognizes that the eternal verities only seem so because we have been taught to regard them as such; that every people, whether it expresses them or not, lives in devotion to verities whose eternal nature is as real to them as are those of Euroamerican culture to Euroamericans. . . .

3. Standards and values are relative to the culture from which they derive, so that any attempt to formulate postulates that grow out of the beliefs or moral codes of one culture must, to that extent, detract from the applicability of any Declaration of Human Rights to mankind as a whole.[54]

In the name of the right to be different, a first statement made an emotional declaration of the authenticity of primitive man. A second invoked this same pluralism and asserted the impossibility that the human race could be unified, loyally hailing the succession of identities to which it gives birth. Faithful to respect for individual differences, persuasive words were written to explain cannibalism in one tribe, stoning of adulterous women or the amputation of thieves' hands in Moslem countries, the sexual mutilation of young girls in Africa and the Middle East, and the segregation and massacre of "untouchables" in India. The argument was: to each his own truth. In the past, the revelation of statistics could evoke a new form of shame, that of being different. But now the aim is to seal each person off within his own uniqueness and forbid him to escape. If this means defending customs that are a little cruel or barbarous, it does not mean that we want to adopt them as our own, but because they show a richness and otherness that are good in themselves.[55]

The cultural development of all social functions, no matter how rudimentary, were deemed to be perfect and complete accomplishments of mankind's potential talents. Everything, from all traditions, is worth preservation, even what is immoral, mistaken, or out of date. Dogons, Yanomamos, Baris, and little villages in southern France are all unique achievements. Each civilization forms a cohesive, organic whole, that is indissociable, to use Toynbee's word.[56] The West is reduced to being one society among a thousand others, and the map of the world is no longer a mixed salad, but a mosaic where each piece must be entirely separate from the others. To maintain the status quo, the struggles of the Third World peoples are to be used against Western influence, because it is a vehicle of unbelief and permissiveness. The ideal principle of the unmixability of cultures imposes a duty on each people to defend its integrity at all costs.

For this idea of differentness as a basic right, each human group or aggregation simultaneously combines both an expression of uniqueness and the idea of legitimacy. Peculiarity is the basis of this right, rather than the other way around. Claude Lévi-Strauss said, "The feeling of gratitude and humility that each member of a given culture can and should feel toward all others must be based on a single conviction, that other cultures are different from his own in the most heterogeneous ways. This is so even if he cannot see the ultimate nature of these differences, and even if, in spite of all his efforts, he only succeeds in understanding it imperfectly."[57]

All expressions of collective will, with their customs and specific language, therefore, deserve our respect from the very moment that differences appear, and judgments about justice, crime, barbarity, and dignity recede before the absolute criterion of the right of individuality. There is no longer any eternal truth, except that which results from naive ethnocentrism,[58] which is the driving force of imperialism. Whoever might timidly suggest that liberty is indivisible and that the life of another human being has the same value everywhere is duly scolded in the name of obligatory tolerance toward other cultures. Other people's lives and sufferings in those societies are not taken seriously once they have been stuck into the ghetto of insurmountable differentness. Their otherness makes us happy because it is inviolable.

Of course, it is good when people come closer to one another, and nice conferences are organized where, for example, Catholics, Jews, Muslims, and Buddhists are invited to exchange their respective creeds, listen to one another's differences, so that they will throw themselves into one another's arms and be friends forever.[59] But these invariably come down to a standard circus act that is like Noah's Ark, in which a cat, a dog, an elephant, a marmot, and two foxes are put together under the vigilant eye of an overseer. Leaping over the walls between rites is not so easy. What usually happens is a crude encounter in empty space, in which priests, rabbis, bonzes, and Brahmans congratulate themselves and cling all the more strongly to their abstract dogmas.

Very quickly, the discussion groups degenerate into explaining parallels where rival references to the Absolute touch one another but do not intersect. Our Muslim brothers are delighted at our understanding of the *sourates* of the Koran, but they would prefer that we undergo a true and formal conversion. Our Christian brothers certainly respect the message of Mohammed, but they also suggest that the best part of Islam is already contained in the New Testament. Our Jewish brothers, with much deference, point out all that the New Testament owes to the Old. As for our Hindu and Buddhist brothers, they are pleased at the attention shown them, and to prove their good will, they willingly add our gods to their own in their prayers. Everyone shows the greatest courtesy, but discreetly repulses the slightest proselytism directed towards him. This is how the discussion conferences between the great religions are transformed into holy alliances of the totally deaf.[60]

Jacques Berque[61] wrote about Islam that "the individuality of someone constitutes his real tie with others," but he ultimately gives us a confused idea of how this different person can communicate with others. It is one thing to boast about the identities of people who have been newly decolonized to explain or excuse the occasionally frenzied defensiveness they show. It is quite another to give one's blessing to insular communities that are closed off to the spread of all new ideas and hostile to all contamination.[62] How is it possible to give one's blessing to differences if they exclude humanism instead of conveying it? It is entirely understandable that a certain number of fundamentalists in Moslem, African, or Asian countries want to rebuild their nations' weakened structures. But it is highly questionable when, in the name of this undertaking, they seal off borders, build a cultural iron curtain between themselves and the outside world, and lock up their citizens in an indefinite quarantine. If we did the same to them that they do to us, there would soon be absolute silence on our planet. In the name of tolerance, we are supposed noisily to approve the intolerance these other societies show toward us! What is being confused here is the approval and the noting of differences. In the immense panoply of customs, barbarism, and hypocritical prohibitions that appear in the colorful movie that history and ethnology show us, what is celebrated is the triumph of the spirit of clannishness and tribalism, a spirit that does not even recognize foreigners as human beings! This deprives us of any ability to distinguish one that might have been able to synthesize this heterogeneity. But different customs now bump into each other like agitated molecules, there is no way to tell the difference between justice and injustice, and the world is given over to capriciousness and arbitrariness.

The celebration of differentness as a supreme norm cannot possibly provide a way of evaluating people; the very idea of human fellowship is undermined here. The quasi-neurotic concern of some regimes for the prevention of all impure contact with the West is warmly supported. We study their ability to conserve the inflexibility of their morals in the face of the invasion of industry. They are strongly encouraged to resist, but our own concern for their future contradicts the very advice we give them. We hold out our hand in friendship, even as they pull back theirs. We try to build a passageway to them, while they boast of having burned the bridges between us. Essentially, we glorify the same behavior in others that we always criticize in ourselves: excessive xenophobia, cultural narcissism, and relentless ethnocentrism.[63]

It is very clear what sort of advantages a tyrannical regime or bloodthirsty government can derive from these areas of silence as soon as they are criticized for violations of basic freedoms. "It is not your fault. You could never understand us."[64] Your Western prejudices have blinded you.[65] You have the right only to acquiesce or be silent, and any objection you voice would be an act of unqualified imperialism. Any time doubt is cast on the justifiability of female circumcision, mass shootings, and hangings and tortures committed by some banana republic, the accused regime or state wraps itself in its differentness like an outraged virgin, screaming that it is being raped and that its motivations are not understood. Under the protection of this sophistry, the most abominable outrages, the most lunatic nihilism can be practiced with the blessing of the great thinkers of the Western world.[66]

In the nineteenth century, the natives were imagined to be so different from us that it was thought impossible to teach them the European way of life or ever to give them French citizenship. At that time, differentness was perceived as inferiority, and the distance between them and us insurmountable. Taken to its logical extreme, this consideration for their autonomy led to discriminatory policies that are lamentably well-known. What else is South African apartheid but the concern for cultural difference taken in its literal sense, to the point where the "other" is so different from me that he does not even have the right to be near me? It is well-known that, in Pretoria, the rule "everyone in his place and everyone will be happy" is a state religion, and that the balkanization of ethnic groups, the segregation of blacks, coloreds, and whites is always justified by a scrupulous concern for preserving differences. Similarly, for racist theorists such as Gobineau, decadence comes from intermingling races and not in racial differences themselves; each has its own genius that commands it not to mongrelize itself. In the splendid name of cultural differences, then, peoples' progress can be arrested, technology and the material means to progress can be withheld from them, and inequality can be established under cover of the beautiful name of diversity. This proves that the unrestrained praise of "distinctive character" and traditions can conceal the same backward paternalism as that practiced by the most condescending colonizers.[67]

Pop Ecumenicism[68]

In the name of respect for diversity, cultural relativism boasts that primitive man is the sole survivor of authentic and happy humanity. On the same premise, it praises cultural peculiarities as so many fatherlands sealed off from one another. Or, again, it rejoices that all cultures are now accessible. At one moment, it builds up barriers and the next it tears them down; separatist pessimism coexists with integrationist optimism. Even as it declares that Chinese or Cameroonese minds are unfathomable oceans, the fluidity of all cultures is loudly asserted. Cosmopolitanism is the supreme slogan of the lovers of differentness, because it gathers under the same flag the troops who want to enrich the European mind with all the ideas from the sunny and tropical lands. Very early in the twentieth century, the idea was born that the great religions of the world could be brought into harmony by the expanding uniformity bestowed by a technology that broke down frontiers, broke up petty nationalism, and reconciled families that had long been alienated from one another.

The list of people who have made ecumenicism the creed of modern times is long—from the theosophical society of Madame Blavatsky to Roger Garaudy, by way of René Guenon, René Daumal, Hermann Hesse, Alan Watts, and Lanza del Vasto. This current of thought clings to the conviction that all great books say the same thing, and that the great faiths are complementary rather than contradictory. It has enjoyed varying success, but it regularly reappears. It attempts to end the negation of other cultures that was typical of the West in its imperialist phase, so that the spiritual treasures of the human race[69] will no longer be sterilely confronted. There is only one religion, and it is the same everywhere in the world.[70] Western man must lend his voice to a conception of the world that is symphonic rather than hegemonic.

Whether as the impulse toward tolerance and against fanaticism (Drieu La Rochelle), a taste for new experience (Daumal), a desire to reconcile East and West (Lanza del Vasto), or a need to reduce the menace of nuclear war (Garaudy), this planetary vision always has the detached attitude of an aesthetic approach to the great religions and finds them all equally beautiful and valid. It refuses to accept any distinctions between them because, from its point of view, it makes no difference if the name of the Supreme Being is God, Jehovah, Allah, Brahma, Buddah, Isis, or Osiris. It is an attempt at worldwide rather than national thinking, an attempt to accomplish voluntarily and in reverse what many Indian, Pakistani, Malayan, African, and North African intellectuals were forced into against their will—double or triple cultural membership.[71] It imagines itself transplanted, multiplied, nothing less than a sign of world citizenship. It aspires to be the sum total of all previous humanism. In its thought are combined past civilizations, which is a claim to be the heir of Bossuet, Lao Tse, Plato, Mohammed, and Rama. The whole world is seen as a theater where it plays successive roles; as Nietzsche said, "I am all the names in History."[72] This is what the worldwide hybrid trumpets—without ever asking how it will reconcile so many contradictory images, how it will ensure the unity of philosophies that are incompatible and dissimilar.[73] This religion has lost all blinders, overcome all fanaticism. It is an athlete of thought and human relations, speaks a sort of super-Esperanto, is the universal ambassador and universal synthesizer of History.

Once again, though, cultural relativism contradicts itself at the same time as it asserts itself. It is positively dazzled by other cultures, but shows little consideration for each one. Let us take, for example, that modern-day prophet Roger Garaudy, whose great success is typical. His program is to "make it so that every person be the home of the culture of all peoples from all time."[74] A noble undertaking, you may say, but it is one that reminds you of the soups that country folk make in the winter, into which they throw all the week's leftovers. In the supermarket of thought, Garaudy is advertising a discount price on all human wisdom, from the beginning of history to modern times—a dash of Zen, two pinches of Taoism, a drop of the Inca Empire, a bit of the Tibetan Book of the Dead, two teaspoons of Tanzanian socialism, a big bowlful of the Chinese cultural revolution, a slice of Iranian Shiite Islam. Let it all simmer for a while, and then the magic potion of salvation is ready.

Garaudy's plan is impressive, but is as foolish as it is ambitious—because without being some non-person of all time and of all places, I cannot understand how I, a Frenchman in 1986, can be successively a Vishnu follower on Monday, Voodoo worshipper on Tuesday, Fidelista on Wednesday, Protestant on Thursday, yogi on Saturday, and Socialist Catholic Jew on Sunday. Not to mention, of course, my own personal beliefs. The naiveté of the cosmopolitan point of view is such that it loses contact with the Absolute idea that inspired it in the first place.[75] It simply forms a badly sewn patchwork quilt of quotations without dates or references, of creeds strung together like pearls without concern for coherence or historical perspective. This gigantic stew combines a total ignorance of tradition, with a deep disregard for it. Garaudy presumes to tramp across centuries and continents, but does so with the heartiness of a bulldozer that is not concerned with details and levels everything in its relentless advance.[76]

Cosmopolitanism can be translated into the following argument: All cultures are equally valid, none more so than any other. It follows that a total person must be the sum of all cultures that were directed against each other in the past. The conclusion is that all cultures are a single culture, and therefore, that no culture in and of itself is better than any other, since it is simply a portion of universal culture. The result is the opposite of the idea that was the premise—every culture must then feel guilty because it is only a fragment of universal culture, since it is nothing without its connection to other cultures. The worship of cultural diversity leads to a passive indifference because, if all are equally valid, then different visions of the world destroy one another as a result of their mutual contradictions. It is one thing to penetrate the subtleties of Chinese, Japanese, Yaqui, Peulh, or Zulu society in order to legitimate an immense enlargement of the scope of human consciousness. But it is quite another to declare that these models are mutually interchangeable, and can be piled up like a stack of saucers. This procedure leads the ethnologist, traveler, and cosmopolitan to dehumanize the world even as they are evoking its richness. They suppress the diversity of cultures even as they pretend fully to recognize it. If Christianity, Islam, and Buddhism must be reunited, this means that separately they are worthless. Each is only a sketch of worldwide religion, for which they constitute the formative stages. The intoxication of discovery gives way to disenchantment with the checkered multitude of postulates of the human race. The crazy variety of piled up rites and gods collapses into a thousand solitary pieces. It is nothing but wholesale holiness, sold by the square yard like cloth. It is a huge, empty barrel whose sides boom hollowly.

The colossal project gives way to a tired "what's the point?" attitude: *I only recognize your difference in order to emphasize how little it means to me. We are all equal because you all look the same to me.* In the name of equality, everyone is pronounced to be the same, and tolerance leads to homogenization. Europe has ceased to be the infallible repository and legitimate dispenser of truth, but this is because there is no more truth at all. This cultural single-mindedness, which was avidly denounced as the responsibility of the West,[77] reappears with all cultural expressions laid out side by side, like so many butterflies on an entomologist's slides. The very possibility of coexistence of national identities is undermined by this encyclopedic mish-mash, because they are added up and stuck permanently on display in a museum. The ultimate stage of humanity is an absolute nothingness. The disillusioned Westerner shuffles through the variegated scriptures of different human attitudes, bidding a sad farewell to a dying civilization, ready to condemn his own to the same destiny. The planetary tourist has used up everything without having understood anything.[78]

I have no intention of being so ridiculous as to condemn or even judge ethnology as a science. It has restored the spirit of new collective life to disintegrating empires, it has revealed to subject peoples their own sacred texts, it has provided native nationalisms with the ammunition they needed to emancipate themselves from colonial domination, to find some measure of dignity and transcendence. Missionaries, linguists, anthropologists, and ethnologists—all have provided arms to the peoples whom their own homeland oppressed and exploited. In return, their studies have had the salutary effect of shaking up European and American worlds that were too full of their own values, and fought against the murderous ethnocentrism of the epochs of conquest. A reductionist ideology, however, was built upon this exemplary work and ended up replacing it. Cultural relativism is the diluted and vulgar substitute for ethnography. It has ceased to be revolutionary or subversive and has spread a kind of conformity of its own. The unremitting effort to put oneself in the place of others, the rite of passage of all researchers, has been replaced by the threefold sin of abstraction, skepticism, and lukewarmness. Imperialism engendered intolerance, but liberalism cultivates indifference. It oscillates between evil universalism and narrow-minded particularism, it sidesteps the tension between single and multiple views, it puts together what is different and calls it identical. In a vicious circle, the immense storehouse of ethnology, through half-baked study, ends up legitimating the very ideas against which the discipline has been fighting from the beginning—spiritual colonialism, general disinterest, and hatred for others. The idea of being open to foreign cultures engendered the intellectual monstrosity of differentness, a catchall that inspired not only starry-eyed conversions but a highly sophisticated form of racism. Our era has learned that Euro-centrism makes its honey from all sorts of flowers, including the most altruistic ones, and that blindness born of humility is no better than blindness born of arrogance. The passion to be someone else requires first of all that you recognize the otherness of what you are searching for. It is not so easy to become a heretic. It is not possible to escape your own society with a wave of the hand. It requires dedication, courage, and perhaps madness, such as all the great thinkers have had. Faced with cultural differences, the "cosmopolitan" European can only look like a slavish imitator or an intellectual actor. A Senegalese proverb says, "No matter how long a tree trunk stays in the swamp, it will never be a crocodile."

4

Thou Shalt Hate Thy Neighbor as Thyself

In 1964 the American anthropologist Colin Turnbull went to Northern Uganda to study the Iks, a tribe that used to be hunter-gatherers, but that had been forced to leave their territory and settle in villages because of the creation of a national park. Turnbull went to the Iks with a single conviction—that there was a natural goodness to African man, particularly when he was a nomad, uncorrupted by Western civilization. Turnbull expected to find "gentleness, generosity, consideration, affection, honesty, hospitality, and compassion."[1] But he was quickly disenchanted. The resettlement of the Iks had been like a Biblical "fall" and had totally corrupted them. The Christian virtues praised by Turnbull in his earlier studies[2] of hunting tribes had disappeared. In less than three generations, these once-happy and prosperous people had degenerated into villagers whose only concern was their individual existence. They had given up all social relations, and lost all notions of hope, love, and respect. The Iks grab food from the mouths of their parents, drive their children out of the family compound so that they will not have to feed them, and let old, sick, and disabled people die with total indifference. Their Garden of Eden had turned into a "hideous world" [op. cit., p. 224], a "band of carnivores" [op. cit., p. 64], always ready to kill one another in order to eat. They excel in "what might be called bestiality if that were not so insulting to animals" [op. cit., p. 270].

Turnbull could not forgive these Africans for having destroyed his Robinson Crusoe fantasy. The end of his book is absolutely astounding. In the degeneration of the Iks, he sees a kind of reverse evolution, and the future of the rich peoples, who are devoted to the vagaries of progress and the cult of technological tricks. His tone then changes to invective. He recommends that the Ugandan government deport and disperse the Iks so that their bad example cannot contaminate nearby populations. Since the government did not do this, he limits himself to hoping that the 2,000 surviving Iks will soon disappear from the face of the earth.[3]

An ethnologist praying for the extermination of the people he studies is certainly a new phenomenon! It is typical, though, of Third-Worldists. The same tendency to shift from praise to condemnation to pass from adoration to hatred when our investments of goodness and gentleness do not pan out is always there.[4] The desire to *control though compliments,* in which the Third World is a neutral and controllable object, changes to impotent rage when the guerrilla, the native, or the primitive is seen as richer than was thought. If the facts do not fit the fantasies, it is because the tropical skies look down on a hell even more abominable than our own. The playground of the angels is really nothing but a cauldron seething with three billion monsters. We have come full circle, and the proof is clear—self-punishment is the highway to hatred of the human race.

The Ambiguity of Western Masochism

Criminal Pride

Several years ago, when the Ayatollah Khomeini declared that France was the Little Satan and America the Great Satan, some intellectuals were tempted to make fun of him. They were wrong, because the declaration of the Imam reflects exactly what the white man thinks of his own society. "From the perspective of history, the West is the greatest criminal of all time."[5] We, the spoiled children of the Earth who "made" colonialism, the slave trade, the genocide of Indians, we who yearly are said to exterminate 50 million people simply by means of unequal economic relations, have a monopoly on murder. Our sick narcissism tells us that we are the worst, in contrast to whom the people of the Third World are the purest.

A century ago, Rudyard Kipling wrote a famous poem in which he exhorted the white man to shoulder his civilizing burden for the greater benefit of the human race. Today, we are proud to carry our burden of sins, and take all evils on ourselves, without allowing other peoples the right to have theirs. There is something ambiguous, though, in this excessive self-injury. The application of superlatives of vileness, sordidness, and hatefulness to ourselves betrays a perverted boastfulness. As kings of iniquity and princes of infamy, we are still at the apex of history. We are diabolical alchemists who spread their misdeeds to the four corners of the earth, and we know that we are still the master race, because the only things that cannot be questioned about us are our absolute perfidy and ignominy. If there were an Olympics of Evil, industrial civilization would win in all events. This is the reverse side of imperialism. The remorseful man always grows in his pathological paranoia because he is a megalomaniac. He perceives the hand of Europe and America in every human misfortune, the better to call himself the Great Master whose fault it is that the planet is in a shambles. He has a macabre egomania, constantly thinking he sees conspiracies which bear a striking resemblance to the old fantasies of Jewish and Freemason conspiracies. This gives him a chance to puff up his aggressive personality to planetary proportions. If you are going to be the guilty party, it is more thrilling to be guilty on a universal scale than on a region-wide or family-wide scale. Civil wars and children with bloated bellies are *my* fault. Clouds of locusts and devastating droughts are *my* fault. Catastrophes, poisonings, tornadoes, butcheries are all *my* work. Paradoxically, this chaos has order to it, because these millions of people are acting according to an invisible logic that emanates from *me*.

We are still at the center of everything, after all. This is the conviction of the Third World-worshipper, the silk purse that has not succeeded in making himself into a sow's ear, and has given the Northern hemisphere an over-idealized image of evil. Colonization affected our superiority complex, but it is no longer in our power to decide the fate of Patagonians, Zulus, or Vietnamese Mois. It is impossible to accept this exclusion, though, and in colossal self-overestimation, Europe is still seen as the center of gravity of the universe. A contradiction in terms has arisen. Our society is not supposed to be particularly special, except in its harmfulness, but in stressing this, in the last analysis, we acquire an extraordinary, absolute uniqueness. Our culture is as poisonous as hemlock. We have fallen back into ethnocentrism just when we thought we had escaped it. This is a double distinction—we admit our fault, but at the same time get a childish pleasure from being the source of all the horror in the world.

The Indelible Stain

When the West is blamed for the evils of the world, three main types of accusations are presented:

Guilt by history: You are responsible for the frightful genocide of colonialism that was carried on against Indians and blacks from the Renaissance to the twentieth century by your ancestors.

Guilt by contagion: You are guilty of being the happy descendants of these unscrupulous freebooters, and you must not forget that your prosperity is built on the corpses of millions of natives.

Guilt by confirmation: You demonstrate that you are no better than your conquering forefathers because you do not react when hunger kills children and new nations are pushed into underdevelopment by your selfishness.

In short, the present is the consequence of the past, and the future will repeat it. The question is not open to discussion—day by day and year by year the list of sins grows longer, sins imputed to a community of people on whom weighs the ancestral suspicion of having fouled the wellsprings of life. Evil is a sort of anthropological curse that attaches to people in countries of the temperate zones. The West is supposed to be cruel and toxic—like cat hairs are to an asthmatic. No matter what we may do, our error remains and we cannot expiate our sins. By a device like that used in anti-Semitism or racism, collective characteristics are cited,[6] and a whole group of people in all their variety are treated as a single person whose criminal nature is ascribed. There are no more human beings, simply entities—the French, the Germans, the Americans—in the same way as one talks of the Jews and the Arabs. The amalgamation of a certain group of people, regime, or government guilty of certain actions with the people they belong to transforms political guilt into metaphysical guilt.

If the West is genocidal by definition (the way ice is cold), if the responsibility is collective and goes back to the dawn of time, what is the point of denouncing its inherent criminality here or there in El Salvador, Brazil, or South Africa, and seeking to protect its victims? What is past is past, irrevocably; why should we be eternally responsible for it? How long will the peoples of Europe continue to be blamed for the atrocities committed by their ancestors? When will it end, this genealogical blackmail that, in the name of reparations and collective interests, would make us the indirect accomplices of slave trading, massacres, and pillage? There is nothing so dangerous as this idea of collective responsibility, which is transmitted indefinitely from generation to generation, and which evokes memories of the worst sort of totalitarian coercion. In the context of French history, our army applied the concept of collective responsibility in Algeria, when, in response to a guerrilla attack, it razed villages, massacred citizens, and tortured suspects. A respect for the past cannot be allowed to lead to confusion of debts and charges. Penance for the wrongs of the past cannot be irretrievably committed to a seamless and endless history. To suppose that Europeans and Americans are naturally or culturally evil is as intellectually lazy and moralistic as to say the opposite. It avoids thinking seriously about contemporary conditions of violence and oppression. It is wrong to declare that the West is guilty simply because it exists, as if it were an insult to creation, a cosmic catastrophe, a monstrosity to be wiped off the face of the earth. The question of Israel is fundamental in this regard. Through non-recognition of the Jewish state, the entire Western World is held to be illegitimate.

The Serene and Guilty Conscience

In the seventeenth century, the French Jesuit priest Louis Bourdaloue distinguished between four sorts of conscience: the good and serene (paradise), the good and troubled (purgatory), the troubled and guilty (hell), and the serene and guilty (despair).[7] Third-Worldism, as we have seen, belongs to the last category. The Westerner can accept that he is the garbage of the world, because it suits him perfectly. By calling himself accursed and pernicious, he affirms that at the same time he is part of an elite, one that in every way resembles an aristocracy of birth. He has done nothing to deserve his denigration, but cannot get rid of it. It has been given him once and for all, because it summarizes what impels him to do evil in all circumstances, including evil against himself. His faults give him a certain dignity, a place in the hierarchy of all time, and he is sheltered under the wrathful gaze of the great tribunal of History. This permanent conceit does not help him to fight against injustice, but to coexist with it.

What is a guilt that refuses to regret but a hardening in sin, a complacency with evil, a way of living cheek by jowl with horror? With great fanfare, Third-Worldists beat their chests, enjoying the revulsion they inspire, cynically rolling in the mud. But the insults to the self are automatic and prattling, like a parrot's talk. This comedy of slurs is a welcome reassurance for their good conscience, a narcotic that numbs it to the slings and arrows of fortune. The ritual judgments passed against Europe are very similar to the booster shots that children get every year. As with a vaccination, a little bit of anxiety and recrimination is injected in order to avoid any moral examination. It is a terrible form of doublespeak. Pathetic rabbis of remorse lose their voices screaming about their hatred of the West and pallid preachers build whole careers on denunciations of imperialism. But the mechanical nature of this phobia makes their ridiculous insults sound like nonsense. Morbid rumination focuses on itself, and the prattling penitents deal with the poverty of the world with a throwaway phrase, and then get back to business. They still love their enemy too much to really want to get rid of him; they continually revive their victim only to kill him all over again. They imagine the CIA everywhere because they would be seized with a desperate rage if, by some chance, their favorite target were to go away. They are like priests of the Black Mass; they spit on and scoff at the Northern hemisphere, but this is in order to affirm it and to retain the all-important position they so cherish. They are persecutors who cannot be reconciled with one another, and thus no longer owe anything to anyone. *The moment comes when moral and metaphysical guilt allows the abdication of all political responsibility.*

In comparison, it is clear that the two positions of good conscience and guilty conscience are equally plausible, and, because of this, they neutralize each other. The man of conviction and the man of contrition no longer have any doubt, and each is absolutely sure of himself. The latter suspects everything except suspicion itself. He has become its dupe after having been its herald. Through an excess of lucidity, he lets the better part of his perceptions melt away in a sour and undignified dishonesty. The mistrust he showed toward the West prevented him from mistrusting his own mistrust. His vigilance was its own blindness, because there is a fanaticism of skepticism that is like the fanaticism of faith. And the hope never to be fooled is perhaps the foremost stupidity of our time. The Third World-worshipper is blind because of his vision and a liar because he is too sincere, and ends up like his enemy, his reflection, the rigid and self-assured conservative. This explains why so many big-shot Maoists or Castroists have now taken openly reactionary or colonialist positions. On the soil of shamefulness, flowers of the good old days have quickly grown up again. One says, "We will bring them civilization," while the other says, "We have sent them to hell," but the results are the same. The mirror-images of self-flagellation and self-congratulation are both totally closed off from the world of other people.

Like self-satisfaction, excessive guilt leads to a shameful disdain of others. We care about the countries of the Southern hemisphere not because of the good they could do us, but because of the harm we can do one another with their help. With a good conscience as well as with a guilty one, one is in the position of never having to question anything, because the whole world is preconceived. To the Third World, we seem permissive, evasive, intransigent, and futile. Our unconditional support for a particular struggle or people cannot conceal the superficiality of our involvement. The illogical sincerity of collective egotism that pervaded Western elites from the 1960s to the 1980s had to lead to the opposite of what was intended. It was impossible really to love the far-off peoples in whose names we were quarreling with each other.[8] The taste for self-abuse was still a taste for oneself, a rampant egotism. Third World worship has never ceased to be militant ignorance about others.[9]

His Majesty the Baby

I am two things that cannot be ridiculous—a savage and a child.
Paul Gauguin

The Third World is spontaneous, sentimental, and just. The West is cruel and rapacious. A whole current of the European Left has built a veritable moral prosthesis on this fundamental differentiation. This brutal dichotomy, though, cannot conceal its own ambivalence, because in order to look at developing countries as innocent, they must be infantilized. In order to see in them the openness of which we are incapable, they must be deprived again of the autonomy our forefathers so cavalierly disregarded. There is a strange coincidence here, which suggests a relationship. In the West, the discovery of the importance of childhood took place at the same time as the colonial adventures and their horrors. It is no accident that Jules Ferry, the founder of public schooling in France, was in favor of the expansion of our overseas empire. Colonial ideology strongly insisted on the immaturity of the peoples subjected to European discipline, and the necessity of educating them.[10] Doctors, psychiatrists, and intellectuals turned with interest to the psychology of the Negro, the Arab, the Hindu, and the American Indian to justify the domination of the European race. Whether lazy or cruel, primitive or charming, the native is always the focus of careful teaching, because he is an exciting experimental subject the conqueror can use for refining his teaching skills. From the rice paddies of the Tonkin Delta to the tent villages of Constantine, the great saga of childish, naive, capricious, or versatile peoples justifies the mission of civilized societies. Africans, Asians, and Arabs need us too much for us to abandon them to their fate. "With the unformed clay of the primitive multitudes, France is patiently modeling the face of a new human race," in the words of Albert Sarrault, Minister of Colonies, in a speech at the beginning of a new year of classes (1923) at the school for training colonial administrators.

It is also no accident that, nowadays, when "pedagogy has become theology,"[11] the child has been given the inverse role of teaching the adult, just as primitive societies have acquired the job of guiding the civilized world. This modern tendency to see adulthood as a form of degeneracy that has not been able to keep promises made in youth is the exact counterpart of the adulation of the Southern hemisphere as the future of the Northern.[12] There is a parallel between Lewis Carroll's *Alice in Wonderland* (1865) in which, for the first time in European history, a little girl was made the center of attention and grownups outside it, and the beginning of the young nations' being praised for their youth and passion. It is a parallel that goes back perhaps all the way to the eighteenth century, and it would require a historian of ideas to measure its scope.

Nothing has really changed in our view of non-European peoples since colonial times; we still look upon them as children. But we have given immaturity such value that it is greater in wisdom and superiority. Third World-worshippers are still captives of this illusion, and the reference point of history remains the basic premise of their belief. The African, the Chinese, or the Peruvian is ahead of us because he is backward. If it is postulated that all growth is a step backward and that all history is decadence, he is ahead of us because he is behind, and backward only in that he is ahead of time. The subordinate is our teacher because he comes from the dawn of the world, while we come from its twilight. Whether seen as a soldier of the revolution by Marxists, as a childlike martyr by the humanists, as a primitive from before the Fall by the ethnologists, man in the Southern hemisphere is a "wise nurseling" (as Ferenczi described him) who, in the depths of his poverty, shows astonishing wisdom and utters hidden truths that terrify the Old World.

The Evil Seducer and the Chaste Virgin

Why is the colonial era, in all its phases, so cherished to this day? Because it duplicates the biblical myth of the fall of Adam and Eve. The time before the European Renaissance was the blessed time of the Hesperides on other continents. It was a time when animals could talk, and Nature poured forth profuse blessings on natural men, who were whole and splendid and did not know the difference between good and evil, between what was yours and what was mine. But then bearded and helmeted creatures came from beyond the sea, carrying fire and slaughter, and Paradise disappeared. Free and happy men were condemned to slavery. Novalis said, "Wherever there are children, there is the Golden Age." To preserve this myth, Third-Worldists persist in talking about the relations of the Southern hemisphere in the same terms that parents use to talk about their children—terms of corrupted rectitude and spontaneity. Like childhood, the Third World is seen as a place of eternal springtime, a fragile kingdom under attack by vicious adults in the guise of greedy capitalists.

In the biblical story of exile from the Garden of Eden there were four components: tempted man, tempting woman, animal tempter, and object of temptation. There were also two communications—between the serpent and the woman, and between the woman (as ambassador of sin) and the man. It was a simple story, in comparison to the many guises by which the West has manipulated and seduced the virginal Third World. The evil of Europe has many forms: pornography, rock music, gadgets, blue jeans, drugs, carbonated beverages, technology, tourism, and money. Satan is legion, he has a hundred faces, a hundred costumes for penetrating the spring-like oasis. This explains the diffuse regret with which we behold perfectly natural changes that these nations undergo as they begin the initial disruptive stages of political life. It also explains our rage against the industrial world, that profane corrupter who begins the transformation of an innocent humanity by stealing away its childishness.

To explain the disasters, repression, corruption, nepotism, and stagnation that ravage the Southern hemisphere, the key concept of *neocolonialism* is invoked. It looks as if Europe has left her former possessions only to rule them better, and so she must assume the blame for the mistakes and errors they commit. It is a wonderful short-circuit—the present once again is only a reproduction of the past, and the ancient accusation can be given free rein again. Is torture routine in the prisons of Iran and Syria and Algeria? This is only because their policemen "are the pupils of our own cops," as Claude Bourdet said.[13] Is Shiite Islam locked into a closed-minded fundamentalism? This is because "the 'solutions' of the West have failed" and condemn certain countries to fundamentalism, as Roger Garaudy said.[14] Is poverty spreading like wildfire? This, of course, is because of the shameful pillage committed by multinational corporations. French colonialists, American imperialists, English overlords, and Dutch, German, and Swiss businessmen are invoked to explain illiteracy, epidemics, wars, falling standards of living, and the despotism of peoples' new leaders. Because, on this earth, there are only two kinds of countries, the "sick countries" and the "betrayed countries," in the words of Roger Garaudy.[15] Instead of taking reality into account, instead of looking for causal relationships, far-off causations that pardon the states in the tropics are preferred. Thus, neocolonialism is the universal sin that becomes a way of permanently dismissing the problems of the real world.[16]

There is another notion that follows from this, and that is that the elites are manipulated by remote control.[17] The bourgeoisie of the Third World are all supposed to be artificial creations of imperialism maintained in power by and for it, in exchange for monetary profit, military support, cheap raw materials, inexpensive manpower, and profitable outlets and markets.

The conclusion is that these social classes and the states themselves are simply conduits—puppets propped up by the CIA, Unilever, United Fruit, or Nestlé. What is suspicious about this accusation is its comprehensiveness. There is no ruling class in the Third World that is not a foreign body, a cyst under the skin of a martyred people, no matter what the geographical, sociological, cultural, or historical conditions of the countries concerned. That's all there is; it's as simple as that. Ruling elites are illegitimate in Ivory Coast, Benin, Caracas, and Taipei. No matter how much vigor or patriotism they show, they will never be anything but parasites and conduits from the outside. Rich Africans, Arabs, and Asians are subject, in fact, to a twofold hatred. They are the object of attacks because they are heretics. These attacks are far more violent than those directed against an enemy, for they are hated not simply because they are bourgeois, but because they imitate foreigners. They are perpetuating in foreign lands the existence of a class whose extinction on the ash heap of history has been predicted by socialists for almost a century. Worse, they wrongly play this role and in the wrong way. They are ridiculous as well as hateful, because not only do they exist, but they are despicable in their aping of our bourgeoisie. All cultural hybrids are rejected as worthless, which is to forget the contributions made by intellectuals of the Southern hemisphere to universal culture. Senghor, Césaire, Gandhi, Nehru, Tagore, and Naipaul are disqualified as uprooted, and they are prosecuted in the name of authenticity, in a populist sort of indictment. The pantomimes of black rulers copying Napoleonic rites, pampered Asians living as if they were English, totally Americanized and rich Mexicans, Panamanians, and Salvadorans are all described in the same terms of ranting hatred that colonists once used for blacks and Arabs who ate in restaurants, drove cars, or wore neckties.

It makes no difference that scholars of Africa or the East denounce or modify this dogma, and demonstrate empirically that the inequality between rich and poor is the result of social structures that date from before colonialism, and that they cannot be explained by the class divisions of industrial societies.[18] It makes no difference that more and more Third World intellectuals are appearing to their own bourgeoisies to take charge of their own destiny and are affirming that the basic cause of the crisis is entirely internal, psychological, and spiritual.[19] It makes no difference that these young nationalist ideologies have found their own means for self-oppression in their search for ways of defending themselves,[20] or that they are beginning to refuse to accept the ideology of diabolical causation that makes it all too easy to attribute the sickness of the Southern hemisphere to outside agents.[21] Our Third World-worshippers will not let go the idea that groups in power, their families, and their relatives are and can only be conduits of outside power, are nothing but "lackeys."

Shut Up and Be Childish!

Because they are former colonial peoples, the Africans, Vietnamese, and South Americans have become like untouchables whose mistakes must all be played down in the name of Western barbarism. But the corollary of this monstrous monopoly is that they are totally powerless to define their own politics. In other words, Third World worship cannot accept that the unhappiness of the countries of the Southern hemisphere could be the fault of these countries themselves. *They do not exist except as a province, a mental protectorate of industrial countries.*

Our pious zealots cannot admit that the emancipation of the Third World might be the job of the Third World itself, any more than Cecil Rhodes, Bugeaud, or Lyautey could admit it. They devote as much passion to embellishing the developing countries as their fathers did to denigrating them, because both currents of thought stem from the same racism, from a view of differentness as inferior or superior, as the case may be. Just as at the height of the Empire, Oriental or African societies must be absolved from the weight of important decisions, and, thus, must be spared the difficulty of their consequences.

The propertied classes are rejected as mere by-products. Intellectuals of the Southern hemisphere are rejected simply because they are guilty of having been educated in Europe or America. The civil service, police, managers, technicians, bureaucrats, and officials are all rejected because, in their arrogance and brutality, they have betrayed the true Africa, the true Asia. What is left is the mute masses of people, brutalized by poverty and suffering, but who are also guardians of the treasure-house of tradition. They have been identified by our dear, paternalistic Third

World lovers as the true Third World, the way another ilk of believers shows off fragments of the True Cross. They project their
stock of clichés on this faceless and voiceless human horde and
make them speak their words. *Like a child, the Third World must
not be allowed to speak so that the Third-Worldists can talk in its
place.* Those who accuse the native bourgeoisies of copying their
counterparts in advanced countries are the same people who try
to put the words they want to hear in the mouths of African and
South American peasants. Imperialism is supposed to be an om-
nipresent monster, like the statues of Shiva with 12 arms and four
heads. It covers the globe with a constant and thousand-eyed vigilance, intervening wherever it wants, as it wants, deposing pres-
idents, generals, military leaders, and regimes as if they were
pawns on a chessboard. The conclusion is that the developing
countries, with no capacity to govern themselves, are innocent of
their own sufferings. They are denied national sovereignty, denied
local power, and even denied moral responsibility. This is the
threefold creed of Third-Worldism and it has all the characteristics of colonialist thinking.

The Angel's Betrayal

*We need a total intellectual revolution to uproot the European habit,
of both the extreme Left and the extreme Right, of doing for us, thinking
for us, deciding for us, the habit of denying us the right of initiative
that is the fundamental right of having our own personality.*

Aimé Césaire, Letter
to Maurice Thorez, 1956

In this universe of victims and vampires, the "other" has only
two roles to play—that of rebel or traitor, oppressor or oppressed.
Asiatics, Africans and primitives are classified in advance, only
tolerated as long as they do not contradict us. Whether they like
it or not, they have to shoulder the burden our leftists have assigned to them. But they are so perfect, so irreproachable, suffering to their hearts' content, like three billion Christ figures,
that we cannot love these disembodied heroes. Instead, we respect them, we take off our hats in their presence as if we were
in a church or a cemetery, we lavish mournful worship on them.
But so many good traits next to our bad ones get tiresome after
a while. Politeness and forced sympathy become trying. No com-

munication is possible, because we are so anxious to agree and conciliate. There is much amiability in Third-Worldists' speeches, but also much resignation. They are not talking about flesh and blood men and women, but birds trapped in a gilded cage of good behavior. Because we cannot recognize that the "other" is really another person, we idealize him, just as our predecessors devalued him. But to seek the perfect other prevents us from seeing the other as he really is. Because he is so loaded down with other peoples' hopes he is inevitably doomed to disappoint those who build him up. We expect of him what we do not expect of real people, and he is not permitted to do what real people do. The ex-colonial is marginal and outside history; he is deprived of the power to make peace and wage war on his own, and amounts to a sum of subtractions, an abstraction that had to be idealized so that we could project ourselves on him. He has now become the victim of a lunatic morality, a faceless man whom we can crush or idealize as we please.

This dogmatic version of the Third World is thus not a place, but an angelic person who has made no compromise with the horrors of the Western World, and who, therefore, assumes the twin figures of the innocent and the hero. Unfortunately, there is somebody unselfconsciously protesting against this adoration, and that is the deified man himself. He has no concern for these prayers or worship, and has the gall to show that he is not superhuman at all. After all, what has been the history of the nations of the Southern hemisphere since the Bandung Conference? It has been one of vigorous resistance and clever avoidance by these people of the enlightened image that a certain ideology has conferred on them. What did the Algerians, Tunisians, and Vietnamese do as soon as they were left on their own? These young republics left the cloistered gardens of childhood and bought tanks, cannons, and other arms. They filled their prisons, declared war, suppressed the rights of dissidents, and set up despotic political structures. The demand to be ordinary, that is, to be states with the same rights and prerogatives of others, also implies the capacity to make mistakes, to set up dictatorships, and to resort to violent methods. This is the price of freedom. The first traitor to Third-Worldism was the Third World itself; it never followed its assigned course, and did its best to overturn the pedestal on which it had been placed.

This explains why our credulous dupes were so indignant.

They could not tolerate the knowledge that the Golden Age had already been corrupted, and that there might be other murderers on earth besides us. "They cannot have done that themselves. Wars between poor peoples are manipulated by the rich."[22] This is a selfish bitterness because, in acting this way, the Third-Worldists are robbing these peoples of their own history, in the same way the ruling classes of the great powers make every local conflict an arena of the struggle between the superpowers.

This refusal to recognize "autonomous disturbances" is a curious confusion practiced by all sides. An American administration will explain political tensions in El Salvador, Guatemala, or Colombia as secretly manipulated by the Soviet Union, while forgetting underdevelopment, the hopeless poverty of the people, and the selfishness and blindness of the coffee kings or banana princes. It is confidently averred that such and such a conflict between two Middle Eastern countries is secretly controlled by Zionism and its allies or that secession in an African country is encouraged and financed by an intelligence organization with a Texas accent. In both cases, people of the Southern hemisphere are patronized as half-conscious agents in a conflict that goes beyond them. It's all very simple: They do not exist as such, and the choreography followed by these blood- and sweat-soaked countries was written by far-off powers. The miraculous irresponsibility we bestow on them is merely the prelude to disregarding them altogether. "It is neither logical nor natural," said Mexican president Lopez Portillo on February 24, 1981, "that the great powers fight our battles as if they were their own."

The Third World Does Not Exist[23]

What is the Third World, in the simplest sense of the term? It is a residual category, and shows the disdainful ambiguity that we have regarding the "other" as soon as we refuse to describe him. It is a convenient, malleable, and serviceable term that can be applied to the whole planet after you take away Europe, America, the USSR, South Africa, Australia, and New Zealand. A leftist Christian tract recently declared, "It is not necessary to go overseas to meet the Third World. We meet it all the time in our everyday life. It is there in our morning coffee, the clothing we wear, and the gasoline we put in our cars."[24] One might well ask if, for propaganda purposes, Guatemalans and Colombians deserve to be reduced to coffee grounds, Saudi Arabians and Yemenis to drops of gasoline, Koreans and Indians to pieces of cloth. This sort of vulgar economism, which takes the place of morality and sees nations only from the point of their specialties, seems like the exact equivalent of colonial greed, which computed the value of a state from the point of view of profit. When Mohammed is nothing but a barrel of gasoline, Abdou a quart of peanut oil, Lopez a cup of coffee, one is very close to a dehumanizing sort of racism. Just as there is anti-Semitism without Jews, there is Third World worship without the Third World, in which the words "Brazil," "Thailand," or "Senegal" do not refer to countries or cultures, but are simply elements of a theoretical and abstract construction. The other is not evoked but invoked, as in a prayer. He is desired precisely because he is somewhere else, and the country in whose name we beat our breasts exists only that we may breathe our bitterness on our own.[25]

In everyday life, the idea of the Third World does not add the slightest scintilla of understanding to the real world. It is nothing but an instrument for pouring invective on one's enemies. Third World worshippers present the curious spectacle of a brawl among priests who are bashing one another over the head with their holy icons. But what they are fighting about exists only in their speeches. The Southern hemisphere becomes an evanescent divinity that recalls somewhat the definition of poetry suggested by Paul Valéry—a purely solipsistic activity the experienced practice through love of the art, leaving it to fools to imagine that they are actually communicating with someone. The phrase "Third World" is a polemical slogan that lumps peoples together and casts the majority of the human race into the shadowy world of statistics, as part of an ossified universalism. At a time when economists no longer see a common destiny for all developing countries and try to adopt more flexible approaches,[26] when the movement of nonaligned nations is falling into incoherent quarreling, the mechanical usage of the words "Third World" is a sign of unprecedented intellectual laziness. Our most important mark of respect toward the nations of the Southern hemisphere should resist lumping them together under the same vague label. *It is crucial to be aware of this: In this commonly accepted term, a whole symbolic battle is at issue, a battle for the mental territory we will allot non-Europeans in years to come. To think of the Third World as terminally ill is to shrink the mental horizon of our contemporaries, and disqualify four billion people for future generations.* In *Heart of Darkness,* Joseph Conrad, when speaking of the blacks of the Congo, described "the extraordinary effort of imagination we need to make to see these people as enemies." But what an extraordinary lack of imagination is needed today, what shortsightedness is required to see Africans, Asiatics, and Pacific Islanders as nothing but patients in some colossal asylum! We must always counter this fiction of a three-dimensional world with reference to specific cultures. Beginning with early education, we must present the idea of the splendid disorder of these continents and how they resist categorization and generalization, not encompassed by the concept of a Third World. In some cases, a deliberate vagueness is as serious as prejudice; here again, verbal preciseness is very important, and things must be shown the way they really are. To escape from colonialism we must escape from commiseration, from the sad poetry of pity, from the bowing-and-scraping complex that sums up our attitude toward overseas lands.

We could dream endlessly about far-off societies, and speculate in approximations, but is it not better to dream about real people? The double fault of Third-Worldist literature is that it portrays Europe in a way that verges on caricature, and that it builds a model of foreign peoples that is both sickly and ridiculously righteous. It is guilty of the stupidity of being inconsequential, and it is hard to tell which is more reprehensible, the doubt that it casts on our own culture or the devaluation it inflicts upon others.

There is no question that it was still the colonial model that prevailed among those who lifted the young nations onto the altar of radicalism. Of course, colonialism was in retreat in leftist circles in France and Europe, but enough of its traces and habits were left that a line whose ultimate logic was the universal uprising of the oppressed still carried its basic traits. So the imperial ideal, far from being vanquished, was reinforced by its opponent and heir, Third-Worldism. I suggest that in the quarrel between these two attitudes there are common hypotheses. They share the same impatience for resolving the problems of others rather than our own, the same tendency to see the entire world as a problem of domestic policy (John F. Kennedy's formula), the same belief in a world of good and evil that has switched from North to South, the same transformation of Africa and Asia into a commercial preserve for one and a stockpile of fantasies for the other, and the same way of maintaining Africans and Asians in a state of political infancy. They share the same proselytism, the same opportunism in defending their position no matter what it does under any circumstances, the same passion for subscribing to the same epitaphs of praise for different societies, the same faith in the educational and progressive values of their respective times, full of a triumphant messianism. Colonialism set up the relationship between teacher and pupil as absolute; Third-Worldism has turned the relationship on its head and made the pupil the teacher. It teaches the opposite of what was taught earlier. What used to be glorified is now fought, and what used to be fought is now glorified. As Saint Rémy said to the chief of the Franks, "Burn what you used to worship, and worship what you used to burn." The reversal means a return to Square One. The criticism is still "a religious criticism of religion," in Marx's phrase, a ritual murder of Western imperialism that begins to look like a repetition of Good Friday—two days later, the dead man rises again in all his glory. These are all elements that make allies out of the two enemies, so that *to fight Third-Worldism today is to continue the anti-colonial struggle of the past.*

The End of Messianism

Dirty Hands

Purgatory is better than heaven or hell, because there is a future in it.

Chateaubriand

It is no longer possible to see the Third World as a savior, as a bearer of hope for the future on behalf of a wandering human race. What was supposed to happen did not happen, and the glorious prophecy was destroyed by unforeseen events. Neither Northern nor Southern hemispheres have a monopoly on truth or horror, and we must sweep away both illusions of our own openness and the perfectability of others.[27] The great trauma of the last 10 years is that the oppressed have also lost their innocence. The people we expected to be resurrected have turned into jailers, torturers, mass murderers, and perpetrators of butchery, as if independence for people meant mostly the right of people to kill their own, with their own weapons, and under their own flag! The former slave must be given his due—he is as good as his former master at subjugating other slaves to his will. The terrible truth that has only recently become clear is that all men are sinners, even those whom centuries of suffering have nominated for the exalted task of redeeming the human race.

The same movement that forbids the West to have a clear conscience ought to forbid its neighbors' innocence as well. If a curse weighs upon the states of the Northern hemisphere, it weighs equally heavily on other great civilizations. There is no society not founded upon crimes, massacres, or conquest of the weak—neither Islam, the great empire-builder by conquest and the sword, nor China, Japan, India, Inca Empire, precolonial African Kingdoms, or the Ottoman Empire. Nobody has the right to absolve himself of sin by invoking the sufferings of others.

To excuse the atrocities of new nations by citing colonialism, imperialism, American influence, or whatever, is to start from an outrageous falsehood. N'Guéma, Sékou Touré, Idi Amin, Pol Pot, Khomeini, Somoza, and Pinochet—to cite only the most bloodthirsty—are vicious dictators who are totally responsible for their misdeeds and have no right to excuse themselves by citing outside factors that are supposed to have determined how they behaved. None of these arguments has any value whatsoever—the lesson of the previous colonial power ["I was taught to do this in England or in France"], the excuse of international politics ["I had to do this because I was surrounded"], the mythical explanations of history ["I had to liquidate the traitors to preserve the Revolution"], the excuse of manipulation ["I was duped by Moscow/Washington"]. None of these arguments explains away freedom of choice; therefore, none explains away blame. And the soldiers, guards, and militias that obey the orders of these tyrants, the people who are their helpers, are equally responsible.[28] There are not two systems of measurement, or a double standard, for two portions of the human race—one for the evil whites and one for the natives protected in their irresponsibility, capriciousness, and naiveté. *The fact that they used to be colonies confers on them no privilege, no passport to absolution, no moral superiority.* Nobody acquires a state of grace simply because of the suffering he has undergone. It is not possible to confer upon him a stamp of innocence dispensing him from moral reckoning that would argue that his interests are one and the same with morality and right. Nowadays, imperialism is evenly spread throughout the world. The "revolutionary" government of Nicaragua is acting with the same brutality and arrogance toward the Miskito Indians as did the conquistadores of old. The new nations already have a history of the same war crimes and the same atrocities that stain the history of the Old World. A fundamental blame is attached to all men who find themselves trapped by power relations that are part of their lives, and the nations of the Southern hemisphere are neither better nor worse than us. Like us, they are capable of the best *and* the worst.

Let us put an end to this image of angelic countries that fix old and sinful Europe with a reproving stare, using the crimes of the West to refashion a whole lily-white history for themselves, and using this cover to perpetrate acts that are immoral. They are not held accountable, since they are owed everything on account of past outrages.[29] If they are forever categorized as angels, they can carry out the worst crimes without feeling responsible to anyone; thus, they sit in judgment on others but do not tolerate the slightest reproach against themselves. They put themselves in a position of protesting in the name of rights they were historically denied, but they deny us the right to judge them, because we are far away from the scene of events—even as our distance preserves us from local passions, and makes us more disinterested and impartial. Muslims say, "You cannot judge me, because you have to be Muslim to understand me."[30] You cannot judge me, says the African, because you have to be black to understand. Oddly enough, Sören Kierkegaard used the same argument to defend Christianity; he said that, to understand Christianity, you first had to convert to it! As soon as a race or a government tries to put itself above criticism, it is close to falling into barbarism. As soon as a people believes itself to be "special" and thinks of this as a permanent quality that cannot be changed by history no matter what happens, it transforms itself and others into biological species as distinct as cats and dogs. It is suspicious and distasteful when any movement or rebellion declares an *a priori* anti-Western stance and assumes the macabre position of a crusade against the white race. *When will the United Nations admit that anti-Western hatred and anti-white racism are crimes against humanity?*

Those who practice selective indignation against the peoples of the Southern hemisphere by giving them most favored nation status in the area of morality,[31] show a condescending paternalism and, in fact, contribute to underdevelopment and to the martyrdom of its victims. To assert that we have nothing to teach them, and nothing with which to reproach them, is the height of futility and permissiveness. To support this moral abdication for fear of helping imperialism is to give in to a loathsome form of blackmail. To criticize a regime is not covertly to support colonialism, and the opposition of a friend who does not go along with the crowd is more valuable than the insults of an openly declared enemy. In short, the Manichean opposition of good and evil falls apart as soon as it is presented. Good is nobody's exclusive property, and participation in history inevitably soils the participants. The Third World had to disappoint us in order to show its authenticity. A page has been turned. The former slaves have rejected their former masters and have found new masters and new forms of servitude. But that does not concern us. They have lost the blessing of the Cross that justified their origins, and have attained national maturity. Let them work it out. Their freedom is out of our reach, and they alone will be the judges of governments they agree to accept or eventually decide to reject. We can do nothing more for them than what they ask, which is the greatest degree of equity in the context of economic interdependence. We can improve the terms of trade in raw materials, create more equal exchange rates, undertake worldwide negotiation on trade, cancel or reschedule debts. But we cannot substitute ourselves or them. We can do no more than to give them a start, and these countries remain free to answer or ignore this invitation, to benefit or not from this arrangement. "The Third World is neither paradise nor hell, but instead is a kind of purgatory, in which a new world is being established, which will be whatever its peoples deserve"[32] (Jean Rous).

The Question of Human Rights

The West did not create human rights. Human rights created the West.
Jimmy Carter

No people can be freed from the obligations it incurs as a member of the community of nations. In this sense, a single moral rule must be used in the Northern and Southern hemispheres—that what is good for one is good for the others. To reject the ideology of human rights because it was born on European soil is to forget that these rights were proclaimed in a poor society—France in the eighteenth century—where people did not have enough to eat,[33] and that they were not proclaimed for one class or one nation, but for the entire human race. The accusation of imperialism in response to assertions of human values assumes that certain peoples, because of their origin or the color of their skin, should be spared the penalties everyone else suffers. It assumes that fear of death and love of life is less in another country, and that an Egyptian, a Malian, or a Guinean does not deserve the same assistance as a European when he is brutalized. It is a glaring sophistry to denounce international human rights policy because "it comes from within the economic boundaries of the OECD, which includes the 25 richest nations in the world, of whom 19 are European," and because "our political freedoms are the bright side of inequality, which condemns three quarters of the human race to the darkness of poverty and the biological struggle for survival.[34] It is squarely in the tradition of mercantilism to pretend that freedom is a limited quantity that can be divided up like a cake, with some people getting the bigger parts and others the crumbs, to make values and justice into products that are subject to cycles of scarcity and abundance like any others. The search for equality, the end of the overexploitation of the Southern hemisphere, and the end of dictatorships supported by the superpowers means working for the greater dignity of man by seeing it alive in the most concrete details of everyday life.

It is impossible to talk of freedom in the abstract, and it is dangerous to subordinate it to some material need. What is the standard of living above which it can be finally agreed that it is time to reestablish freedom of the press, allow workers to strike, and permit different parties to flourish? Civil liberties are not a luxury for pampered peoples, but a minimal condition for an increase in wealth. To suppress the metaphysical purity of principles under the pretext of more important tasks—for example, the absolute necessity for fighting against hunger[35]—is to compound the injury. It means ignoring the fact that all dictatorships are costly and that it is wasteful to employ resources for repression, oppression, torture, surveillance, and deportation that could be put to better use. And that the cold monster of totalitarianism does not simply make martyrs of men, but perpetrates famine, underdevelopment, and anarchy. No necessities but insanity and evil could justify the horrors committed in China, Cambodia, Iran, Uganda, El Salvador, and Lebanon. Neither torturing poets in prison, murdering children, nor making mutual spying into a civic duty has ever given a single mouthful of bread to hungry people. The careful observation of democracy in a local election in the French countryside has nothing to do with human slaughterhouses in Africa, and the suppression of minorities and massacre of political opposition has done nothing to generate wealth and raise the standard of living.[36]

Regis Debray said, "For there to be free men, there must also be slaves."[37] He was wrong. Slavery and disdain for law produce a vicious spiral that goes on forever. In the dictatorships of the Southern hemisphere, there is always enough money to buy machine guns, cannons, bayonets, and barbed wire, to pay torturers and spies, and there is never enough for investment in agricultural, industrial, or health-related expenditures. There is a necessary link between the poverty of democracy in the states of the Southern hemisphere and the economic poverty of those states.[38] Repression and the rampaging of soldiers becomes the only luxury allowed to penniless countries. This leads to a worsening train of events in which vengeance calls for more vengeance and material poverty leads to a thirst for blood. Democracy is not some miraculous state that is achieved once a certain per capita GNP is reached. It begins with itself; and just as children learn to walk by walking, respect for democratic rights is learned through respecting democratic rights. It is a principled search, because democracy must be built, day by day, through little steps and small victories, as freedom must be learned. It cannot be achieved at the right moment when people are finally ready for it. In this case, action takes precedence over desire. How is it possible to build a future of well-being and independence when these values are denied in the attempt? How is it possible to pretend to act in the name of the masses when states are exalted at the cost of the peoples whom they govern? What guarantee is there that freedom, after it has been so long trampled underfoot, will somehow spring up again at the end of the process? This is why a few formal liberties are worth more than seamless totalitarianism. A few steps toward social progress, even if they occur alongside pitiless exploitation, are preferable to a total absence of the rule of law. Anything that can save mankind from inhumanity is an opportunity that must be seized. Parliamentary institutions are certainly not a magical formula that must be applied to all regimes. However, in spite of their imperfections, they are superior to dictatorship, the autocratic rule of a *caudillo* or a political party, the omnipotence of political and military elites.

Some would argue that, because democracy has its ambiguities, it is an illusion. Because the freedom of rich countries coexists with dictatorship in poor countries, this freedom is nothing but a facade that conceals a system of extortion, and it must, therefore, be destroyed. This is a perverted kind of logic that would deprive everyone of freedom in order to redistribute it to the greatest number of people possible. And this leads to an all-or-nothing dead end. Either the entire human race will rise up from its chains some fine morning, or it will continue to groan under the boot of some all-powerful state. In the name of some radiant future, the opponents of human rights and civil liberties are the active agents in bringing about a new Stone Age.[39]

Universal Human Rights[40]

People refuse to understand that Zaire has the right to be be different. Before, we had 44 parties and seven unions. That led Zaire to chaos and anarchy. I said, "Throw the 44 parties into the river. It's over."
Mobutu [41]

It is believed that the rights of man can be forgotten because the West violates them, even as they wave them on high like a flag. Though these values were born on European soil, they are no longer Europe's exclusive property. Oppression has been carried out by Spain, Portugal, Holland, England, France, and the United States, but the moral progress made by these same nations is the property of all peoples. Individual rights, like scientific discoveries, are neither Western nor Eastern, neither African nor American. There are only two ways to treat a man, with respect or with violence, and there are no exceptions to this rule. We must first postulate the humanness of everyone, and then characterize him as Chinese, Greek, or Yemenite, because in every social order there are common needs that derive from the concept of humanity as the ultimate and final reality. Everyone carries within him the same unmodifiable essence, and no cultural difference can change it. Rich countries may indeed violate the principles they preach by exploiting certain regimes in the Southern hemisphere, but these great principles are still valid. The West, as the cradle of moral values, could do without the people commonly called Westerners—which really comprises the white race. This is because it has no skin color, and could just as well speak Ivoirian, Chinese, or Malian, as well as German or English. It is not Europe that is triumphant, it is a part of the European spirit that has been detached from its country of origin and has become the common heritage of the human race.

The rights of man are a privilege that belong to all, and no bloc or camp has the right to arrogate them solely to itself. Any other state has the right to reproach Europe in the name of another European tradition we may have forgotten.[42] One Eurocentrism opposes another, just as the people of the colonies, in demanding independence, were turning against their masters the same principles that were used to subjugate them. To put the great powers in opposition to one another wherever their greed leads them to intervene overseas is to work to make this external confrontation into confrontations within the regimes themselves. In this sense, international morality is the same as vigilance, the right of the community of nations to criticize any of its members who violates the basic rules of law, so as to diminish the inevitable disparity between the virtues a society preaches and those it practices.

Condemned for Being Like Us

In a fascinating work,[43] the Ivoirian philosopher Abdou Touré describes with despairing irony the extent to which the Ivory Coast is culturally dependent. French table manners become the ultimate in good conduct; huge expenditures produce copies of Avenue Foch or the Tour d'Argent restaurant in Abidjan; French is learned to the detriment of local languages; the couple is chosen as the ideal form for a family; Parisian artists, painters, and jewelers are adored as if they were on a cultural mission to Abidjan; and the white woman is held up as the ideal of feminine beauty. These are all signs of a serious crisis in the national imagination which, because it cannot invent anything, must import everything. It is as if, 20 years after independence, Ivoirian elites were still good little students and the French were still the only ones with the brains to know how to live well. This phenomenon of imitation is common in many countries of the Southern hemisphere. An article in the *New York Times* on January 13, 1982, described with astonishment the total fascination of Mexican middle classes for the American way of life. National television (which is privately owned) shows nothing but Superman cartoons, American football games, and commercials in which vapid blondes praise the merits of Coca Cola and Mustangs. Cultural alienation is such that little children know by heart all the imported brands of potato chips and cornflakes, but are incapable of recognizing the Mexican national symbol or the monument to the Revolution.

Many young nations, such as Iran, have reacted against this latent form of cultural colonialism. Decolonization has meant that they were emancipated at the cost of disappearing as separate cultures. They have entered the modern world via a course of development that puts together independence from and similarity to the West. The danger of losing their identity—which is particularly acute in countries that have carried on a policy of rapid industrialization—and the mystique of pursuing their cultural roots, impels regimes in the Southern hemisphere to erase any similarity it has with the hated West. The propaganda of these governments accuses others of being corrupt imperialists, meaning that they carry the sign of an accursed kinship. These mutual antagonisms carry preponderant importance in local conflicts. It explains why Morocco spends fortunes in its struggle with Polisario, which, in turn, is supported by Algeria or Libya, the hostilities between Egypt and Libya, the continuing conflict between Iraq and Iran, Syria's occupation of Lebanon, and Iran's exportation of its revolution to the Arab Emirates. All have a single enemy, a convenient alibi in the evil foil that is the tiny state of Israel. This explains how countries that are identical can fight each other savagely: the worldwide leveling of differences has aroused hatred against the West, which has become both a universal obstacle and a universal model, and from now on it is to be persecuted as the very incarnation of evil.

The forceps delivery of an infant national identity from tribal and ethnic and religious identities is always characterized by hatred for the Northern hemisphere. It leads to reprisals, massacres, and civil wars every time a neighboring state or a member of the community is accused of giving in to the enemy. Through a cult of purity and authenticity, as in Zaire, or tradition, as in

Iran and Indonesia, governments in the Southern hemisphere hope to avoid any risk of Satanic contamination. The mistake made by African, Pacific, Asian, and Muslin nationalists when they invoke their cultural heritage against the West is that they do not prevent this very insistence on purity being taken up in the organization of the Western world anyway, and that, while they think they are rejecting it, they are playing a part in its drama. The stupid imitation of consumerism is quite rightly condemned, but then they walk right into another equally disastrous kind of imitation, that of the West's criminality, horrors, and violence. They show a real talent for copying the worst faults of their former oppressors. This is their fallacy—to escape from the consumerism and permissiveness of the West, they imitate its totalitarianism. Their terrifying accumulation of certainties is accompanied by a deep hatred, so that the more their hatred for advanced countries is proclaimed, the closer they are to the vilest parts of our past. Even the rhetoric used to vilify the West is a subdialect of Third-worldspeak devised in Europe, a secondhand language from the old days, as if it were impossible for them to assert themselves without copying us.

The great dictators of the Arab, African, and South American worlds are nothing but third-rate, vulgar imitations of the tribunes, Caesars, and colonels of European history. What is Qaddafi but a Bedouin version of Mussolini? Khomeini is a Robespierre disguised as Ali Baba and a Torquemada who knows how to manipulate the media. Bokassa imitates General Boulanger and the ridiculous ceremonies of Napoleon Bonaparte. Mobutu is a little taste of absolute monarchy flavored with French sauce. Pinochet, Castro, Galtieri, Stroessner, and their pals are mixtures of mafiosi and mini-Hitlers with Spanish spicing. Those who treat freedom as if it were a crime are little tyrants, bloody braggarts, Frankenstein monsters of the tropics. They are recreating the bloodiest episodes of our own history, and they are nothing but second-rate actors. Everywhere, the devaluation of Europe and its democratic traditions is a sign of gratitude toward values that are viciously trampled underfoot. Because they are deceived by the logical fallacy of choosing a Western remedy against the West,[44] every one of their curses and condemnations is an act of respect for a part of the world they hate.

Each time democratic principles are rejected as stained with imperialist filth, in the name of negritude, the Vedas, Inca so-

cialism, Hispanicity, or the Koran, it is usually to revert to forms
of despotism that democratic tradition has already confronted and
conquered. For example, there is a slogan, "Neither East nor
West, but an Islamic Republic," that is common nowadays in the
Persian Gulf. What is this two-headed monster, this mongrel of
theocracy and secularism? Under the pretext of rejecting the West
in its socialist and liberal forms, it is happy to contradict both
Islamic and republican respect for law, and justifies an arbitrariness that has no relation to the mercy of the Koran or the principles of republicanism.[45] By squarely opposing its religious heritage to scientific and technical thought, the Third World makes
itself into a bastion of backward thinking, and adopts values, doctrines, and ideologies Europe has already tried and rejected. The
vision of "going beyond" Europe is only a pretext for unleashing
violence to suppress the people. The result is a crude Marxism and
mindless fundamentalism, monstrous mutations, reversions to the
mistakes that Europe has already made, inspired by the idea that
these will serve as part of the anti-European arsenal. The ridiculous plea of Frantz Fanon was to "go beyond" Europe, but the
result was a wallowing in unconscious imitation of the most de-
graded aspects of industrial society. It is impossible to "go beyond" democracy. Peoples of the Third World, you must accept
this little bit of the West so that you can more fully be yourselves!

European Thought Is Critical Thought

Doubt is the modern crown of thorns.
T.E. Lawrence

If there is one lesson Europe can teach others, it is self-criticism,
something that we have practiced systematically. Europe alone
has risked its own identity by uniting its cultures in anxiety and
doubt, offering the sole example of a mosaic of ethnic groups and
societies that have been able to prosper through questioning
and the constant threat of self-destruction. The unique conver-
gence of geographical and cultural territory explains how, along
with divisions of region and religion, there is the fundamental element of each person's division within himself.[46] Europe was
scarcely born when it began to oppose itself, and because of having placed its own enemy within its heart, could open itself to

other cultures without being swallowed up. It is the only culture that has been capable of seeing itself through others' eyes (even though its perceptions may be mistaken). Because there has been no doubt about its identity, it has been able to grant a great deal to other cultures.

This little peninsula on the tip of Asia is the only civilization in history to have been able to reflect on its own misdeeds. The naive hope of renewing the European continent through hatred of Europe has been a typical Western tendency since the Renaissance.[47] This pleasure in pillorying one's own country, in violently and skillfully manipulating the scalpel in one's own heart is only seen in our part of the world. What appears to be a renunciation is really only a stronger allegiance; the blasphemous revolt of the intellectuals looks like anti-Western feeling, but is really an ambiguous phenomenon that is part and parcel of what it denounces. The success of this criticism suggests that the "evil" of the West is only one of its aspects, and does not negate the remarkable elasticity that allows it to direct the strongest criticisms against itself. By revolting against his own society, the critic proves that it is not what he says it is, because he himself belongs to the society, as well as to its alternatives.

So the enemies of Europe are also its friends. When it is wounded, the wound is one that heals, and a traitor is only a different sort of partisan, since he opens a critical way that denies mainstream thought the monopoly of truth. After all, the war in Algeria and the war in Vietnam were brought to an end by public opinion in France and the United States. Peace demonstrations in Paris and Washington, the respect for democratic values by the military and the deterioration of the American army contributed to the end of the fighting as much as the courage of the FLN and the Vietcong. In democratic countries, it is difficult for brute force to prevail over conscience. Attacks on the system are part of the system itself, colonial history was reinforced by rabid anticolonialism all the way from Las Casas and Montaigne to Sartre, because Europe comprises not only an ethic of expansion and profit but a territory of tolerance and pluralism of thought and faith.[48]

The Third-Worldist would like to call himself an enemy of our society, but he is really only a shamefaced supporter of it. He cannot escape from Eurocentrism, because self-criticism and openness to other cultures are themselves the historical activities of Europeans. His existence is an affirmation of Europe, he flourishes in the midst of the very doubt that would deny Europe. To be European means always, in one way or another, to be one's own enemy. The West is not *in* crisis, it *is* crisis; it is a basic dissatisfaction, a confusion that seeks itself and is based on endless and constant self-questioning. We can say of the West what Borges said of Shakespeare, that in the intimate core of his being, he was nobody, even though he taught himself to pretend to be someone. Europe is a great mass of contradictory thoughts living under a single roof like some noisy and quarrelsome family. It is a squabbling spectrum of cultures, none of which has been able to eliminate the others. Nazism, whose contemporary equivalent is Soviet communism, is the only historical movement that tried to destroy Europe as an antagonistic entity. Europe has never been an empire itself, even though some European nations have been imperialistic. It is therefore impossible to say that the West is nothing but colonialism, just as it is impossible to say that Islam is the same thing as Iranian massacres or China the horrors of Mao's cultural revolution. A civilization that is guilty of the worst atrocities as well as the most exalted accomplishments does not deserve to be called by a single epithet, because it has never subsumed its existence as a single principle. Genocide is far from being an invention of the West. On the contrary, it was the West that first made it possible to think of certain crimes as if they were crimes against humanity.[49] The West, and the West alone, gave a precise meaning to the word "barbarism."

The superiority of Europe can only be denied in the name of another idea of Europe that is infinitely dynamic. Its main benefit is to have produced anti-colonialism, which is only one other way of being Western by way of criticism. *The Old World's example has made it impossible for any nation today to escape from the obligation to criticize itself.*[50]

European Chauvinism Is Still Chauvinism

Europeans themselves, however, need to be reminded of a basic truth. No privilege can grace the 30 nations of this continent by bestowing on them a purity they never had. The perfectly valid affirmation that underdeveloped countries are no more exempt from sin and violence than we does not diminish the frightful genocide of Indians in Latin America, the murderous wars of imperialism and decolonization, the unbearable scandal of the gulf between rich and poor. All this is monstrously unjust, and cannot be undone. It would be depressingly dishonest to try to reduce our responsibility by comparing us to the human race in general.

To repeat: A guilty conscience is an illness that is worst when it is absent where it ought to be present. In the uncertainty of an unpopular war, a massacre, or some bloody bungle, the first duty of a democracy is to distribute images that show it in a bad light, to communicate the facts that condemn it. It is frightful that some administrations, political parties, and intellectuals express unconditional praise for the "free world" and with a stroke of the pen conceal the fact that the glorious European flower grows from soil soaked in blood, slavery, and butchery. A country like the United States has paid dearly in recent years for the dream of pious simplicity preached by the founding fathers—the unshakable conviction that the USA is the land of the best and the brightest, the naive belief that what is good for Uncle Sam is good for the world.[51] The stupidity and blindness of some rulers of advanced nations, who keep bloody Caligulas chained in their backyards, who have no respect at all for the most elementary of human rights, are more dangerous to the West than the noisiest critics. By coddling deranged dictators, they abet the decline of democracy and open the way to Communism. Narrow-minded politicians who confuse the cause of liberty with that of an oligarchy, who defend the "Western World" through thick and thin, are playing the game of the Kremlin in spite of themselves. A little part of the world can no longer base its lifestyle on a disproportionate sharing of the world's resources. What is good for Europe but bad for the rest of the human race is a crime.

We can feel only the deepest repugnance for those who claim a mission of redemption for the whole world for a single people or camp, a single language, or the region it comes from. The newly minted apostles of the free market—who are usually former staunch Fidelistas or Maoists that all agree on how much the Third World has let them down—have changed the aim of their typewriters and are now on the firing line for free enterprise, multinational corporations, and Christianity. But in doing this they are simply tipping over the game board and going back to Square One. The free-floating and boastful chauvinism of Western World-worshippers of all stripes is worth no more than the simplistic formulas of the Third-Worldists. Double-duty fanaticism is the opium of fools, and its most important characteristic is to be reversible like a jacket, to be useful to any cause at all. There have been

enough intellectual prostitutes in the writing of history already.
Both sides shamelessly maim and manipulate the facts, using them
up until nothing is left. Such ideological frenzy is simply the pillage and suppression of reality. If we want to break the deadly
circle of hatred and malediction, we cannot begin the game of bad
feeling all over again, attacking newly independent nations to
make ourselves look better, as if in the reckoning of gains and
losses between the two worlds the balance was now even. In the
Kingdom of Parrots, all speech is equally senseless.

If we are proud of our country, of its technical and cultural
accomplishments, why should we try to play innocent every time
someone does something repulsive in our name? Every Westerner
carries the historical responsibility for his culture. If he claims a
part of its greatness, he must also acknowledge his kinship with
its worst representatives. The flame of anger and indignation must
always be kept burning in the fight against passive guilt. To mourn
colonialism today does not mean cloaking it in sanctimonious oblivion, but teaching children about it in school, teaching them what
infamous deeds our country showed itself capable of, the pile of
corpses our republic was built on, who were the torturers and who
were their accomplices. The mistakes of the past cannot be erased
by forgetting them, but by facing them and uncovering all their
worst details. Who would dare to deny that France owes a debt
to North Africa and black Africa, England to India and East Africa, the United States to Latin America? Just because there were
evil episodes in our past, and periods of shame and horror, we do
not have the right to bless and perfume them, to make our happiness depend on our indifference to other people. The shadow of
death is still attached to the most dramatic achievements of Europe and the New World.[52]

The Dangers of Self-Hatred

He who hates himself must be feared, because we will be the victims of
his vengeance. Let us therefore take care to teach him to love himself.
                                            Nietzsche, *Aurora*

The foregoing teaches us this: that hatred of the West is really a
hatred of all cultures concentrated on a single one. In the beginning, one finds nothing loveable in oneself, but in the end, one

loses the ability to love others. If the value attached to other cultures is in proportion to the disdain for our own, it is certain that this fascination will decline as one is reconciled with one's own society, or at best will linger in a kind of esthetic eclecticism. A doctrine that preaches the liberation of the human race cannot possibly be based on the hatred of an entire civilization. Man does not work to diminish but to increase himself, and there is every reason to mistrust a form of humanism that begins by leaving out a quarter of the surface of the globe and calling for the consignment of a whole society to hatred and oblivion. The great religions, philosophies, and belief systems are so linked to one another that to reject one is to reject all.

It is futile to hope that the systematic cultivation of shame will miraculously open us up to far-off societies, and wipe away misunderstandings. Some may say this sense of guilt is our last chance to retain some modicum of respect for the oppressed. But this is pure cynicism, because it means admitting that, aside from a vague feeling of unease, there is nothing that ties us to them. The proclaimed abandonment of Eurocentrism is still an involuntary act, and the first precondition of the acceptance of others is a consensus about our respect for our own culture. Let us become our own friends first, so that we can become friends of others again. If we are tired of our own existence, others are of little use. To love the Third World, for it to have a future, does not require a repudiation of Europe, and the future of industrialized countries does not require that they forget the nations of the Southern hemisphere. Every self-destructive wish carries with it a generalized negativity that envisions the end of the world.

Conclusion

"There is only one remedy for love: to love more. . . ."

—Henry David Thoreau

He who sees the light glowing from the East seeks out the East; if, for him, it glows in the West, he should seek out the West. My desire is for the light itself in all its glory, and not for the places it touches.

Ibn Arabi

Our Faith Is Built upon Discord

If the vigor of your undertakings at times conceals atrocities from me, I am doubly confounded, because your misdeeds paralyze me with horror, and your virtues fill me with admiration.

Diderot, "Discours pour Reynal," 1781

Because we reject both a dishonestly clear conscience and sterile self-denigration, the only perspective we can bring to our world is one of discord. Admiration for and distrust of Europe, which are both based on real experiences, seem to pose an insurmountable contradiction. Each would like to be a universal belief, and looks at the other as a kind of blindness, but their common truth lies in their mutual dependence. In other words, both the anti-European Inquisition and aggressive Eurocentrism must be affirmed together. Because it is impossible to avoid choices that by themselves could tear us apart, to be legitimate we must practice both skepticism and allegiance.

We must, therefore, become defenders of a twofold tradition, that of solidarity and criticism. Our contemporary history still presents a daunting accumulation of scandals. But we must re-

149

member that all the great accomplishments of Europe have been carried out in opposition to established powers in the name of an ideal Europe. Repulsion is accompanied by an irresistible passion, and with regard to Europe we cannot help being insanely in love and insanely indignant as well. Incompatible feelings can coexist because both are deemed necessary by the person who feels them. In itself, the duty of perseverance implies a critical distance. The more I respect Europe, the more I challenge it; the more I challenge it, the more I reinforce it. It is a continuous circle that opens and closes, but each time at a higher level. The headlong pursuit of self-hatred does not allow us to escape from shame, it simply makes it more bearable by depriving it of that arbitrary element that would make it a subversive emotion. Also, a European who has learned to be critical has not stopped loving his own society. He is attached to Europe while remaking the lessons of history. The "negation of negation" does not mean that there is no more negation. Doubt remains a quiet voice in the midst of the plenty that maintains our privileges, through a sort of controlled error.

A secret voice whispers in our ear that neither of the two positions can be held separately. A position of gratitude must be maintained toward values that are being trampled underfoot. If there is hatred there, it is expressed in the name of greater love. It is love of Europe that leads us to have a careful hesitation about military or colonial adventures she would like to have us engage in. This emotion requires that, in the name of Europe, we condemn the actions and errors of certain Europeans.[1] The excitement of love is never so impetuous as to be beyond self-examination. And self-examination cannot wipe away affection. European identity comprises these alternating convulsions.

We must pay attention to these two values, and we must remain faithful to the admirable genius of the Old World, without denying the sacrifices required by every search for justice. We must tread a path of vigilant affection, equidistant from suicidal nihilism and self-satisfaction. Perhaps the only way to combine the critical effort of the Enlightenment and the inventive capacity of the Renaissance is to maintain an iconoclastic and rebellious way of thinking, along with a conservative one. The way to affirm the force of reason and the power of the imagination, to be absolutely modern while being absolutely traditional, is to maintain a way of thinking that commemorates and preserves along with one that is deviant and analytical. Only the reconciliation of our founders, who were men of action, and our critics, who are men of second thoughts, will give us a perspective that may be full of drama, yet is exciting to explore.² The European must not put an end to the war that is within him; he must translate his uneasiness into an overarching principle. Where there is a desire for disunity, he must show a deep-flowing continuity; where there is respect for tradition, he must perceive the emergence of innovation. The vicissitudes of history, conflicting interests, and the greed of different alliances, have all long required that we love our cultures as unhappy lovers, obsessed by the evil of our companion but unable to leave her, compelled to find fault with her where we would prefer to adore her. To be European nowadays means to speak with doubt and enthusiasm at the same time. Our perplexity must always offer the chance for salvation, so that we will not inflict lasting scars. To love ourselves without being conceited, we must constantly swing between faithfulness and separation.³

There Will Always Be "Others"

> *The rebirth of the human race in each of us leads immediately to the recognition of the pluralism of humanity. Man is the only animal who speaks, but there are millions of languages. Whoever forgets either of these two facts will fall into barbarism.*
>
> Raymond Aron

It might seem that I have undertaken the reassuring job of demystification as if I finally had the right attitudes about the "other." But I have no light to shine, nor am I pretending to announce the radiant dawn of true brotherhood. It is too easy to make fun of one utopia that has been substituted for a dream that is just as elusive. Unmasking is a mask itself, and when it is tried in relationships, it can only lead from one mistake to another. There is no point in replacing the various forms of Third-Worldism with another analysis that would also think of itself as infallible and that could reign over the universe. The radical criticism of different Western leftist attitudes toward the countries of the Southern hemisphere does not lead us to a new level of knowledge, but to a new state of uncertainty. At the beginning of any relationship with the "other" comes misunderstanding.

For there will always be "others." No matter how tolerant

and liberal Western culture becomes, it will never make differentness into another form of sameness. There will always be "others" in the world, and identities that are different from ours will always diminish our existence. That is why exoticism and racism will continue to thrive; to eliminate them it would be necessary to eliminate the foreignness of others that they thrive on. Every culture is, for itself, an absolute that assumes uniqueness and self-sufficiency. So cultures cannot be complementary, but must be supplementary, competing and overlapping and interweaving like the vines in a jungle. There is no harmonious cosmos, because there are too many distinct parts of the human race. The pretense of each one that it is sovereign must lead to tension. The universe is hostile to me because I am not the whole universe, and differentness leads to mutual repulsion. War, misunderstanding and invasions are not so much the fruit of human evil as the result of the proximity of the multiple expressions of the species that is frightened and maddened by their proliferation.

Of course, there is such a thing as the human race as a biological entity, a characteristic common to us all. That all men are brothers is an abstraction of faith, as long as I have not experienced fraternity with a flesh and blood man. Such a relationship is filled with ambivalence, because we imperceptibly share hostility and attraction. All friendship for a stranger walks the path of a necessary reserve—no matter how open-minded or big-hearted I am, I will never eliminate the outsideness of another person. Even if the globe were a sealed chamber in which the essences of North, South, East, and West were to mingle, I could not apprehend them all without selecting and transforming them. It is not true that peoples and nations can reconcile and understand one another on basic principles through dialog and good will. Differences in belief and race will always stand in the way of perfect communication. The "other" remains impenetrable, neither so different nor so similar as is believed, and this is why the revelation of the human race to itself is an unrealizable dream.

This proposition, however, must be immediately turned around and completed thus—the foreigner is the selfsame source of fear and wonder. The door between us is also a bridge that unites us, and at this level, it is hard to tell the difference between conviviality and conflict, because all discord is a kind of linkage. It is not true that "Western society is a miracle," as Broyelle said. What is a miracle is the flourishing of many societies side by side, without regard to qualities that might make one culture or another particularly attractive or fascinating. The world is wide, languages are different, and fatherlands are many, and these factors will always lead men to oppose and sympathize with one another. My first feeling of gratitude toward the African, the Asian, or the South American other stems from the fact that he is different from me. The babel of languages and races is both a horror and a gold mine. We are confronted by a world to which we do not have the key, and we can neither absorb nor ignore it. Perhaps, it is time to accept the outlandish fact of "otherness"—and to set it on a new course that is no longer based on deprecation or idealization. The affirmation of the perfectability of the far-off foreigner was certainly a necessary step in the aftermath of the unjust mutilation carried out by colonialism. But it is not possible to base a movement permanently on a counter-truth.

Passionate Attraction

> *This immense "other" has saved me more than I myself would have wanted.*
>
> Maurice Blanchot

Why must our sympathy always be directed toward suffering people, only to forget them once they are no longer stricken with misfortune? Why is our attention focused only on countries where freedom is menaced, children starving, and dissidents tortured? We should remember that no lasting relationship is based on pity. It is no more possible to fall in love with a beggar than with an economic growth curve. Philanthropy is worthless if it does not start with a passionate attraction toward one nation or another. Moral universalism must always be sustained by an emotional particularism. The ethical level is not above or below the esthetic level; rather, they reinforce one another and coexist in the mystery of differentness. My sense of moral responsibility can be sustained only by an admiring fascination for the other. Beyond pathos there is still love, and there is no moral relationship that is not first emotional. Neither generosity nor duty is enough to establish strong ties, and the dictates of conscience are not what usually motivate people. That is the danger of any overly exclusive human-rights policy, of a sense of justice that is disinterested and dispensed dispassionately. It cannot value one culture more than another, and is satisfied with being applied wherever there is pain, nightmare, and blood. The impersonal character of this sad, unspontaneous and unsympathetic virtue risks giving countries of the Southern hemisphere a false image of misery. The conviction necessary for the achievement of a great cause certainly cannot stem from self-deception and egotism, but it cannot stem from charity alone, either.

Nothing could push us outside the gates of the Old World if there were not some aspect of the human race out there that excites and intrigues us. Nobody would leave his borders if the far-off other were not, above all, seductive; if he were not, in and of himself, enough reason for me to seek him out. I am not sufficient unto myself, and enchantment comes to me only from the outside. A foreigner inspires me before he fills me with pity or astonishment; my obligation toward him springs from an irresistible magnetism. He inspires me because he is the avenue by which I will escape from myself and the terrible self-absorption that is our lot.

How can we not seek sustenance, dreams, and hope from beyond the seas? We do not admire China, Morocco, India, or Japan through condescendingly good will or purely archeological curiosity, but because the respective cultures of these countries are works of art so beautiful that they bring tears to our eyes. Overseas, we are side by side with people whose intelligence, refinement, and grace are dazzling. The tropics are not simply an object of study, but the dreamed-of place of another possible destiny. What other criticism can be used to gauge the legitimacy of a choice, other than the possibility of a new life? They could be called countries that are becoming *developed*, but could just as well be called countries by which we are *enveloped*.

We have discerned the outside world through decolonization. How can we make sure that the taste for discovery will survive the end of colonialism? For Europe, mourning its empire does not mean getting rid of its possessions and retiring into its northern fortress, aggrieved and afflicted. It means forming ties of friendship with its former subordinates; it means substituting emotion for domination. Rather than penitence, melancholy, or self-hatred, a new sort of contact is needed for a better relationship between cultures. Friendship toward other peoples is more than simply tolerance of one state for its neighbors; it is a certain will on the part of a people to construct concrete ties with others. In a field opened up by good will, politics and polemics wither, while understanding and love take root.

In Defense of Eurocentrism

If a Christian were to come to me full of enthusiasm for the Bhagavad-Gita, and say that he wanted to convert to Hinduism, I would reply that the Bible has just as much to offer as the Gita. But you have not really tried to find it. Make this effort, and you will be fully Christian.

Gandhi

Why should people study foreign languages?[4] Why travel to Africa or Brazil? First, to learn that we are not alone in the world, to cross-pollinate ourselves by finding our opposites. But we also want to feel that we are not at home everywhere, and that we cannot escape our attraction to our native land. To approach the other is to mortgage our integrity and deepen our solitude. *In other words, having only one national culture is deadening to the spirit, but not having a national culture is, too. We have to answer and deny the two needs at the same time.*

On one hand is the stupidity of a self-sufficient community that protects itself against the best things the rest of the world has to offer. On the other is a casual and amiable eclecticism that is accessible to the most diverse messages because it is eminently uninterested in any of them. Only the reaffirmation of a persistent identity allows us to escape from the here and now. Any contact requires a basic center, a fatherland, as the elementary condition of cosmopolitanism. The same imperative that commands us to remain aware of "others" also commands us to live a bit for ourselves. The "rolling stone" is cosmopolitan, not in spite of the fact that he is a European but because he is European. While he may be entirely closed off in his cultural differentness, he is still much more international than he is French, German, or Danish. The fixed point of national attachments is also a starting point that gives expatriation its dynamic nature. Without a mother tongue and a place in the country where heart and mind can develop naturally, without this place in our memories, family ties, the neighborhood where we grew up, there would be nothing to arouse our curiosity, to push us in one direction or the other. I can fall into or out of love with one or any nation because I am not attached to any of them. The essence of my enthusiasm for the world is that it is a force reined in by its bedrock, and that overcomes obstacles by throwing itself at still others. My attachment to Europe greatly sharpens my taste for leaving it, because it is a fixed compass point, whereas I follow all the others as my wandering leads me. Cosmopolitanism is at best nothing but a utopia that deprives us of the blinders of overbearing nationalism, a fertile contradiction that remains inaccessible and tries to instill a maximum of uprootedness with a minimum of identity.

If being torn away from domestic security were not a painful and long-lasting deprivation, there would be no such thing as migration, and it would be possible for people to travel in all cultures with no problems, the way blood circulates in the veins. In this case, difficulty is the condition for accomplishment, and the small-town mentality is what encourages people in their impulse to flee. The unbearable truth that all travel abroad murmurs to us is that each person must live and die within the limits of his own culture. But also, the experience of being in another world deprives me of the ability to live naively, freezes the assets of my roots, and forbids me to remain attached to my own country, like a bulldog to its bone. We are not beings eminently adaptable to any climate, food, or language. This is why the future of the world for us is here in the heart of good old Europe, even if we try to put the whole planet between it and us. Europe is our destiny, our lot. More than ever, our personalities develop through the respect for its borders, its traditions, and its territorial integrity. Appeals to elemental forces, and the call of *Blut und Boden* that inspires all simple-minded patriotism, are no more dangerous than an interplanetary lyricism that stacks up maxims and philosophies, and that would have black and white and red march in our parade like so many interchangeable carnival acts.[5]

Let us therefore be done with the absurd dilemma that would equate a love of the West with ignorance of the customs of the Southern hemisphere. Through reconciliation with the West as a culture, rather than as a militarist and imperialist master, we will be able to open a way toward other societies. We must love the Third World, but this sort of Third World loving must not take place by hating Europe because of its accomplishments. Today, to ignore our own history, or to falsify it, is the way to ignorance of other peoples, to denial of their contribution. How can a Frenchman or a German understand anything about the currents of Islam or the metaphysical creations of Asia if he has not first become familiar with his own religious heritage, even though he may be an atheist? By delving into the treasure of his past without complacency or malevolance, the European will remain a man of many loyalties, penetrated by foreign cultures, and speaking Greek, Arabic, or Hindi while he is still a son of the Seine, the Thames, or the Tiber. He will remain a European, even in his falsifications and betrayals of Europe. Any undertaking that sidesteps the balance between loyalty and disloyalty would revive the arrogant ethnocentrism of the Empire or the foolish masochism of Third-Worldism.

We Must Be Open

. . . Madness . . . would be near the man who could see things through the veils at once of two customs, two educations, two environments.
T.E. Lawrence, *The Seven Pillars of Wisdom*

In short, we have to avoid two illusions: that we have nothing to learn from others, and that we have everything to learn from them.[6] Both assimilation and preservation can be practiced through avoidance of intolerance and of self-punishment, the safeguard of respect for oneself because respect for others is placed above all. Total closure would be spiritual death, but total openness a disaster. If the West were left entirely to its own immobility, to vain gloating over its riches, it would cease to grow and begin to diminish, to lose its edge. It is in the West's interests to give the countries of the Southern hemisphere not merely the means to criticize it but to compete with it, to raise itself to our own level of wealth and prosperity, because if it buys tranquility at the price of others' suppression and suffocation, the price will be high indeed. The oil crises of the 1970s are perhaps the best illustration of this. The less intelligent Westerners are, the more foolish other countries appear to them, and the xenophobia of the former is in direct proportion to the fanaticism of the latter. At a time when crisis requires us all to be saved together or perish together, protectionist self-sufficiency is not an option. The West must be required to expose itself, to run risks with others, and to live continuously in the bright spotlight of the outside world. The vitality of a culture can be measured by its capacity to escape from its own destiny, to comprise more than it can extract from itself alone.

What Lévinas called "receptivity to the contribution of the other" implies that we get outside ourselves because we are already inside ourselves, we set out from a private domain to which we can retreat at any time. I am not able to take on at will any skin, climate, race, or language. There must be a possibility of gathering together against the universal fact of our dispersion, of a retreat into ourselves that ensures the preservation of memory and the feeling of historical continuity. But at the very core of this intimacy, I must be wrenched away from animal self-satisfaction, and the desire to resume contact with the outside.[7] Of course, I cannot escape from Europe. But that is not the same as being convinced of this without trying to expose myself, without trying constantly to lose myself far beyond my own borders.[8] Opening a window to the outside prevents my being rooted within a narrow horizon and lets me float freely, whereas the preservation of a place to return to provides the other with a land of asylum. The oscillating alteration that must regulate our relations with the outside world requires that we forget ourselves without abasing ourselves, that we know how to care for the other, but also to ignore him.

We must substitute the idea of a separateness that avoids absorption for the idea of a planetary whole or a "universal civilization." Our distance from "others" must not destroy our relationship with them, nor our relationship with them the distance between us. Any society that is too receptive is in danger of losing its identity, just as any excessively closed group soon degenerates and rots on the vine. The state of the world does not allow any country to close itself off, and each must find the distance between closure and openness that it needs to allow productive surprises, intriguing dissonances, and fruitful contradictions. Asking foreign cultures to join in the problems of the industrial revolution does not mean melting them all together into some common matter, but adding their voices to all the others. If we begin to add up what the West owes to foreign cultures today—such as the rediscovery of our bodies, religious consciousness, or a taste for dancing and music—we will discover many contributions without which our era would have no spice, no genius. Beyond fighting and mistrust, it is these magic imports that more than anything else argue in favor of holding out our hands to the other. If a form is created together, taken up by some, and modified by others, this is true communication.

Faithful Betrayal

Do not measure our attachment to France by the renunciation of our own fatherland.

                                        Jacques Rabemanangara, Poet of Madagascar

Any attraction we may feel toward a society has little to do with its intrinsic value, and has nothing to do with whether that society deserves it. There are some great civilizations that leave us cold, while there are second-rate tribes about which we cannot stop talking. To love a particular foreign culture is an unfair choice that excludes lots of others, but not loving any foreign culture at all is a terrible sign of spiritual avarice. There is no attraction unless my freedom of choice has been affected by some special relationship, some particular tone. To enjoy Eastern music, or South American literature, or Buddhism, there must be a preference for a certain melodic line, a baroque storytelling style, a particular sort of meditative peace. Once I come to know them, I integrate these forms of expression into my cultural heritage and they become necessary to me, and beneath its obvious richness, I find gaps in my national culture that seem intolerable. To love Arab music more than any other does not mean I have entered the Arab world, and it certainly does not mean I have become like the other people who listen to it. It means establishing a common taste between "the Arabs" and me; it means sharing a common domain, bridging a gap that allows me to become more involved with them. Two universes that abut each other are suddenly joined by the magic of a common passion. Of course, it is only a partial communication, but it is much better than a mutual distaste.

I will never know all artistic or literary forms in the world, of course. I will never visit all the continents. I will never be able to embrace all religions and will never be a friend to all men. But in my loving some other people, learning one or two foreign languages, choosing one country to be fond of that is thousands of kilometers from my home, I give a personal but indirect homage to the principle of outsideness. Somewhere in the world there will be a country that chooses you as you choose it. By making a specific choice—of Masais, Indians, Lapps, or Australian aborigines—I preserve the universality of foreignness; I cultivate transcontinental energies that do not conform to borders or races.

The chasms that separate cultures are also the result of an emotional geography and one of preference (that varies according to fascination or fad) and also of an underlying equality. Any of them could be chosen at any time. So if there is no gratuitous interest in other people, if we do not study with impunity Islam, African art, or the way of life of the Trobrianders, with no connection to our own feelings, my preference for this one or that in no way is a sign of the inferiority of the others. It does not contradict the moral principle of the equality of all men; it keeps the principle of equality from slipping into one of identity. By maintaining such a difference, I am defending the very fact of pluralism, without concealing the arbitrariness of my selection. Love that does not make a choice between people is so grandiose that its value must be diminished, and it is foolish because this sort of affection does not go well with ecumenicism. Every culture is in fact the most irreplaceable, because all others can lay claim to this quality. What is essential is that I live outside myself, that I build bridges that are neither compromises nor cop-outs. What is essential is that fascination put us on the road and carry us toward a land where we were not born.

Thus, the genius of our land is the genius of flight. The multitudes of human beings that live next to us make it impossible for us to live in our native country as if in some promised land, where truth is fixed once and for all. To untie the bonds that attach us to one spot implies that we live in our homes with an unfaithful attitude, straining toward somewhere else, men of many alliances, capable of the greatest affinity as well as the greatest dispersion. There is no confusion at all between my cultural, linguistic, and romantic homelands and my organic home or ethnic membership. The wind from afar allows us to open up to each other like flowers far from their gardens, and teaches that *exile is today a way of finding our roots.* To know how to separate oneself from what one is close to in order to rejoin what has been left behind means that our country becomes foreign and that a far-off land has the sweetness and charm of our native soil. A double or triple cultural membership that dramatically characterized the destiny of some intellectuals from outlying countries after decolonization must now be recognized as a good thing. Asian, North African, and African critics and artists have a lot to teach us.[9] The situation of the half-breed and cultural mongrel, which used to be an anomaly resulting from colonial annexations, should be the norm for contemporary man, who must live in several cultural universes, and who must forge a contradictory alliance between the particular and the indeterminate. The best way of preventing the standardization of customs, the monotony of a single language, or the domination of imperialism, is by being a go-between who breaks down the walls of misunderstanding, and who savors the differences between customs and ceremonies. What the world most needs today is cultural turncoats who go from one universe to another, break up classifications, diminish contradictions, and make communication flexible. Just as the utopian Charles Fourier glorified the nectarine as the alliance of plum and peach, and childhood as the third emotional sex that was neither man nor woman, today we must accept the "beauty of the half-breed," as Guy Hocquenghem described him. The man of many languages and roots is the only person capable of protecting us from the barbarism of unquestioned ideas and from a cold turning inward as a nation or a part of the world. This is how we develop a hostile love for the home where we were born, the language we speak, the cherished places where we formed warm relationships. From the heart of our native land we seek a place beyond, and from beyond we discover the spice and diversity of our home country.[10] I hate Europe, or France, or Germany, but that means that I leave them only to return; I only marry them to leave them. Europe is the springboard from which I leap out to the world, and the world sends me back to Europe. . . . [11]

Fellowship Must Be Relative

We embrace everything, but we catch only the wind.
Montaigne

Third-Worldism constantly confuses guilt and responsibility. Guilt indicates that there is an exact fault, that a crime or some serious act has been committed. Responsibility implies the obligation of each man to all others, a feeling of common membership in the same species. Are we to blame for the famines of the Third World

in the same way that a murderer is guilty of his crime? Until it
has been proven, we are not. But we are responsible, because the
duty of every man is to help others to live when others have been
reduced to abject need. I cannot remain insensitive to the fate of
my brothers, because I am concerned with their suffering as if it
were my own. So an absolute requirement arises: Even though I
may be ignorant of the troubles of the world or the twists of history, I am equally responsible for the injustices that are committed, the murders that are committed on other men.

Here again, though, our analysis must be refined. A universal
and angelic and limitless fellowship would be disembodied, insuf-
ficient to deal with the misfortunes of any particular category or
group of people. Through large-scale institutions, unions, political
parties, and associations, I can reinforce and enlarge it to global
dimensions; and through them I am obliged to make gestures of
abstract charity in the form of food, medicine, and money, to countries whose names I do not know. But we choose our causes as
our causes choose us, in an inner encounter with the outside world,
in which the world proposes as much as we dispose. This is why
we cannot honestly embrace all causes, and also why we cannot
be disinterested in any of them. When we express concern for
Poland, we may be scolded by those who would have us also remember El Salvador, Lebanon, or South Africa.[12] We must reply
that a thousand causes for outrage are only so many reasons to
do nothing, and that if we are urged not to prefer one struggle
over another, East or West or South, we are being pushed toward
an involvement that has no limits, which is really a complete lack
of involvement. It would mean the fairyland of solidarity with no
content: I feel solidarity, period, like some mystical and bloodless
love that floats in the air.

To be effective, solidarity has to be circumscribed and chan-
neled. Other solidarities can be based on it, but only as aims sought
by other people. To be effective, responsibility must choose a limited field of action and a specific geographic area (which is not
related to its distance). Without this, it is indeterminate, blind.
Our need for political action and sympathy beyond national borders must be tailored to the scale of causes in a particular area,
beyond which there is nothing but the hubbub and babbling of the
news media. In this respect, too much generosity is suspicious. A
fellowship that expresses itself in general terms and that is incapable even of saying the name of those people whom it helps is

the solidarity of armchair windbags. It dies of its own purity, from choosing everything. It is nothing but a grandiose slogan, like the postwar label "existentialist," which was invoked everywhere and anytime. It gives support to the most dissimilar causes with the same enthusiasm. The same people who support Poland in December support the PLO in July with similar arguments, and six months later will support some other guerrilla movement. Details are minimized in all cases, and common denominators are sought where historical details should call for exact analyses, strict attention to facts. It is a purely sentimental attachment to people in the outside world, and Cambodians, Palestinians, and Lebanese all march through the square marked "Victim"; it is the same preordained ritual for different participants.

This kind of solidarity is for mercenaries of the news media, who must impartially cover all the active spots on earth. Let us not ask more of the media than what they already do quite well—make us aware of human problems. Our sort of attachment to the outside world cannot follow the rhythm of the news, even if we do care about it. We must learn to detach ourselves from the hassle of the headlines and hot stories, so we can take root somewhere on earth. Newspapers and television cannot possibly serve as a guide to action because, when the TV screen stops talking about a country, it continues to exist. If we based our attention to the world on the pattern of the news media, we would develop the flexibility of public opinion, which is too apt to take a stand for one group one day and another the next. That is a kind of technological solidarity for the busy man who wastes his effort and spreads himself too thinly. A hand held out in this way will soon be pulled back; reflex solidarity provides aid, but then takes it back again.

Universal brotherhood, then, makes for cool relationships. The indispensable division of labor commands us always to live out our idealism through friendship, to give up the desire to be everywhere at the same time. I am not a friend of mankind unless I form close ties to some at the expense of others. What prevents us from loving them all is what allows us to help some of them. Being partial is inconsistent with altruism, and yet altruism presupposes a partiality that is its opposite and also its precondition. The narrowness of a choice is the guarantee of its specificity. This detachment is not just a way of limiting our attention, it is the focus of our joining the rest of the world; it both limits and eases things. Concentrated attention to a friendly country is not a straitjacket.

This course, as soon as I embrace it, reveals infinite depth and richness. No solidarity stands by itself, and behind each one is an unfair bias, an irreducible arbitrariness, a selfishness. This is the ambiguity of support or refusal. It leaves each person the freedom to choose his place and indicate the worldwide dimension of living together through the way in which he makes these differentiations. Universalism is the constant concern of such selective philanthropy, because it always urges universalism to take some concrete form and go beyond the level of good intentions. Other men, of course, call for help and solicit my good will but, because I have limitations, I cannot give myself to everyone. If I overextend my giving, I can only make a gesture, a premium paid against others' accidents and misfortunes. What is left, aside from accidents and misfortunes, is what is important—faithfulness and constancy.[13] There is no solidarity without a choice made by conscience and limited by comparisons, confined in the network of its own relationships.

The Southern Hemisphere—Playground of the North

It is an accepted fact that "travelers are cool invaders" (Sartre), former colonizers who have come back as vacationers to the scene of their crimes. They are "watchmen scattered beyond the seas, across the vast and moving girth of our Empire," as Pierre Benoît said of the soldiers of the colonial army. The multinational corporation of the world's pampered folk pours forth charter flights full of people in shorts and suntan cream into the cradles of ancient civilizations. They descend on the Mediterranean, Kenya, and Central Asia like a swarm of flies. For people from rich democracies, tourism is like a feudal adventure in dictatorial and poor lands. It is a geographical and spiritual escape, an intoxicating experience for a German clerk, an English secretary, or a Parisian laborer to become a great lord two thousand kilometers from home.

Tourism does favor the economic predominance of a few international giants (airlines, hotel chains, travel agencies); it is accompanied by direct cultural penetration, which native traditions and social structures can scarcely resist;[14] it is a violation that encourages a rottenness and "worldwide prostitution" that looks at "sunshine, artistic heritage, cultural treasures, clear air, sand, countryside, wild animals, and young women of the Third World" as if they were so much "raw material."[15] Yet those who attack tourism would at the same time have us love the "Third World" without our ever going there, would have us be concerned about the people of the Southern hemisphere but not visit them. The trauma of invasion is still with us, as if a single white foot placed on African soil were a soldier's jackboot, as if the camera were a modern version of a gun and a safari a manhunt in disguise. They cannot have it both ways. Either isolation is to be extolled, and rigid and insurmountable frontiers reinforced between the Northern and Southern hemispheres, or the free circulation of people and ideas must be encouraged, along with the intermingling of cultures, no matter what the cost. Of course, tourists are ridiculous creatures who, after spending a night on a sleeper train or bouncing in air pockets on a cut-rate charter flight, alight in Morocco, Egypt, or Brazil thirsty for Ektachrome and "real communication." Yet this stampede in search of Moors, Arabs, or primitives is a symbol of a mystery that gives it legitimacy. It is the mystery of contact with the "other," the search for a broader life by means of a tightly organized itinerary, even if the search does get lost in the usual couscous in the sky. There is obviously a great temptation to react by closing off borders, selecting visitors, making more people get the visas required for travel, setting up a *cordon sanitaire*, allowing only visits by experts, providing official hosts, and thereby setting up a whole legal code for international travel. In short, the temptation is to set up conditions and restrictions, to reestablish isolationism and supervised travel of the kind in the Soviet Union or China. This is really a classic type of tourism, because it guarantees that no tourist will speak to a Russian or a Chinese outside of official channels. The consequences of this sort of system are inevitable—spying, noncommunication, prohibition of unofficial contacts, establishment of forbidden zones, schedules overloaded to discourage the curious, etc. True, our sumptuous tourist palaces somewhat resemble asylums, where crowds of retards crouch in ignorance and brutishness. And sunbathing, beaches, palm trees, nice weather, and dancing are a distressingly impoverished experience. But amid this mediocrity, a calling may develop, and feelings of sympathy can be born.

Prior to mass transportation, travel was a restricted monopoly reserved for the elite. Tourism has given travel the nature of universal suffrage. The art of wandering was previously the preserve of rich heirs and family offspring, but tourism makes it a general public practice. Is that so bad? While we should always point out the drawbacks of the tourist industry when it seriously disrupts cultural or ecological equilibria—this problem is just as serious in advanced countries—we should also point out its positive aspects, for it is the price of travel. The same system that provides a youngster from a middle-class or poor background in Berlin, Paris, Liverpool, Madrid, or Zurich with the unheard-of chance to travel at modest cost and in a few hours to continents thousands of miles away also makes it possible for him to adopt an arrogant or illiterate attitude once he gets there. In the past 20 years, in spite of all their distortions and stereotyping, in spite of the bias imposed by group travel, travelers have been able to rub shoulders outside the walls of their political, linguistic, or professional ghettos. Think of what restrictions on travel, and pulling people back inside their own borders, would mean in terms of the vitality of the world. Think of the obscurantism behind this sort of measure, making misunderstanding of others a normal thing, a return to a form of barbarism the Middle Ages never saw. It would strike at the very heart of peoples' desire to travel and communicate with others.

Authentic travel is not the opposite of tourism; it is its continuation by other means. It transcends armchair fantasy, transcends itself through human contact, joins together the security of what is known with the exaltation of novelty. From the secure base of the vacation village or the luxury hotel, the tourist pushes out feelers into the unknown and restores a complexity to the country being visited that was not apparent at first sight. When the unexpected happens and the expected does not happen, an illuminating frustration takes one's horizons in a different direction and beyond expected paths. It may be necessary to clean up the behavior of roistering people on paid vacations to tropical countries, but this must not be at the price of more restrictions and limitations. At a time when the illusion of knowledge spread by the media would have us believe that we never have to leave home, tourists are a heretic band, ordinary men and women who keep open our windows on the world. The more complex our understanding, the more we need the skeptical and curious mind of the traveler who, in spite of all propaganda, goes off to see things as they really are and accepts little of what would compromise him in a foreign land. If we want to increase the number of people who understand the Third World, rather than increase peoples' guilty consciences, we should lower air fares around the world and make cheap flights available to all. *The charter flight is still the best vehicle for friendship between peoples.*

The Ambivalence of Exotic Tastes

Perhaps it is futile for people to try to establish a unity between them.
By attempting this, they only enlarge the chasm that separates them.
E.M. Forster, *A Passage to India*

A taste for the exotic gives out mixed signals, which make it both fascinating and dangerous. It always runs the risk of degenerating into the fetishism of folklore, which prefers the artifacts of the "other" to a personal relationship with him. It can fall into a second-rate sense of the picturesque, which prefers decor to people, which would rather fill the landscape with stereotypes—the artisan, the fisherman, the tailor, the sorcerer, the marabout, the bonze, the sadhu, the donkey driver—so as not to see real people. Law is seen as custom, art as spectacle, religion as superstition. It highlights the difference of the other precisely when it is inoffensive. It is a symptom of something worse, because it was essentially the backbone of the colonial system, the favorite recourse of minor authors from Claude Farrère to Pierre Benoît, who were only too happy to embellish the tropics in order to devalue the natives and justify their subjugation. Exotic literature was never so great as when it portrayed the failure of colonialism. The colonizers departed, yet the tropics are still enchanting.

It is worth wondering whether this ambiguity is the dark side, the trap that is inevitable in any communication. Another person gives off a vague aura that allows me to objectify him. To approach him, I need a basic stereotype that permits me to capture its reflections in objects he creates or the functions he fulfills. What portrays the other can also prevent us from seeing him. Exoticism always has the irritating inexactness of a universal grammar of diversity. The savoring of the strangest aspect of the stranger, and the familiar in the distant as well as the unfamiliar in what is near, did not begin with the adventure of colonialism, because Westerners had shown the same tendency in Europe in the seventeenth and eighteenth centuries. Frenchmen and Germans nowadays enjoy visiting the Orient, but they originally did the same in Europe; the English visiting Italy and Greece, the French visiting England, Spain and Poland, and vice-versa.[16] Exotic is whatever is Out There. The gift of interacting with the other comes by way of the perception that he is different, of being sensitive to the disharmony between us. Roads, villages, and utensils carry in them the mark of human activity, and give off an aura of foreign humanity. The otherness of another person accumulates in things, it inhabits them. My perception of him arrives through the anonymous vehicle of technique, a construction, an artifact, a work of art. Now I can be entirely content with this vehicle alone, preferring objects to subjects, landscapes to people.[17] No law can force us to move on from the level of consumption of these symbols to the level of intersubjectivity. So exoticism will always be touched by a fundamental duplicity. It is both magical and doubtful; it is uncertain. And the ambiguity of its symbols will always lead people to attack it vigorously.

To rebel against the pitfalls of exoticism and refuse to experience the glamor of the unexpected, however, is to attack the very root of differentness, the way in which the other displays the sign of his foreignness in the world. There is no "bad" exoticism—on the one hand, one that is the territory of the shameless white man, and on the other, true communication. There are simply differing degrees of strangeness, while it is understood that no one can require us to move on from appearances to people themselves.

To travel, therefore, is above all to be astonished at the inexhaustible variety of the senses; all objects appear before my eyes with a sort of innocent purity. I avidly taste the goods and riches that these far-off lands shower on me. I am a creature overwhelmed by an unknown world whose anomalies excite me. I seek the unfamiliar in everything. I throw myself into a passionate praise of what is different; I am enraptured by what is unheard of and avoid what is familiar—a particular quality of light, the shocking sights and smells of a jungle, the exquisite burning of a spicy dish, the sounds of a new language, the reflections of a rice paddy. Deliciously free of any civic responsibility, I wander carefree, to gather pleasure from a nation of which I am not a member, and where I am only passing. And, of course, I could stay like that, limiting my experiences to superficial contact at the level of services and purchases. I could very well gorge myself to the point of nausea on golden minarets, lateen sails, mangrove swamps, atolls, pirogues, odalisques, junks—all the paraphernalia that soon simply look like so much trash. This endless plunge becomes boring if it does not develop into a concrete relationship with people. Instead of pure contemplation, people prefer the development of ties between them, their complications and mystery. The traveler understands the foreign land through its inhabitants, he does not understand the natives through their habitat, monuments, or temples. The only real diversity is among human beings themselves. If I go outside of what is typical, a weakness shows up in the realm of my happiness: These fields, forests, and proliferating plants are the setting of other men's customs and countenances. The nature I see is partly cultural. Whether such magic works or not in the tropics, by going there we learn primarily that we are separate from it, and that to stay means we would be emigrants without a common past or future.

I once believed that I could contain a certain country in the most striking symbols of its personality, but I am left with nothing but a shell. And the longer I stay there, the more that initial familiarity recedes. The exotic consists in the unusual power certain places and objects have to contain a marginal space within them, a sign of something they are not. It is the rich or poor skin that the other agrees to shed in response to my hunger. Through it, he also demonstrates that he is forever outside my grasp. Through the medium of photographs and purchases of clothes and works of art, I am trying to capture a spirit that eludes me. Exoticism has above all an "opening spirit," to use Pascal's term; it is the anticipation of the face to which it leads, and this anticipation becomes most acute when the other escapes his landscape and appears in all his naked glory.

The Traveler in Midstream

The excitement that travel produces, therefore, is based on a communion that turns out to be impossible, and this gap is there from the start. My extended stay among a people and its culture and language is a relationship. Sometimes it is delightful, but more often, it is stormy. It does not lead to cool disengagement, but to passionate involvement. It is impossible to spend several years of one's life with Shiite Islam, the Balinese, voodoo, the Peuls, or the worship of Shiva without going through stages of convulsive enchantment or rejection. This confrontation is a contact that spares me neither indignity nor glory, neither the overwhelming desire to prostrate myself, nor sourness and bitterness. I encounter the other in a troubled world of tension and in a framework that alienates me. My desire to love and be recognized is accompanied by the hope that I will be recognized as a brother, if not as an equal. But the more I find a fellow striver and sufferer in an Indian, a Chinese, an Argentine, or a Congolese, the more his foreignness is impressed upon me. A motivation of affection toward a culture combines an endorsement and a reserve. Or rather, my integration into a foreign world is but a particular type of exclusion from it. The simultaneous search for the greyness of the void and the intimacy of knowledge do not expand our understanding of a tribe or a religion; rather, they enlarge our areas of vulnerability. The main effect of escape abroad is to remystify the earth, and to give a certain richness to our knowledge of countries that a superficial visit seemed to exhaust. It follows that this enrichment leads to power. Discovery does not lose its secret quality, and *the way in which a culture or people show themselves shows a lot about what they are concealing*. By our making friends and learning a few phrases of the language and a few shreds of history, the country that was distant and abstract to us when we set off becomes distant and concrete.

This explains the peculiar sadness of a person who tries to become an expatriate. He feels impelled to question, but gets no answer. He came to seek another center, but finds himself totally eccentric. He leaves behind foreigners whose existence has become more intimate, but who are still an enigma. He thought he would achieve some understanding but only deepened his confusion. His search, as far as he has carried it, is testimony to his alienation from others. The emotion he invests in it is the price he pays for this disunion. He is enraptured and devastated because of a distance that recedes into infinity. The voyage to the other strives for a meeting, but fails in its promises. The world can be seen through the prism of many educations and languages, and the superimposition of these normally closed-off worlds ends up by confusing rather than making them all the same. A piercing contact and unforeseen shortcut have disrupted the iron barrier of national boundaries. In a moment, a traveler can believe he has the magic aura of a person cut off from the rest of the world, an anomalous being who fits no categories, kinship, or descent. But such a flimsy bridge, built across incomprehension and mistrust, does not end his solitude. He has no place in this land where he was not born, and loving it is like loving a woman who is courted by many but cannot give herself to anyone other than herself.

I have described this as a relationship of love, but it is more like romantic than erotic love. Travel is a sort of caress that trips and wanders without an aim, and that never touches; there is no hope, even an illusory one, of any joining. The more I seek him, the more the "other" escapes me. Thenceforth, my peace is disturbed by a secret torment—the self-denial I have subjected myself to has ended with the poverty of non-knowledge, a lack of possession. The stranger has nothing to reveal, because his secret is so deep. Neither the light of knowledge, habitation, or cohabitation, nor conquest and murder are enough to penetrate his essence, to tap his inner reserve. The nomadic traveler is away from his homeland but is not there in others, and remains suspended between two worlds that escape him. Stopped in the middle of the stream, he has left the security of the shore where he was born, but sees the other riverbank retreating even as he tries to reach it.

Love for Our Fellow Man

The only worthwhile kind of travel is one that leads us toward other men.

Paul Nizan

The very failure of travel is its success. No discomfort can diminish my hunger for going abroad, or bring down the fever that rages in me. The more the other reveals himself to me, the more I push toward him without reaching him. Soon, the witless desire to be the other gives way to a desire for the other insofar as he is not me. Of course, this is still an illusion, but it is the best one to be under. In his passion to promote the unity of the human race, the traveler is right: He knows that loneliness in interaction is better than isolation in mutual hatred; that imperfect communication is better than a hostile silence; that a single fruitful conversation is better than many sterile monologues; that all speech that touches another person loses its bitterness and entails manifold affirmation; that to make people give up their arrogance and forge a thousand bonds of friendship it is more useful to magnify everything by hyperbole than to demolish it through rancor; that the wanderer who is always eager to escape himself is always more in the right than one who sits at home.

Thus, traveling means coming to welcome the other on his own territory. It means declaring that a man is more my neighbor than people like me or my family. It means giving up the required identification of race, camp, party, ideology, and language in favor of the free choice of a country I want. It means giving priority to uncertain relationships rather than hereditary ones, borrowed identities rather than kinship and citizenship, choosing an intimacy of the heart rather than one of flesh and blood. Travel is, therefore, the homage that friendship renders to distance. However fragile it may be, it is proof that no spiritual or physical distance can overcome the similarities that impel people to meet and gather together. I have only to choose between two postulates that are both contradictory and necessary—I cannot be involved in the fate of this far-off other, but I cannot live with him, either. I am obsessed by people whose existence obliges me to leave my country, but I am unable to blend into their way of life. And so, I am caught in the emotional situation described by the adage, "I can't live with them and I can't live without them."

This is why we must consistently repeat the exhortation to travel to generations that effortlessly crossed borders and found Europe too small. In spite of misunderstandings and narrow-mindedness, keep traveling to East, South, and North, in search of remarkable people. We may be tempted to lose faith, but we must have faith in "others." What questions humanity also inspires it. Let other lands beckon and tantalize. Be consumed by the other without losing your freedom, without fear of losing it. All travel is a gamble on others' generosity, a search for good will, because the world is livable only in a state of constant interchange. The attractions and illusions of far-off people in the tropics are calling with their myriad voices: Come to us! Come to what? They do not say. The world out there is not a promise, nor is it a prayer. It is a call.

Notes

Prologue

1. Maurice Renard, *Les Mains d'Orlac* (Paris: 1910).

Chapter 1

1. Christopher Columbus, *La découverte de l'Amérique*, Volumes I & II (Paris: Maspéro, 1979), 1, 61.

2. Columbus' discovery is admirably described and analyzed by Tzvetan Todorov in *La Conquete de l'Amérique* (Paris: Seuil, 1982), 20–55.

3. This was the phrase used by Basil Davidson in *Les voies africaines* (Paris: Maspéro, 1965).

4. Jacques Berque, *Depossession du monde* (Paris: Seuil, 1964). "This uprising . . . is pulling the whole human race into its struggle."

5. For example, Georges Montaron wrote in *Temoignage chrétien* (November 27, 1973): "If they [Christians] give greater attention to the Third World, it is unquestionably because these people are the "Poor Man" whom Christ talked of. It is also because the poor are the victims of a system of domination that is based upon the law of the survival of the fittest and the power of money. And it is because the poor are engaged in a struggle for dignity that is a struggle for the whole human race, one that is basically our own struggle, as well. This is why we declare our solidarity with Chileans, Vietnamese, Palestinians, Angolans, and Cambodians against all forms of imperialism."

6. Yves Florentin, *Le Monde diplomatique* (September 1981), "The world is not divided into five parts, but two—the one that wins every time and the one that is losing again and again." Michelle Loi, *L'intelligence au pouvoir* (Paris: Maspéro, 1973), "As Luxum maintained

173

throughout his life, there are not several ways to look at the world, there are only two. Whoever refuses one accepts the other."

7. Frantz Fanon, *Les damnés de la terre* (Paris: Maspéro, 1961).

8. "The infant who has become an adult sees that there was blood in the bottle that nursed him. In looking at his past, with an eye sharpened by psychoanalysis, he no longer sees his childhood the way Kipling described it, like that of Mowgli playing in the jungle with callow laughter, but like that of a young and metaphysical murderer" (Berque, op. cit., p. 47).

9. When the writer Jean Genet was asked by Tahar ben Jelloun about his long visits to the Palestinian camps in Jordan and Lebanon in 1970, 1971, and 1972, he replied, "Why the Palestinians? It was entirely natural that I should live among people who are not only the most deprived, but who most purely crystallize hatred of the Western world" *Le monde diplomatique* (July 1974).

10. Jean Ziegler, *Main basse sur l'Afrique,* collection "Points Actuels" (Paris: Seuil 1980), 74. It is remarkable how in this book Ziegler, in a pattern the opposite of aristocratic titles, stacks defect upon defect with the intention of drowning the subject under the flood. But the effect is the opposite, and this excess of denigration exonerates the United States because it is overdone; each epithet crowds out the other, and what is supposed to cause outrage inspires laughter. This is the fault of all ritual formulae; they are like religious incantations.

11. Yves Florenne, *Le Monde diplomatique* (November 1972).

12. Eldridge Cleaver, *Sur la revolution américaine* (Paris: Seuil, 1970).

13. "It seems to be an obvious and elementary fact that the leadership in the United States, because of its dominant position and counterrevolutionary efforts on a planetary scale, was alone in being to such an extent the instigator and manager, or material and moral supporter, of the most terrible bloodbaths to have occurred during the years following the Second World War." Noam Chomsky and E. E. Herman, *Bains de sang,* collection "Change" (Seghers/Laffont, 1974), 34.

14. François Manasta, in *Le Monde diplomatique,* in 1971, described the American system in this way:

"More than 600,000 dead in the Civil War, more than 5,000 blacks lynched from 1860 to the present, a crime rate that continues to grow, almost 35 percent of black teenagers unemployed in the third trimester of 1970, in nearly every household a firearm ready for use, an arrogance of power toward other nations, waiting lists of over two years of psychiatrists. . . . "

15. René Dumont, *L'Utopie ou la mort,* collection "L'histoire immediate" (Paris: Seuil, 1973), 73.

16. In a communiqué issued during the American bombing of North

Vietnam in the winter of 1972–73, the World Ecumenical Council meeting in Bangkok proclaimed, "Even if the fighting ended today—which it should—the human family will have been witness to a 'demonic' experience that will have to be exorcised; guilt will have to be expiated and poisoned relations will have to be made healthy again" (*Témoignage chrétien,* January 25, 1973).

17. "American imperialism is not a myth . . . it is violence incarnate, the law of the strongest made into a dogma, the arrogance of the self-satisfied rich" (Georges Montaron, *Témoignage chrétien,* May 1970).

18. In this sense, anti-Americanism is a phenomenon very similar to anti-Semitism. See the elegant analysis made by Vladimir Jankélévitch in *Quelque part dans l'inachévé* (Paris: Gallimard, 1978), 136ff.

19. "I saw so much inequality, injustice, and loneliness there [in the USA]; so much sickness of life and insecurity, even among well-to-do people. Is that our own future? The society of the psychiatrist and the tranquilizer?" (Marie-France Mottin, *Cuba quand-même,* Seuil, 1980, p. 11).

20. "Saigon, the city of sexuality and opulence, with its gangs and sewage, the scum of the armies and deserters, is being liquidated. . . . The villages have joined together to overwhelm the evil capital. . . . I would not go so far as to say that the victory of the Vietcong is one of good over evil. But it certainly represents the revenge of cleanliness and dignity against filth and disorder" (Xavier Grall, commenting on a televised feature on the fall of Saigon in *Témoignage chrétien,* June 12, 1975).

21. "Day after day, the Vietnamese people are giving us a priceless lesson in the spirit of sacrifice, perseverence, and revolutionary humanism in its struggle against the worldwide representative of oppression and repression" (Che Guevara, "Lettre sur Vietnam," quoted by Rudi Dutschke, *Ecrits politiques,* Bourgois, 1968, p. 91).

22. The same ambivalence toward the United States and her allies can be found in the present-day slogans of the Iranian revolution. Here, for example, is a message sent by the Iranian revolutionaries to the blacks in England during the summer 1981 riots: "Down with rotten, bloodsucking English imperialism."

23. *La révolution surréaliste,* No. 4, 1925.

24. In *Modeste Contribution aux discours et cérémonies officielles du 10e anniversaire de 68* (City: Maspéro, 1968), Regis Debray reminds Europeans that they still "have the ability to chip away their own little piece from the stones of the West's fortress by giving aid to the 'barbarians' attacking our own sophisticated barbarism from outside the walls" (pp. 89–90).

25. Compare this remark of Claude Julien, one month before the overthrow of the Allende government in Chile, "If the bell were to toll

today in Santiago, it would be tolling also for the humble people of the West" (*Le Monde diplomatique,* September 1973).

26. "Butchering a European is like killing two birds with one stone, because it means eliminating both an oppressor and someone who is oppressed. What remains is a man who is dead and one who is free. And the survivor can feel his country's own soil under the soles of his feet for the first time" (Sartre, preface to Fanon, op. cit., p. 20). Several years ago, the Angolan poet Armando Guebusa wrote, "There is a message of justice in each bullet I fire."

27. "There is a straight path from the struggles of people for their national liberation to the organization of popular uprisings in the imperialist mother countries" (pamphlet of the Gauche proletarienne, distributed in Vincennes in 1972).

28. Leszek Kolakowski, *L'esprit revolutionnaire,* Editions Complexe, 1978.

29. This shows up among leftist Christians as the figure of Christ himself: "Jesus Christ is a Palestinian refugee," proclaimed the editorial of Georges Montaron on December 18, 1969, in *Témoignage chrétien.* Among other things, he said, "Jesus Christ is with the Palestinians, whether they are Moslems, Jews, or Christians, from the moment they become poor . . . the refugees themselves are the real holy places of Palestine, the true witnesses of the living God."

Three years later, when the Americans were bombing Hanoi, the very same Jesus showed up again in Indochinese costume, in almost the same terms: "As Christians who have been for so long caught up in a crusade for the so-called free world, we must declare aloud that today Christ is among those who are suffering in the rubble of Vietnamese cities and villages. For our liberation" (Bernard Schreiner, *Témoignage chrétien,* December 28, 1972).

30. In this regard, see the admirable *Portrait du colonisé* of Albert Memmi, 1957.

31. *Le Tiers monde et la gauche,* a collection of essays edited by *Le Nouvel Observateur,* (Paris: Seuil, 1979).

32. "It was not a ramshackle fantasy or baseless Utopia that sent a handful of guerrillas off into the forest and—without losing their modesty or sense of humor—chose as their ultimate goal the final liberation of a continent of 300 million inhabitants" (Régis Debray, *La Guerrilla du 'Che',* Seuil, 1974).

33. "The Chinese were really in search of something on our behalf," said K. S. Karol in *Le Tiers monde et la gauche,* op. cit.

34. Jean-Pierre Garnier, in *Le Monde diplomatique,* August 1980, once again condemned "jet-set writers who had the ability to raise delicious thrills of exoticism in a reading public that was eager for vicarious

escape, be serving up neatly wrapped vignettes of the most astonishing poverty present in countries that were not called underdeveloped yet."

35. The Biafrans are an example of this. An anthology should be made of the insults and calumny heaped upon them by the French intellectuals, supposedly because they were supported by the big oil companies.

36. "In the hearts of all the poor people of the Arab world, the Fedayeen are heroes, the living image of liberation. Like Che Guevara in Latin America. The Palestinian resistance is a flame that shines upon the oppressed, and grows nearer and nearer. Much more than for us, the Resistance for them is a synonym for revolution, and it has an incalculable messianic power" (Georges Montaron and A. Vimeux, *Témoignage chrétien*, December 25, 1969).

37. On this subject, see Gerard Chaliand's excellent *Mythes révolutionnaries du tiers monde* (Paris: Seuil, 1979).

38. Harry Magdoff, *L'Imperialisme* (Paris: Maspéro, 1979).

39. Pierre Jalée, *L'Echange inégal* (Paris: Maspéro, 1964).

40. Régis Debray was absolutely right when he wrote in *Le Débat* (January 1981), "The mystery of the disembodiment of the national word is related to the fact that, perhaps for the first time in our history, a whole generation is obliged to experience its age by proxy, in the form of ideas, or sheltered by signs or symbols. As an idea, the Third World *is* 'Third Worldism'. As an idea, China *is* Maoism."

41. *Les Confessions,* Book IX (Paris: Gallimard, 1981).

42. "To live by your wits is not to imitate the hustler, who is a low-class capitalist, but rather the Latin American guerrilla, who is a low-class socialist" (R. G. Davis, ex-theoretician of guerrilla theater in the USA, quoted by the *San Francisco Express Times*, March 21, 1968).

43. In fact, there was a two-way trickery at work. We were overjoyed to find phrases in the mouths of Cubans, Vietnamese, and Angolans that we ourselves used, because it showed that oppressed mankind was part of a single community bound together by the same interests. But this was because the Western model—socialist or liberal—had spread so far afield and had so penetrated the "liberation" movements that we could pretend we were discovering ideas among them that they had borrowed from us in the first place. There was a twofold imitation: Westerners aped Chinese, Cubans, and Vietnamese who, themselves, had learned from Western sources. We were not willing to see that Lumumba, Nkrumah, Mao, Castro, or Ho Chi Minh were so inspired by Europe—remember, many of them had been students in France or England—that they could speak the same lingo to European leftists.

44. *L'Idee de l'Europe dans l'histoire,* 1965, quoted by Andre Reszila, *L'Intellectual contre l'Europe,* Paris, PUF, 1976, pp. 8, 9.

45. See Maxime Rodinson's excellent short book, *La Fascination de L'Islam* (Paris: Maspéro, 1980), 100ff.

46. "The taste for the exotic led colonialist politicians to try to preserve quaint customs to ally themselves with native conservatives, and to denounce both reformist and revolutionary nationalist intellectuals, whether socialist or not, as pale imitators of Europe, motivated by ill-understood and abstract ideas to destroy their own cultural heritage" (Rodinson, op. cit., pp. 96–97).

47. It is a fact that the French Communist Party has a long tradition of support for colonialist policies. The Party condemned the uprising in Constantine in 1945 as a "provocation by Hitlerite agents," voted credits to support the war in Vietnam in 1947, and did not grant the Algerians the right to run their country without French supervision until very late in the game. On this subject, see Jacob Moneta, *Le PCF et la question coloniale* (1920–1963) (Paris: Maspéro, 1971).

48. On this point, the positions of different political families vary. The French Communist Party, faithful to its policy of alignment with Moscow, has always supported the allies of the Soviet Union—Vietnam, Cuba, and Nicaragua—to the point where it supports the most questionable actions of these countries, no matter what. The Socialist Party, basing its position on an anti-imperialist declaration of principle, is more moderate and subtle, and uses a different analysis for each situation, to the point where it contradicts itself. The various Trotskyite sects, as guardians of the treasure of permanent revolution, have given a special place to guerrilla warfare, particularly in Latin America. The Maoist far left is basically divided between Marxist-Leninists, the careful imitators of the Chinese Communist Party Line, and the "proletarian Left," an intellectual movement that has used Mao's Little Red Book as a tool for reviving the French workers' movement, which has been frozen by "revisionist tendencies." (Cf. their theme of the "new Resistance.) And in both the Maoist clan and the Christian Left, the myth of a single Afro-Asian-Latin American territory has reached its most surrealistic heights.

49. See, for example, what Father Cardonnel wrote in *Le Monde diplomatique*, November 1974: "There is an affinity, a common bond, between the universality of contradiction preached by Mao Tse-tung and that of a Christ freed from 'Christianity'—a love that shows itself in what it calls forth, not for the ratification of things as they are, but for insurrection against obedience." Father Cardonnel repeated himself two years later in an article entitled, "People's China and Faith." After setting forth the hypothesis that Communist China could "turn from bright red to pink," he went on: "The Chinese revolution takes seriously the resurrection that part of the 'Christian' West professes with its mouth. . . . With acts that correspond to the words of the apostle James, a people who have only known Christianity as the handmaiden of colonial powers

cries aloud to us, 'You have faith. We have works. Show me your faith without works and we will show you our faith.' (James II, 18)" (*Le Monde diplomatique,* February 1976).

50. Josué de Castro, *Le Monde diplomatique* (December 1969).

51. Michelle Loi, *L'Intelligence au pouvoir* (Paris: Maspéro, 1973), 20.

52. "In a world in search of money, comfort, and pleasure, there is China alone, which still so hotly burns with the ideal of austerity, work, self-sacrifice. . . . China used to be a paradise for thieves; nowadays, a visitor cannot misplace anything without it being returned to him. . . . They have an unbelievable chastity—because the Party demands it. Movies are 100 percent moral. When you go from this spotless country to Hong Kong, you suddenly enter the eroticism of our own world, with its newspapers crammed with filthy stories, with opium, gambling, and prostitution. . . . " (Robert Guillain, quoted by Jean Toulat, *Témoignage chrétien,* January 8, 1970).

53. "In China, they take care of themselves before they get sick. They take care of themselves so that they will not get sick, usually through sports" (Michelle Loi, op. cit., p. 70).

54. "All of China is remarkably clean. I do not know what the city streets and village lanes were like before, but today they are astonishingly tidy. The mud and dirt of the fields do not get into the villages or the cities, which are often paved and tiled and carefully swept. And in alleys behind factories, and in schoolyards, there is not one scrap of paper on the ground" (op. cit., p. 69).

55. After visiting a school for young deaf mutes, our indefatigable Michelle Loi was overcome with enthusiasm, and wrote to her family, "I actually heard deaf mutes singing! I'm serious. This country is a world like I have never seen" (op. cit., p. 79).

56. In *Le Monde diplomatique,* November 1974, Georges Frelastre seriously asks if Albania is not on its way to being "the perfect society." And he quotes admiringly the statement of the Albanian Communist Party regarding the reduction of inequalities of income: "The day will come when we will achieve absolute equality. Perhaps this will be at the end of the century, in 1990 or 1995. We dream of the perfect society where nobody will have reason to envy his fellow man because everyone will be in the same situation."

57. The Cultural Revolution "forged anew the link between manual and mental labor . . . restructured teaching from the primary grades to the university level, and made of it a system of education that works on a synthesis of theory and practice. The result is that *homo sapiens* and *homo faber* form a complete entity, a total man" (M.-A. Macchiochi, *De la Chine,* Seuil, 1974, p. 6).

58. "The Chinese Cultural Revolution [is the] only socialist revo-

lution that does not borrow its premises from the individualism of the bourgeois revolutions of the West" (Roger Garaudy, *Pour un dialogue des civilisations*, Denoel, 1977, p. 210).

59. The Cultural Revolution "contributed to the destruction of the myth of the supposed 'superiority' of experts and technicians. Thus, the masses became aware of their own capacity collectively to master complex techniques. They achieved this mastery thanks to their practical experience and with the help of technicians, but without the latter playing a dominant role at all. Rather, it was the other way around" (Charles Bettelheim, "Vers une nouvelle morale proletarienne," *Le Monde diplomatique*, November 1971).

60. In the Summer 1972 edition of *Tel Quel* magazine, sociologist Jean Daubia gave the following interview:

"Question: 'What do you think of the anti-Chinese campaign that is going on in the West, such as, for example, the book *Les Habits neufs du President Mao* (by Simon Leys)?'

Answer: 'The book you mention was written by one of the "leftist" critics of Maoism. Let me say right off that it is not very good. It is a collection of rumors that have been going around in Hong Kong for years, and which unquestionably come from a particular source in the United States. It is very significant that the author hardly dares cite his sources. . . . That borders on charlatanism.'"

61. "Regarding the Chinese, everybody asks (and I was one of them), 'Where is their sexuality?' . . . And it occurred to me that sexuality, insofar as we talk about it, is a product of social oppression, and the evil history of mankind" (Roland Barthes, *Roland Barthes* Seuil, 1975, pp. 167–168).

62. Back when he was a Maoist, Philippe Sollers, supported by Alain Peyrefitte, told Pasqualini, who had just spent several years in a Chinese Communist prison camp, that he should not criticize civil liberties in China, because these yellow people do not have the same needs and demands that we do . . . (broadcast on *Apostrophes*, January 25, 1975).

63. "Civil liberties? The Chinese aren't even aware of being deprived of them, because they have never known them" (Alain Peyrefitte, quoted by Claude Roy, *Sur la Chine*, Gallimard, 1979).

64. "The Otherness of China is invisible unless a Westerner puts himself in a place where the monotheistic and capitalist fabric of our society is torn" (Julia Kristeva, quoted by Claude Roy, op. cit., p. 129).

65. "The Chinese mind has powers that psychoanalysis knows nothing about" (*Tel Quel*, quoted by Claude Roy, op. cit., p. 130). Claude Roy rightly recalls that, on the theme of Otherness, Dr. Colonel Legendre, in order to justify the mistreatment of coolies, wrote in 1900, "The functional power of the different organs of the yellow race is inferior to that of the white race" (ibid.).

66. In *Le Monde,* November 16–17, 1975, the Very Reverend Henri Fesquet explained the lack of security mechanisms around the machines in Chinese factories by saying, "You see, the Chinese are extraordinary acrobats." The use of coolies attached to wagons like animals inspired him to write, "[The Chinese people's] physical strength is constantly exerting itself. It can be seen when, along the roads, this human power is used to move enormous loads, balanced miraculously on two-wheeled carts" (quoted by Simon Leys, op. cit., p. 64).

67. "In Shanghai, I hear the Chinese singing from daybreak onward. . . . Children pass by singing aloud. . . . There is music in the trees, everywhere, as if it were a festival day, when the Chinese do their exercises. This atmosphere lasts all day long. At first, I thought they were preparing for a national holiday, but they weren't. Everywhere I went, people sang, called, chanted, and intoned. They sang 'Navigating the High Sea' and 'The Red Women's Detachment' and taught me 'The Internationale'" (Michelle Loi, op. cit., p. 16–17).

68. According to two philosophers, Jambet and Lardreau, the Christian cultural revolution that began in the fourth century and Chinese cultural revolution "struck down in the skies of Mongolia" (by the death of Lin Piao in an airplane accident), both mobilized masses of people who were motivated by the same demands, "the radical rejection of work, the hatred of the body, and the denial of sexual differences" (*L'Ange,* Grasset, 1976, p. 100).

69. "Millions of dedicated militants will arise throughout China, an unstoppable tide. They grew up during the cultural revolution, and passionately studied courage, heroism, devotion, loyalty, sacrifice, modesty, and disdain for death. That is the milk that has nourished them. Such a sum of virtues that it makes your head spin" (M.-A. Macciochi, op. cit., p. 377).

70. "The problem with the way in which we are informed (or not informed) about China is not a Chinese problem, but a French problem. Ever since Voltaire, China for the French has been a magical world, at times marvelous, at times abominable, but always chameleon-like. . . . So the only really interesting question is why, over the last few years, the Chinese chameleon has taken on such magnificent colors, thanks to the pen and brush of representatives of the French press and intelligentsia" (Claude Cadart, *Regards froids sur la Chine,* Seuil, 1976, p. 40).

71. "I have said that we must apply the thought of Mao Tse-tung even when we don't understand it" (T. Grumbach, *Les Temps modernes,* April 1972, quoted by Claude Roy, op. cit., p. 98).

72. "It makes no difference if it is at the cost of religious 'fanaticism' or moral 'terrorism' of a medieval sort. For better or for worse, it is undeniable that a ritual viciousness, one that is not at all outdated, a tribalism that does not accept Western models of a free society, can pose

a real challenge to such a world order. . . . Iran is the only active de-
stabilizer of the terrorism and strategic monopoly imposed by the two
superpowers" (Jean Baudrillard, *Le Monde,* February 13, 1908).

73. Jacques Berque, *L'Islam au Defi* (Paris: Gallimard, 1980), 62–
63. It is true that Berque modifies his praise with several well-meant
qualifications regarding the reactionary nature and brutality of the new
regime.

74. "Islam today is always on the offensive. Arabs, the Third World,
and Islam are in combat with us. A historical truth is at work, and will
certainly emerge from this combat" (Jacques Berque, op. cit., p. 37).

75. In *Témoignage chrétien,* February 19, 1979, Claude Bourdet
wrote: "Now everything is different in the Persian Gulf. The orientation
of the new regime is unimportant, because no matter what, Iran will no
longer be the policeman of the United States and the accomplice of
Israel."

On February 19 of the same year, Georges Montaron wrote: "Of
course, the methods used by the Iranians to achieve these ends are
shocking to us. But violence is not practiced only by the government of
Teheran. Washington overthrew Allende with violence. . . . What is important is that these students have issued a challenge to America that
is to be condemned in its form but justified and unanimous at its heart."
(See the excellent collection that the magazine *Esprit* put together regarding Khomeini's revolution and the reactions in the French press,
January 1980.)

76. When he was asked by Marc Kravetz, in *La Magazine litter-
aire,* February 1982, about freedom and tolerance in the new Iranian
regime, orientalist Vincent Monteil replied, "The Islamic Republic and
Revolution is a response to an eternal desire for justice, taking the side
of the have-nots. And the Kurdish problem is not new. Thirty years ago,
I saw it for myself. To simplify somewhat, it is still a combination of
foreign involvement and the old devil of separatism. No state anywhere
can tolerate that. As for the Bahais, they are not Moslems, and above
all, they made the mistake of having their holy places in Israel and the
United States, and sometimes, under the old regime of the Shah, of having let themselves be manipulated and gotten rich. Every revolution has
its innocent victims."

77. The same type of solidarity showed up during the Falklands
War. Because it was between a Latin American country and England,
it was thought to be a case of the age-old conflict between the imperialist
Northern hemisphere and the downtrodden South. In the name of this
division between good and evil, all the leftists of South America, as well
as of Cuba and the Soviet Union, made common cause with the thugs in
Buenos Aires, who were still murdering their opponents a few weeks
before the war broke out. As long as North and South are seen through

a theological perspective, with damnation on one hand and redemption on the other, this sort of reactionary collusion will continue.

78. " . . . Western readers who are the least familiar with China will discover a truth that remains inescapably hidden from believers in the Yellow Peril, as well as from the mythmakers of Red China—that the Chinese are also human beings. To put it a little differently, we are all Chinese" (Simon Leys, *Images brisées*, Laffont, 1976, p. 116).

79. Our categories of right/left, progressive/conservative were and still are projected on every movement or organization in far-off countries. This is wrong on two counts. Not only does it mean that we are writing the history of these countries with our ideas. It means that we are imposing our played out categories on these countries, giving them a second childhood in exotic lands, as if they were second-hand tools that were certainly useless in Europe but entirely appropriate for "those people." Remember, for example, that during the Lebanese civil war, the good "progressive Palestinians" were venerated, as against the evil "conservative Christians." In fact, this was a religious war of a medieval type, rather than a confrontation between right and left.

80. Editorial of *Le Nouvel observateur*, December 4, 1978.

81. Thomas Hardy, *La Bien aimée* (Paris: Gallimard, 1981), 85.

82. *Les Nouvelles littéraires* of July 20, 1981, with regard to an article by V. S. Naipaul, spoke of the Third World as a "tyrant factory."

83. J. F. Khan, in an editorial in *Les Nouvelles littéraires*, August 6, 1981, wrote: "Beyond the borders of Europe, what do we see? Once Iran had gotten rid of the dictatorship of the Shah, it rejected capitalism, which kills in Guatemala and keeps Chile in a coma, and also rejected Marxism, which keeps Russia in chains and nails China to a cross. It was thought that a triumphant and imperialistic Islam offered a way out of the age of the Gulag and the Holocaust. Now, after two years of experience, Iran is rediscovering the Gulag and reinventing the Holocaust. Where should they look for examples? To Lebanon, which yesterday was covered in phony wealth and today is being torn apart by its own passions? To Israel, whose admirable democracy is struggling with religious extortion, to the point where these two complementary estates are today tapping their ultimate resources in the negativity of one and the aggressivity of the other? What are they to learn from the convulsions of India, the spasms of Bangladesh, the madness of El Salvador, the somersaults of Morocco, and the craziness that, from Carthage to Suez, has seized the helpless masses who seek, in a return to inflexible religion, the salvation the modern world has not been able to provide them?"

84. Simon Leys, *Images brisées*, op. cit., p. 184: "Western Maoists cannot conceive of the possibility that one can go to China simply out of affection for the people and the land. Such feelings are obviously foreign to people who know nothing of either, to the exclusive benefit of a handful

184 NOTES

of bureaucrats who are monopolizing power in Peking. Without Mao, China and the Chinese people would not hold their attention for a minute."

85. The title of the edition of *Les Nouvelles litteraires* on China on October 1980 was, "On nous a trompés"—"We were tricked."

86. Bernard Kouchner provides a good example of the disenchantment and abdication of the left in his book, *L'Ile de lumière* (Paris: Ramsay, 1980).

87. With regard to the terrible repression in China today, J. F. Khan correctly asks, "Where are the protest meetings, the petitions, the sitins in front of embassies, the declarations by intellectuals, the indignant editorials, the meetings of dissidents? Where? What is scandalous between the Elbe and the Volga is acceptable on the banks of the Yangtse. It's plain old racism—'They're only Chinese.'" (*Les Nouvelles litteraires*, October 1980).

88. Without getting too involved in a controversy that is still going on, there was less interest in the events than in their interpretation. On the one hand, there was a desire to describe Israel as criminal in the tiniest of actions and to expel it from the community of nations. Certain periodicals went so far as to talk about genocide with regard to the bombing of Beirut. On the other, the vigilance of many Jewish intellectuals focused exclusively on the language employed by the media, to the extent that they soon refused to pay attention to facts, so as to concentrate on the way in which they were communicated. In the words of Jean Daniel, they preferred to "observe the observers" rather than pay attention to reality. On both sides, it seemed that the divisions and reality of the conflict had been forgotten. The anti-Israeli hatred of the Communists (the firm position of the Socialist Party prevented the majority of the government from falling into an anti-Israeli frenzy that bordered on anti-Semitism) was met by the obstinacy of some in terrorizing journalists by calling them liars. It took the extraordinary moral upheaval among the Israelis themselves to remind the former that Tel Aviv was not the capital of a new Middle Eastern reich, and to remind the latter that no state, even that of the Chosen People, could avoid moral responsibility.

89. Is Sartre really a Third-Worldist? A persistent legend presents Sartre as the champion of Third-Worldism, a sort of extremist on behalf of young nations, the natural godfather of the abandoned and voiceless of the planet. Now, what does a look back at the life of this philosopher reveal? Aside from showing real courage during the Algerian War—remember the climate of violence that hung over France at the time, and the physical threats against the "pope" of existentialism—Sartre's attitude toward the Third World was a strange mixture of masochism and indifference. His masochism was in his famous "Europe is finished" in

the preface to *The Wretched of the Earth* by Frantz Fanon, which must be remembered as a treasure-trove of theoretical nothingness, historical falsehood, and hateful demagoguery. It was the masterwork of a new theology, of Third-Worldism with its black and white redistribution of fault, in which the shortcomings of Europe derive from its very nature, while the mistakes of the countries of the Southern hemisphere are simply the result of circumstances.

After the damning of Europe and the whitewash of the newly decolonized regimes by the vehicle of Fanon, Sartre went back to his studies and his work on Flaubert. Look at Sartre's biography. The author of *Les Mots* rarely traveled outside Europe, and only when he was invited on some official visit to somewhere like Cuba or Hanoi. Read his work. There is nothing or practically nothing about the great philosophical systems of Asia, about African or South American literature, about non-European religion. By and large, in contrast to Malraux, upon whom he heaped insult after insult and the universal scorn of being the last proponent of bourgeois consciousness, Sartre is a fantastic throwback, particularly in light of his own pretensions. A man who strove in his every move to involve the whole human race remained the most uncritical and naive Eurocentrist. Reread his astonishing analyses of colonialism and neocolonialism in *Situations V.* His incompetence with regard to the countries and matters he deals with, and his total ignorance of foreign cultures, contrast with Malraux's constant wish to think of Europe in the perspective of other civilizations. (Whatever you may think of his myth-making and his verbal acrobatics, Malraux went into the field, always wrote with understanding, and, consequently, was rarely wrong in his instincts.)

Sartre declared that the West was rotten, but after this beginning, was concerned only with the West. He made peace with his conscience after paying a little tithe of guilt. He made believe that he left the uncertain ground of ethical decision-making so as to undertake the infallible implementation of his knowledge, but he washed his hands of how this knowledge was applied. He wasted a great part of his talent in the esthetics of violence and Stalinism, and with regard to the Third World, ended up by showing himself to be not only dogmatic, but inconsequential. The hard-liner was in reality a deserter. Let us remember that he came close to justification of the massacre of Israeli athletes by members of the PLO in 1972. He gave way before revolutionary regimes, just as he gave way to the Maoists, giving his name to ideas and actions that went against his innermost convictions. But, deep down, he did not take them seriously. This follower of the Third World did not accept it unless it fulfilled the familiar role of the victim from whom he had nothing to learn. This preacher of universal involvement, this maniacal devotee of petitions, had no real affection for anyone but members of his own tribe.

A steadfast internationalist, he scarcely concealed his own comfortable provincialism. This curious detachment helps us to understand many forms of activism by intellectuals of his time and afterward. The weakness of the master was made a regular practice by his followers. The only thing of Sartre's that they kept was his penchant for abstract brotherhood, his habit of making generous and over-general formulations, his lip-service to others, his propensity to see the Third World as a charitable work for which he felt much contempt.

The antithesis of Sartre today is Naipaul, with his disenchanted recognition of facts, his desire to grapple with real flesh-and-blood human beings rather than pure ideas; in other words, his active and critical sympathy for nations of the tropics. It is true that Naipaul, an English-speaking Indian born in the Caribbean, is a man without a country. Sartre, alas, was only French, with all that implies about congenital navel-watching and "deep-seated indifference to everything foreign" (This was the title of a book by Jean Claude Guillebaud, published by Seuil in 1978).

What is revealing on this point is the condescension with which Sartre always treated expatriate writers. In *Situations I,* he reproached Nabokov for not belonging to any culture. Later on, in an interview, he found Samuel Beckett and Eugene Ionesco guilty of "being outside our language and our society" (quoted by Denis Hollier, *Politique de la prose,* Gallimard, 1982, p. 34). In stigmatizing what was not French, Sartre always had his eyes fixed on no horizon farther than that of the Vosges. His tone was like that of a Barrès or Maurras.

Chapter 2

1. Pierre Herbart, an old Communist organizer, remembers a similar experience from when he was researching on behalf of the Party in Indochina, the misdeeds of the colonial administration in the inter-war period. "My travels took me to Vinh, the center of the famine. The beggars had already gnawed the bark from the trees, and had gotten to the point where they were eating dirt. Then they wandered off along roads that took them to the better part of town. For the last time before dying, they wanted to look at us miscreant Europeans eating at the hotel behind a picture window; and the children looked at us without daring to move because they would have been chased away, and they wanted to see how people ate" (*La Ligne de force,* Gallimard, 1958, p. 48).

2. The idea of enlightenment through education is the child of 19th century pedagogical optimism. It presupposed two things: That evil and exploitation are the result of ignorance, and that education alone is enough to mobilize good will, banish misunderstanding, and reconcile mankind. Plato said long ago that nobody is intentionally evil. Now, what

such a brief on behalf of knowledge ignores is that even educated people are perfectly capable of evil.

3. Michel Bosquet, "La grande bouffe des affameurs," *Le Nouvel observateur,* October 17, 1981.

4. Figures from the United Nations FAO for 1981.

5. Pierre Marcilnacy, "De Passy à Cancun," *Le Nouvel observateur,* November 17, 1981.

6. René Dumont, *Le Monde,* October 14, 1981.

7. Jean Ziegler, *Main Basse sur l'Afrique* (Paris: Seuil, 1980), 19.

8. "The famished stare that the hungry people of the Southern hemisphere focus on the riches of the North are a permanent danger to peace and stability" (Preamble to the motions of the 13th meeting of the Socialist International, Geneva, 1976).

9. "We are told that tens of thousands of human beings are dying or will die because of an unjust throw of the dice, or the vagaries of nature. We say that they are dying to keep up capitalist profits and that all of us in the rich capitalist countries are more or less accomplices in this system of pillage, to the extent that we receive crumbs from these profits" (Comité Information Sahel, "Six Heures contre la famine," *Politique-Hebdo,* June 13–19, 1974).

10. Exactly the same phenomenon can be seen in science-fiction movies. They grab our emotions, they have to concoct ever newer forms of horror, and rely on special effects.

11. It is well-known that the newspapers and television were swept up in a thirst for sensationalism when they presented Beirut under Israeli siege in the summer of 1982 as a new Stalingrad. The shock value of pictures and slogans has taken over from a concern for the truth. The slogan of *Paris Match* is "The weight of words and the shock of pictures," but it is clear that we cannot respect such a slogan. If the photographs retain their impact, it is because words no longer have any weight.

12. He was talking of the book by Nicolas Born, *La Falsification* (Paris: Gallimard, 1981).

13. This shows how laughable is the righteous indignation of François Schlosser, who, after having quoted an FAO report that the real nutritional level of half of the people on earth was deteriorating, wrote: "We understand why this frightening news is only doled out in little drops or suppressed entirely in rich countries. It is because the nutritional decline suffered by half the human race is in proportion to the growth of profits that multinational corporations derive from their flourishing agribusinesses" (*Le Nouvel observateur,* October 17, 1981).

What exactly does "the West" do? Who is "the West?" Numerically, it is the peoples of the Northern hemisphere. Politically, it is a series of democratic governments. Sociologically, it is the middle classes. But who in the West exploits the Third World? A few companies that possess an overabundance of wealth? Yes, certainly, but that does not give a consistent picture of the exploiter, and so we are all equally guilty. But that is an enormous condemnation—is the worker as guilty as the boss, the tramp as guilty as the clothes-horse? (The economist Samir Amin argued this point in the 1960s, during a famous debate with the French Communist Party.) Of course not. They are victims of their particular bourgeoisies, who are the guilty ones.

The imprecision persists, because "the West" is identified as a tiny elite of corporation heads, top officials, and big leaders, or encompasses all the peoples of the industrial nations, going from the unity of all against a few to the antagonism of all against all. In some cases, the guilt is shifted to some scapegoat, and in some cases it is taken on oneself. What is irritating about the term "the West" is its lack of precision, the absence of a tangible enemy. There is constant shifting between a faceless West and a West like me, of which I am the carrier. What is contradictory is that we are only tools of the multinational corporations, but we are all responsible for their actions. Everyone subtracts his guilt from all the others by instant imitation, and then the group reunites in hatred of the ruling classes. Either the evils suffered by the human race because of "the West" stem from the sole responsibility of big corporations that ought to be broken up, or I take on this responsibility and become my own enemy. "The West" is the name for this precise and cloudy entity, a pinhead or a dark mass, a whipping boy or an entire continent. The word must be left enormously ambiguous so that guilt can circulate freely, as in a well-irrigated organism, and so that everyone will feel a little guilty without knowing exactly why. This makes it possible, when a disaster or a plague strikes, to accuse each Westerner individually, so that he will feel involved. It is the accuser's finger pointed at those of us who are cool and indifferent: "What are *you* doing about this, Westerner?"

It is a flexible idea that is particularly malleable. When I hear "the West" I can say to myself that those other people are the ones at fault, until I am struck with the accusation that I am as guilty as anyone else. "The West" is an insulting epithet that makes us all criminals without our being sure exactly why. Living in the Northern hemisphere is enough of a crime for us to be willing to pay the penalty at any time. "The West" is really a surrealistic character.

14. Is it possible to do without the media, this megaphone for use against hardened selfishness, without even worse results in the end? No, of course not. But the news can show and disseminate all possible moral points of view. It can bring a feeling of urgency to some catastrophes, but it cannot make us act. It justifies neither the fears nor the hopes that have been placed in it. By the same token, every attempt to manipulate it into setting an example or doing good is wasted. Its immensity and its limitations cannot be changed.

15. It might seem that we are reusing the threadbare image of verminous and poverty-stricken India. This is, in fact, how we are looking at it. Calcutta is certainly not the only poor city in the Third World. But, because of its own history and of the number of refugees that moved there after 1942, and then after the Indo-Pakistani war of 1971, it is a symbol of destitution to Westerners. Whether this image is true or false is not our concern; we accept it as an image. Since Calcutta is only a point of reference, everything that follows applies just as well to cities as diverse as Manila, Jakarta, Seoul, Cairo, Bogota, Lima, and Sao Paolo.

16. Claude Lévi-Strauss wrote in *Tristes Tropiques* (Plon, 1955, p. 151): "Beware of laughing at this, or being irritated, because it would be almost sacrilegious. It would be pointless to condemn and criminal to complain about these grotesque gestures and grimacing lurches, because they are clinical symptoms of agony. A single haunting fear, that of hunger, inspires this desperate behavior. It is the same fear that drives streams of people from the country to the city . . . and stacks up the refugees in the corners of the railway stations, where they can be seen from the train at night, asleep on the platforms and rolled up in cotton robes that are their garments today and will be their shrouds tomorrow. It lends its tragic intensity to the beggar's stare that meets your eyes through the bars of the first-class compartment that were put there—as was the armed soldier kneeling on the running board—to protect you against this silent demand of a single man, which could be transformed into a howling mob if a traveler's compassion overcame his caution and led these living corpses to hope for some charity." I must repeat that, of all the books written about the Third World, none are as beautiful, truthful, and correct as *Tristes Tropiques*. It is so burningly real that whole pages should be read to children in school.

17. Interview with Mother Theresa on the occasion on her receiving the Nobel Prize for Peace, in *Newsweek* International Edition, August 18, 1980.

18. "In Europe," wrote Tibor Mende, *L'Inde devant l'orage* (Paris: Seuil, 1951), 69, " . . . poverty has a depth and a dimension, or at least our imperfect methods of statistics allow us to gauge and measure it. The accumulated poverty of the great urban centers on India is desperate beyond description, and its dimensions are almost incomprehensible to an observer who is used to Western norms."

19. "All that you have is a few carefully learned and hoarded attitudes of outrage. To pay your dues. You could say that you have a voucher for outrage" said Nicolas Born, in *La Falsification*, op. cit., 160.

20. "Compassion and pity were not at issue, because these are simply refined forms of hope. What I felt was fear. What I had to struggle against was dislike," wrote V. S. Naipaul about his reactions to Indian poverty in *L'Inde sans espoir* (Paris: Gallimard, 1968), 46.

21. Describing the famine that struck Calcutta in 1942 after the

English army blockaded Assam and East Bengal against the Japanese advance, the Indianist Alain Daniélou reported, "In the cities, well-fed Europeans (there was never any rationing for them) disgustedly stepped over the skeletal women, children, and men who were strewn about, to get to their clubs or official dinners" (*Le Chemin du labyrinthe*, Laffont, 1981).

22. "I had succeeded in separating myself from what I saw, in dissociating the pleasant from the unpleasant. . . . I had also learned that I could always get away and that, in every Indian village, there is a place where there is relative calm and cleanliness, where one can recover and regain one's self-respect." (V. S. Naipaul, op. cit., p. 47).

23. On this point, see the excellent travel book about a Calcutta slum by J.-C. Guillebaud, *Un Voyage vers l'Asie* (Paris: Seuil, 1979).

24. Writing about America in 1930.

25. Henri Lauret wrote in *Le Matin*, October 22, 1981: "With 700 million inhabitants, the Northern hemisphere created a GNP of about 40,000 billion francs in 1980. The Southern hemisphere, with two billion people, has had to do with a productivity of about 7,000 billion francs (not including OPEC, China, and the Comencon Countries)."

It is worth adding that the foreign debt of the developing countries has reached 600 billion dollars, part of which is owed to private banks and the rest to states and international financial institutions.

26. Paul Bairoch, *Le Tiers monde dans l'impasse* (Paris: Gallimard, 1971), 249.

27. For the first school of thought, see Paul Bairoch, op. cit.; Jean Labbens, *Sociologie de la pauvreté*, Gallimard, p. 265ff.; Raymond Aron, *Plaidoyer pour l'Europe decadente*, Laffont, 1977, p. 273ff.; and Charles Rangel, *Le Tiers Monde et l'Occident*, Laffont, 1982. For the second, see the writings of Pierre Jalée, Jean Suret-Canale, and Samir Amin. For example, there is the question of whether or not the wealth that Great Britain drained out of the Indian subcontinent after the middle of the eighteenth century made its industrial takeoff possible. Even if there were a clear relation between the two, this sort of speculation is clearly fruitless, as Jacques Berque points out. The real trauma of colonialism "was of another order, another scale, and another quality" (*Dépossession du monde*, Seuil, 1964, p. 103ff).

28. Nietzsche remarked, in *Le Voyageur et son ombre* (Gonthier, 1975) that, "Our time only tolerates one sort of rich people—the ones that are ashamed of their wealth. If one hears about someone who is very wealthy, one is immediately seized with a feeling like the one felt in the presence of a repulsive sickness that bloats the body, dropsy, or an excess of fat. One must make an effort to remember one's humanity in order to be able to associate with a rich man without letting him see one's feeling of disgust."

29. Maurice Merleau-Ponty, *Signes* (Paris: Gallimard, 1960), 47.
30. News report at 8 P.M. on Antenne 2, October 14, 1980.

In 1926, while he was investigating the misdeeds of mining companies in the Congo, André Gide wrote, "I cannot just say to myself, as others often do, that the natives were more unhappy before the occupation of the French. We have taken on responsibilities to them that we cannot escape. Henceforth, I am full of discontent, for I know things and I must take a stand. What devil made me come to Africa? What did I expect to find in this country? I was contented, but now I know I must speak out."

In the past, the truth came out through the way in which it was revealed. André Gide in the Congo, Albert Londres in the prison of Cayenne, Vidal-Naquet and Jacques Servan-Schreiber in Algeria—all went under the surface, behind the scenes, to find what was hidden there, even though it might be frightful. And it was this "frightfulness" that they brought to light every time, and which aroused the indignation of their readers.

Nowadays, we are overloaded with horrors and repulsive pictures, thanks to media bombardment, and our capacity for surprise is dulled. Thanks to the means of communication, the world now has its own observer, so that each person experiences the shock of happenings from the other side of the planet. Voices are transmitted instantly, even though they disappear just as fast. We are used to expecting the worst, particularly since the genocide in Cambodia, and we are always ready to overestimate things because we want to avoid underestimating them. At least in democratic countries, we add a tragic view of public life to a surfeit of disasters and suffering. The revelation of too much agony and evil has led to our senses being overloaded.

I am certain that the experience of suspicion will continue to dominate our relationship to the world for a long time. Tyrannies continue to live by lies, and by words that no longer mean what they once did because they have been so overused. Thus, we experience the combination of totalitarian domination and media hysteria. On the one hand, regimes survive thanks to the systematic disinformation, while indifference grows amid incessant, babbling calls to action. This means that there are two basic principles for journalistic ethics—to uncover things without puffing them up, and to tell the truth without drowning the listener in catastrophes. It means rediscovering the virtue of all incisive reporting: moderation. Honesty is always preferable to dishonesty, but when it is combined with subtlety, it has a power to awaken and shock people that is much stronger than gut appeals to cheap sentiment and emotional overkill.

31. Jean-Yves Carfantin and Charles Condamines, *Qui a peur du tiers monde?* (Paris: Seuil, 1980), 42.

32. Pamphlet compiled by *Frères des Hommes* and *Terre des Hommes*, "Ici Mieux se nourrir, là-bas vaincre la faim."

33. Ibid.

34. Claude Julien, *Le Monde diplomatique*, October, 1974.

35. Francis Pisani and Gerard Viratelle, *Le Monde*, October 25–26, 1981.

36. "Ici Mieux se nourrir, là-bas vaincre la faim," op. cit. These figures were restated by Jean Ziegler in *Le Monde diplomatique*, November 1981.

37. Interview with Joel de Rosnay in "Ici mieux se nourrir . . . "

38. Susan Georges, introduction to *Comment meurt l'autre moitié du monde* (Laffont, 1976). This book, though, is one of the best and most intelligent commentaries on the problem of hunger.

39. Maurice Lelong, *Témoignage chrétien*, March 1966.

40. René Dumont wrote, in "Problèmes de la faim dans le monde," *Le Monde diplomatique*, July 1967, "Faced with this horrifying tide of poverty, how can we go calmly to sleep at night?"

41. The accumulation of horrors over time is not usually what outrages people, or gets them to act. Remember that, during the war in Vietnam, a single photograph, of a Vietnamese girl (Huynh Cong-ut, 1972) running naked and screaming in pain from a bombardment, caused more damage in American public opinion than all previous television reports.

42. René Dumont wrote, in a special edition of *Tricontinental* entitled "Famine and Poverty" (Maspéro, 1982, p. 96), "Our excessive eating of meat is a form of cannibalism, because our livestock eat one third of the grains [grown to feed human beings] and tens of millions of tons of feed . . . all of which are products that can feed people directly."

43. Vincent Leclercq in "Ici Mieux se nourrir . . . " op. cit.

44. Jean Ziegler, *Retournez les fusils!* (Paris: Seuil, 1981), 47.

45. "The reader in a rich country," explained René Dumont and Marie-France Mottin, *Le Mal-developpement en Amérique Latine* (Paris: Seuil, 1981), "must remember that he is equally responsible for and benefits from the horrifying poverty that we are about to describe, even if many people refuse to recognize this."

46. "We Westerners, either in spite of our efforts or with our silent collaboration, are all accomplices in imperialism's tasks of domination, exploitation, and death. We are collaborators with the oligarchies of our own countries, of France, Switzerland, and elsewhere, in the daily destruction of what defines us as men: the awareness of our common identity with all other human beings" (Jean Ziegler, *Main basse sur l'Afrique*, Seuil, 1980, p. 14).

47. "The West improves its methods of cutting trees, and develops single crops, and the result is the deforestation of the slopes of the Hi-

malayas, floods in Bangladesh, and famine in West Africa. Inexorable scientific and technical progress have led to 50 million people dying of hunger in the Third World in 1980. And these figures are already out of date—85 million people will die of starvation in five years. You can't stop progress!" (Roger Garaudy, *Promesses de l'Islam*, Seuil, 1981, p. 75).

48. In an article in *Les Nouvelles littéraires,* October 29, 1981, about the sexual mutilation of thousands of women in Africa and the Near East, Simone de Beauvoir accomplished the remarkable rhetorical feat of absolving Islam and the natives of this crime against the female sex, by suggesting that the problem comes from neocolonialism, i.e., the West. "Most of the voices raised in the crusade for the abolition of the mutilation are the same ones that make common cause with neocolonialism." They make common cause with the Northern hemisphere, therefore, the Northern hemisphere is guilty, because it conceals their depredations. QED. So, now, the circumcision of young girls is also portrayed as our fault.

49. "The main accusation that Brazilians hurl at other Brazilians and foreigners is a wordless one, but one that is suffocated by suffering, "You are inhuman, criminal, you do not allow us to exist," said a declaration of the bishops of Central-Western Brazil, quoted by René Dumont and Marie-France Mottin, op. cit., p. 20.

50. In *Le Nouvel observateur,* June 6, 1981, Michel Bosquet wrote, "The causes of famine in the world must be sought on our dinner tables; that is to say, in a political system that allows multinational corporations to stuff us with exotic delicacies, and to maintain Western-thinking and Western-acting oligarchies in power in the countries they are starving to death."

51. René Dumont arrives at the following conclusion when he writes, at the end of a long sermon against famine, "Sauvy says to Europe, 'Have more children or you are lost.' But a rich Yankee consumes 400 times more energy and rare metals than the poor peasant in the tropics. What really threatens the world's environment is the squandering and waste of its riches. . . . Because the ruling economic system has not succeeded in reducing this cannibalism—15 million dead per year— it is in our interests to reduce the number of rich people, and in the long run at least they should lose power" (*Tricontinental,* op. cit., pp. 96–97).

52. "In an unhappy universe, there can be no happy men," said the situationist Raoul Vaneigem in *Traité de Savoir vivre à l'usage des jeunes générations* (Paris: Gallimard, 1967).

53. In *Vies politiques,* Hannah Arendt shows how, ever since Robespierre, compassion has been the main motivating force of revolutionaries, and shows the damage it has done to modern revolutions through its zeal for pariah peoples.

54. For example, Henri Perroy aptly points out, in a remarkable

book, *La Charité aujourd'hui,* a collection of writings by theologians, "I think we must be very careful before we say that we see Christ in the face of the hungry, the thirsty, the imprisoned. We will see it in the end; at the beginning, we should start by practicing charity, before trying to find formulas that justify our actions and run the risk of transforming charity from what it is into something that is humiliating for others" (Editions SOS, 1981, p. 196).

55. Malcolm Muggeridge, *Mère Theresa de Calcutta* (Paris: Seuil, 1973), 121.

56. This is the expression of Edgar Haulotte, *La Charité aujourd'hui,* op. cit., p. 113.

57. With this exception: If a communist country is being considered, its good points and a positive balance sheet must be put forward. But when a free-market or democratic society is being considered, the slightest drawback is pitilessly emphasized. Not one of our great Third-Worldist preachers has ever been known to analyze the unequal relationship between the USSR and its overseas colonies, such as Cuba, Angola, and Ethiopia. There is a typical blank spot in their curiosity when it comes to these things.

58. The supreme example of this yammering nonsense is still *Le Massacre des innocents* (Editions J'ai lu) by Bernard Clavel, a cry of alarm "about the abysses of suffering into which children are thrown by war and poverty."

59. Michel Bosquet asks, in *Le Nouvel observateur,* October 17, 1981, "Are you ready to eat less, but better, if that will reduce hunger in the world?" He adds, "In Norway, 20,000 people are voluntarily experimenting with cheaper ways to live, and are paying all or part of their savings to programs in the field in the Third World."

60. Marie-France Mottin notes, with a straight face, "In Cuba, there are homosexual habits, which are leftovers from Yankee colonization" (*Cuba quand même,* Seuil, 1980, p. 194).

61. "We have broadcast our needs and means for satisfying them," wrote Charles Condamines in *Ici Mieux se nourrir . . .* op. cit. "The damage has already been done. The seductive power of money and progress has spread its poison to all corners of the universe. Coca-Cola, potato chips, transister radios, nude women, neckties, and paper money are already in the minds of all men, even if they are not in their hands. Nowadays, the windows of supermarkets are the same in Hong Kong, Rabat, London, Nairobi, Sao Paolo, or Abidjan."

62. "Your eyes are burning with the light with which you want to keep all people from sleeping as long as a single child continues to suffer" (Bernard Clavel, op. cit., p. 53–54).

63. "Nowadays, a writer cannot write about everything," says Elie Wiesel in *Le Nouvel observateur,* November 28, 1981. "There are too many causes to uphold, and too many victims."

64. The inventor of this abstract universalism is certainly Jean-Paul Sartre: "Each one of my choices has expanded my world, such that I no longer think of their implications as limited to France alone. The struggles with which I identify are worldwide struggles" (Interview with Tito Germani, quoted by Simone de Beauvoir in *La Cérémonie des adieux,* Gallimard, 1981).

65. See the excellent critique by Kolakowski in *L'Esprit révolutionnaire,* Editions Complexe, 1976, pp. 37–38, regarding the fruitless attempt by the left to find a common root in all struggles.

66. In *Le Monde,* October 31, 1981, an advertisement on page 4 asked readers to contribute signatures and money to a protest against American intervention in Central America, and for Central American rights to self-determination. On page 9, another advertisement, entitled "This outrage must be stopped!" implored us about the plight of slaughtered dogs in Southeast Asia, dogs sent bound and muzzled with tin cans on their snouts to slaughterhouses where they are butchered for food. Of course, the reader may agree with Lévi-Strauss "that the respect we wish to obtain from a man for his brothers is only a special case of the respect he should show for all forms of life" (Speech to UNESCO, 1971). But this juxtaposition of Nicaraguans and dogs inevitably looks strange. The same evening, I suppose, the reader will see televised pleas on behalf of Haitian refugees, Vietnamese boat people, the French unemployed. And all these appeals to good conscience will end up being interchangeable and canceling one another out.

67. "There are two kinds of pity. One is soft and sentimental, and in reality is nothing but the impatience the heart feels to get rid, as soon as possible, of the painful emotion that seizes it when confronted by another man's suffering. This is not compassion at all, but it an instinctive, defensive movement of the mind against suffering in another country. The other, the only kind that counts, is an unsentimental and creative pity, which knows what it wants and is resolved to persevere to the uttermost limits of human abilities (Stefan Zweig, *La Pitié dangéreuse,* Grasset, 1939, p. 159).

68. It is scarcely necessary to puncture the gross puffery of statements like this one, by a hack writer in *Le Matin,* "In the depths of the eyes of these children [in Egypt], in a marketplace smothered in dust in an alley smelling of donkeys, anise, and sesame, you can read the unbounded misery of a Third World that has been abandoned. Every time I travel there, I am overcome by the same feeling of disgust. When will we ever be done with our lazy, pampered babbling? Or with our cozy thrill bought at 7 francs for a news magazine? Rather than buy a paper, it would be better to feed seven hungry mouths for the same money. Instead of succoring a world that is dying, we insufferable egotists reread the pitiful dimensions of our fears. Are we not already stinking rich enough, stuffed to the gills by a society of abundance? All that we de-

serve is a nuclear war, a richly deserved punishment for the third-rate Sodom and Gomorrah of the West" (Jean-Edern Hallier, December 3, 1981).

69. During the summer of 1981, good folk were upset that Amnesty International, Médecins sans frontières, and UNESCO chose to sensitize public opinion by means of billboards. How could so many atrocities be dealt with by means of the same medium as beauty products, panties, or detergents? How could they transform an urgent ethical question into one of esthetics? What was shocking was the brutality of the media, that enlightening explanations were relegated to secondary importance or omitted entirely because of costs. We were treated to the usual tear-jerking: a simple face, a short inscription. ("His crime: thinking. If you forget him, he will die," says the prisoner for Amnesty International. "Five hundred million non-consumers," complained the poster for "Action internationale contre la faim"). And the results showed that the campaign was effective. Humanitarian projects show clearly that pity is an uncertain emotion and that philanthropy is too capricious. Passersby must be constantly reminded by fifty-foot-square billboards, with methods of insistent repetition that have succeeded in advertising. Morality sometimes gets lost, but the business of charity showed its effectiveness.

70. *Le Nouvel observateur,* October 17, 1981.

71. Many have happily embroidered on the theme of our evil eating habits. "Our dinner plates have now become the final link in a more and more complex system that extends its ramifications into the remotest areas of the planet so as to appropriate the work and wealth of all mankind" (Ici Mieux se nourrir, . . . op. cit.). We can only admire the modest, "more and more complex . . . " that caps the argument, so as to convince us of the accusation: You have to accept your guilt, because the process that has engendered it is so complex that there is no point in explaining it to you."

72. What does this mean in plain language? That 700 million people in underdeveloped countries are feeding 60 million Frenchmen who are twiddling their thumbs. A wave of a magic loaf of bread has made French farmers disappear! Such ridiculously oversimplified formulas are used for propaganda purposes, and contribute even more to people's confusion.

73. "Ici Mieux se nourrir, . . . " op. cit.

74. "Ici Mieux se nourrir, . . ." op. cit. "Manioc from Thailand to feed French Pigs" (pp. 33–34); "The Dictatorship of the Peanut," about Senegal (pp. 36–37); "Brazilians Can't Make Butter by Selling Soybeans" (pp. 38–39).

75. This is what a passage by Charles Condamines suggests in this same publication by *Terre des Hommes,* "The reality of life for people in the Third World has become tragic. There is enough food there to satisfy

their hunger, but without money they cannot get it, and their land is used more and more to feed our cattle and pigs. And if they resist or revolt, the forces of order massacre them or throw them into prison" (p. 15).

76. In *Le Monde,* March 24, 1982, Gilbert Etienne, professor of graduate studies in development at the University of Geneva, revealed that the United States of America accounted for more than two-thirds of the world exports of secondary grain, corn, and sorghum, which is used to feed large and small livestock, after which come the Common Market countries, Canada, and Argentina. He concluded, "The feeding of our livestock is primarily a matter of business between wealthy countries." For its part, the daily newspaper in Dakar, *Le Soleil,* wrote about this campaign, acknowledging the generosity of its intentions, but that, "Presented as a sort of therapy, it is overly optimistic, and falls apart because of the mistaken diagnosis that produced it in the first place. The fact that there are constraints does not allow us to think of breaking off trade, particularly when this is aimed at the boycotting of cash-crop cultivation. What would happen to the Senegalese economy if overnight it was suddenly deprived of the revenue from the export of peanuts, its main commercial crop! . . . Aside from being grossly oversimplified, this call for a boycott would produce a situation far more catastrophic" (Sidy Gaye, in an article published in a supplement to *Le Monde,* October 7, 1982). For final proof, Francisco Vargara, in an autumn 1982 special issue of *Tricontinental* magazine dealing with conventional wisdom about famine, wrote: "The figures cannot be disputed: The Northern hemisphere is getting fat on food it produces itself, and it exports more food to the Southern hemisphere than it imports from there. But the food that is exported by the North does not reach the ill-fed masses" (p. 101).

77. *Le Monde diplomatique,* November 1981, p. 10.

78. Ibid., p. 17.

79. Ibid., pp. 18–19.

80. Ici Mieux se nourrir, . . . op. cit.

81. See also, Susan Georges, op. cit., on the fruitlessness of reducing consumption of meat.

82. This is the ideal missionary, but in parody form. Mother Theresa says, "To be a real missionary of Charity, you must be a victim full of happiness," and later, "We could not understand and really succor those who are in need of everything if we did not live like them" (*La Joie du don,* Seuil, 1975, pp. 29, 34).

83. Jean-Claude Guillebaud, Jacques Meunier, and Marc Kravetz dared to write that the women and girls of Culcutta are "impeccably elegant, neat, and clean, as if there were not filthy sewers, buffalo turds, garbage, and slime all around them"; that "the happiness of the children in Bogota is clear"; and that, in a Kurdish guerrilla camp in northern

Iran, "a little girl in a bright red dress stared off toward a horizon of desert mountains, ceaselessly combing her long black hair." For this, they were excoriated by the Trotskyite Jean-Pierre Garnier in *Le Monde diplomatique,* August 1980, for portraying misery as beautiful, and for being the latest lackeys of Western imperialism. Garnier combines the ignorance of the armchair revolutionary and the stupidity of the militant, and his criticism proves in what low esteem he holds these Third World peoples with whom he claims brotherhood, since he denies them a minimal humanity that comes from the right to smile and be dignified.

84. Pope John Paul II, quoted by Max Scheler in *Nature et formes de la Sympathie* (Paris: Payot, 1971).

85. The Third-Worldists claim that 50 million people die from hunger every year. But in *Le Monde,* March 24, 1982, Joseph Kletzman explains that, in 1981, 48 million people died around the world, from all causes put together.

86. "Far from our civilization, look at these people dying from hunger before our very eyes," was a typical statement by a fifth-grade student in a poem published on the occasion of Third World Day, organized at schools by UNESCO and UNICEF on October 23, 1981.

87. Note that none of the analyses of the causes of underdevelopment agree. When one condemns multinational corporations, another praises their positive role. One advocates food assistance, while another denounces it. They agree neither on the diagnosis, nor on the remedy.

88. If all poverty is hell, to use Marx's expression, this hell has different degrees, from absolute poverty to a sort of survival that is precarious but constant. To omit mention of these crucially different degrees on the individual level is once more to bury information under propaganda.

89. A song "700 million Chinese and me and me and me"; lyrics by Jacques Lanzmann, music by Jacques Dutronc, expresses this idea.

90. Poverty in rich countries is never considered. But, according to the latest figures of the Common Market, there are 30 million "people in precarious circumstances" in the European community.

91. Why do all campaigns against hunger end up talking about elaborate feasts? Doubtless, to give our meals the atmosphere of banquets held before the Deluge.

"Let's help them conquer hunger." What can be the impact of such a slogan, when it is repeated on billboards a thousand times? It does prevent our meals from being taken for granted, because if people are dying of hunger, our full dinner plates are a miracle, a gift of God. And so, our generous eating combines the double aspect of abundance and fragility. Rather than make us sad, the child with the swollen belly gives zest to an otherwise monotonous diet. He symbolizes our privilege, according to the principle that a rare pleasure is a precious one. In short, we need to remember rationing in order to enjoy our brioche and fear famine to savor steak, hot dogs, and bread.

92. Over the last few years, since the tragedy of the boat people in Indochina, there seems to have been a great improvement in the appearance of an ethic based on other people's needs. It is an ethic that does not distinguish between good and bad victims; it saves communists as well as counterrevolutionaries; in short, it replaces the "cold-war mentality" in our minds, as André Glucksmann put it.

It is clear, though, that this ethic of human rights, in refusing to choose between the good and the bad, still depends on our whims, just as, in the past, it depended on our political convictions. When almost two-thirds of the human race scarcely has access to the bare necessities for survival, we are presented with a situation of desperate need every day, every minute. Our response to destitution is always arbitrary. Why should we choose to help Vietnamese refugees today, when, for the last 10 years, the population of Bihar has been regularly decimated by famine? Why the Haitian boat people, rather than some Amazon tribe massacred by Brazilian freebooters? Obviously, our pity depends on the effect of the media which, in turn, is a function of the degree of freedom of the press in the countries involved. Today, a really good massacre is one that is on television. A slaughter that a camera has not filmed barely deserves mention. And always forgotten are the deprivations that are just as urgent but which the television screen and the newspapers do not mention. The extent of suffering is always greater than that of good will.

We must realize that, in this regard, everyone divides up the world according to his own preferences. South America is the territory claimed by those hostile to the United States. Asia is becoming the turf or newly-minted anti-Soviets, particularly since the invasion of Afghanistan. Africa is equally divided up between those who denounce the imperialism of the United States and its little French brother. Apolitical people choose countries that are relatively far-removed from the influence of the great powers. *There is really no objective need other than the one I myself have chosen.* Only we decide whether a situation is intolerable, and we all have our favorite areas of interest. We pretend that the choice was imposed on us by absolute necessity, because this is the high-flown manner of speaking used to attract the public to our little sectarian interest. Even an ethic of extreme need cannot avoid being discriminatory. That is the scandal of charity provided from the outside for the unfortunate it has chosen to help. We always help some hungry and downtrodden people more than others. It makes little difference that the grounds for these preferences are not political. Today, as in the past, we still choose some poor people over others.

Chapter 3

1. George Orwell, *Burmese Days* (Penguin), pp. 36–42.

2. Quoted by G. E. von Grunebaum in *L'Identité culturelle de l'Islam* (Paris: Gallimard, 1973), pp. 184–195.

3. This is the title of a book by Fanon and published by Gallimard in 1952.

4. A slightly abridged version of this chapter, with the title "Der Wallfahrt zu den Quellen," appeared in the German magazine *Palaver* in May 1982.

5. Regarding Orientalism, see the book of the same name (Paris: Seuil, 1980), by Edward Said. It is a good synthesis, though highly questionable in its conclusions.

6. Quoted by the Pakistani poet Mohammed Iqbal, *Le Massacre de l'Orient*, Les Belles-Lettres, 1956, p. 19. This beautiful collection of writings (which matches the *Divan occidental-oriental* by Goethe) comes from these lines by Heine.

7. "We must breathe, breathe afresh, refresh ourselves at the living wellsprings of eternal renewal. Where else can we find this but in the cradle of our race, on the sacred heights from which the Indus and Ganges flow, the torrents of Persia and rivers of Paradise?" wrote Michelet in *La Bible de l'Humanité* (1864). And Nerval, in his *Voyage en Orient* (1851), wrote, "I must unite with some pure damsel of this sacred land, which is the first fatherland of all of us; I must bathe myself anew in these streams, which will revive the human race, and from which flowed the poetry and laughter of our forefathers." In 1927, René Guénon, who ended up converting to Islam, took up the same idea when he wrote, "To restore our lost tradition, to really breathe new life into it, we need to make contact with the living spirit of tradition, and, as I have said, this spirit is only really totally alive in the East" (*La Crise du monde moderne*, Gallimard, p. 49).

8. On the hippies, in French there is the interesting book by Michel Lancelot, *Je veux regarder Dieu en face* (Editions J'ai Lu, 1971), the 1970–75 issues of *Actuel*, the magazine *Rolling Stone*, and the excellent reporting by Alain Dister from San Francisco from 1966 to 1970. Of course, the best source is our own personal recollections.

9. Why did the attraction for the Orient focus more on India or Southeast Asia than on Islam? There are several reasons. As a monotheistic religion, Islam is still too close to Christianity and Judiasm to really seem exotic. The tradition of hospitality in countries such as India, Ceylon, Thailand, Nepal, and Indonesia allowed the establishment of many colonies of Europeans, and the authorities did not bother them as long as they remained apart from the people themselves. But the most important reason, perhaps, lies in Buddhism and Hinduism. As they were

practiced by the hippies, both religions retained an individualist dimension that was familiar to Westerners. This made it possible for anyone who was more concerned about his own salvation than the establishment of a community of spirituality and belief to adopt or imitate them. See the excellent analysis of the "Hinduized hippy" in Louis Dumont's *Homo hierarchicus,* (Paris: Gallimard, 1966), 299.

10. "East is East (in the English sense of the Orient) and is still the seat of the Supreme Being. This is certainly why it can be said that the Occident, in a neat match of words, is concerned about the accidental, while Asia is concerned about the easy" (Jean Biés *L'Inde, ici et maintenant,* Devry Livres, 1979, p. 236). Roger Garaudy uses the same play on words in *Promesses de l'Islam* (Paris: Seuil, 1981), 17: "The Occident is an accident. Its culture is an anomaly." It is clear that this transposition of words makes no more sense than the statement, "Roger Garaudy is very gaudy."

11. "The desire to find absolutes that appear in historical periods has been one of the salient traits of modern times since the Renaissance," wrote von Grunebaum (op. cit., p. 105).

12. "In the fairly near future," wrote the Indian author Gita Mehta in *Karma Cola,* (Delhi: Penguin Books, 1979), 20, "When an Indian wants to find out about his own country, he will have to go to the West, and when Westerners want to remember themselves as they once were, they will have to come to us. Another name for this is rock 'n roll."

13. This gave rise to the famous annoucement of a hitchhiker from that era, "I had tea with an Afghan!" It was a way of admitting how hard it was to make contact with Orientals and the total lack of communication, which consisted of sharing a cup of tea at a table with a stranger.

14. "The mantra that India slips into our hearts can be contained in one word, simplicity. The most difficult thing is to learn how to be simple all over again; that is what she is telling us: The simplicity of life with these thousands of simple people, whose being is right there before your eyes" (Jean Biés, op. cit., p. 46).

15. The utopia of the hitchhiker was never anything but a colonialist dream, one of living cheaply or for free, among the poorest of the poor, and if necessary taking advantage of their hospitality by stealing from them. But unlike colonialism, the values of these wanderers did not include thrift, exertion, and work. As thief or parasite, they were closer to the European vagabond of old than to the colonialists of the past century.

16. Inevitably, the dream of rebirth turned into an epic of self-destruction. The junkie came to know the depths of autism, closing himself off from others, including his fellow wanderers, in a society not his own. He started off with a black and white vision: the good East and the evil

West. He ended up in a world where the degree of evil surpasses anything seen in Europe. The junkie is an outcast to everyone, despised by
his compatriots, hated by the locals, and tolerated only as long as he can
pay for his meals and his hotel. He is exploited by the drug dealers, with
no friendship other than the furtive one of a shot or a trip, and always
on the lookout for his suppliers. He comes to slip into a sort of semi-
delinquent state to survive, joins the local gangs, where he is still re-
garded as an outsider, exploited in the most degrading ways, and handed
over to the authorities when his services are no longer needed. His life
is one of total solitude, coupled with total insecurity. His dependence on
a powder or an acid, his mistrust of everyone and everything, the proces-
sion of mental and physical illnesses that attack his weakened body, make
him a pariah, and lead him to join with communities of other wraiths
that gather from Goa to Katmandu, from Bangkok to Denpasar. He slides
down a slope toward insanity, from one depth to the other, until death
by exhaustion or overdose in some stairway or street. He dies in a unique
and abject way in the vast sewer of a shanty town, or goes mad and is
locked up in an asylum that rips away his last shreds of sanity. He goes
on until he arrives at the last circle of hell by a road that is long, quiet,
and inescapable. On this subject, read the astonishing autobiographical
account by Charles Duchaussois, the first person to be returned from
Nepal for health reasons, in 1969, *Flash ou le grand voyage,* LGF, 1975.

    17. Three or four great messiahs now share the European clientele
in India. There is Maharishi Mahesh Yogi (the former guru of the Bea-
tles), the brilliant inventor of "transcendental meditation," whose empire and its revenues extend to four continents. Bhagwan Rajneesh, the
most lunatic of the charlatans of Asia, went into exile in the United States,
with a colossal fortune and a community of almost 20,000 followers.
Swami Muktananda, whose austerity is more and more sought out by
followers in the international jet set, divides his time between Los Angeles and Ganeshpuri, north of Bombay. Because they bring in enormous
amounts of money, these gurus are not only tolerated, but coddled by
the young Indian republic. For more information, see my article in the
weekly *Le Point,* "Gourous du troisième type," June 1982.

    18. "Never before had the Void been pursued with such optimism
and vigor. Everyone felt that whatever Americans wanted, Americans
got. Why not Nirvana?" (Gita Mehta, op. cit. p. 7).

    19. Maharishi yogi guarantees his followers that if they meditate
for 20 minutes in the morning and evening, they will be able to practice
levitation after a few months. . . . There is clearly a competitive side to
this holiness, which leads every guru to be envious of the others. This
leads to their outbidding one another in the production of magical effects
and inflated promises and miracles, in a battle for attracting and seduc-

ing disciples. Since each one claims a monopoly on the Revealed Truth, the way to heaven becomes an orgy of greed, a merciless competition among manufacturers of beliefs.

20. Very few Indians are allowed in the ashrams that are reserved for Westerners. This is under the oh-so-philanthropic pretext that Indians are not advanced enough to share the spiritual nourishment of whites. This is part of the endless phoniness of the expatriate. He is a foreigner who has come to settle in these countries because he has hard currency. He ends up displacing the native, and arrogating to himself the privileges of the ashram at the expense of those who have a right to be there. Of course, the guru makes up for this usurpation by charging high fees, or practices shameful extortion the way Rajneesh does in Poona. In a way—and contrary to the colonial situation—the privilege of being among white people is very costly. This privilege is, therefore, a mixed one, and is all the more odious when it takes the form of segregation within the country itself. It is true that in recent years the Indians, in their turn, have begun restricting Europeans' entry into certain ashrams, and have abandoned the trade in spiritual tourism to their more unscrupulous countrymen.

21. In Europe and the USA the growth of the hippy movement gave rise to an extraordinary growth of sects. As early as 1966, Timothy Leary, inspired by the "gentleness and naive faith" of the hippies, announced the establishment of a new religion in New York, which he called the "League for Spiritual Discovery," an allusion to the initials LSD. His example gave rise to other sects all over the country, such as the New American Church of Arthur Keleps in Miami, not to mention the psychedelic religious communities in which LSD was used as a sacrament. This then led to an immense flourishing of little groups, a large-scale extension of the communications market, to the opening of supermarket chains selling Zen and intimacy, the degradation of religion into a form of psychology, and the Church into an adjunct of the hospital. On this, see Alain Woodrow, *Les Nouvelles sectes* (Paris: Seuil, 1977).

22. Here again Bhagwan Rajneesh knew, better than others, how to use all the twentieth century recruitment methods in his various centers. He is a veritable genius at manipulating people, and his ashram has been transformed into a laboratory of coercion by consent.

23. There is a strange division of labor in this area with regard to the European community in India and Nepal, which numbers between 20,000 and 40,000 people. Whereas rich Calvinist Europeans (Germans, Swiss, and Scandinavians) largely populate the ashrams, particularly in the Himalayas, Catholic Europeans (French and Italian) tend to choose illegality and crime, such as the drug traffic and buying and selling stolen passports and jewels. What explains this division of labor? There have

also been recent arrivals on the spirituality scene in the last three years, the children of South American ruling elites—Argentines, Brazilians, and Venezuelans.

24. As Christopher Isherwood said in *My Guru and His Disciple* (New York: Farrar, Straus, 1980), 49: "I was repelled by the English words I had been taught in childhood and was grateful to Vedanta for speaking Sanskrit. I needed a brand new vocabulary and here it was with a set of philosophical terms which were exact in meaning, unemotive, untainted by disgusting old associations with clergymen's sermons, schoolmasters' pep talks, politicians' patriotic speeches."

25. Not to mention the almost obsessive sanitary preoccupations of Europeans in Asia. In the homeland of the gods, they care only for their intestines, examining their tongues and watching out for their digestion. The hitchhiker sets out, toilet paper in hand, to elevate his soul, but ends up concerned only about his stool and the gurgling guts that disturb his meditation.

26. Here again is the confusion between drugs and mysticism. It was to be the era of the Great Change thanks to hallucinogens, announced by Jean-Jacques Lebel in 1967 (quoted by Michel Lancelot, op. cit., p. 286). Precise doses for reaching enlightenment were given by Timothy Leary in his book, *L'Experience psychédélique:* "Column A shows the dosage that is enough to send an inexperienced person into the transcendental world described in this manual" (quoted by M. Lancelot, p. 133). This stems from the illusion by which the opium eater or acid taker can arrive rapidly at states of consciousness that meditation can bring only after several years of practice. The consciousness obtained in this way is extremely fragile, and coming down is seen as a sort of fall. This leads the drug-taker to double the dosage so he can stay high. And the desire to achieve an acuteness of mind degenerates into passsivity and total lethargy.

27. Of course, there are ashrams that one can escape from, and religious initiations that are worth undertaking, as long as one takes care to differentiate and not try to lump together the different cultural contexts and diverse references to the Almighty. There must also be no time limit to the quest, and one must seek out foreign religions from a starting point of knowing one's own, so that the shock of discovery is also one of exchange. This is why, by and large, the most authentic cultural exchanges are conducted by priests and clerics. Vatican II is well-known to have given great importance to cultural contact, particularly the perspective provided by Father Arupe, the former director of the Jesuits, who had spent several years in Japan. On this subject, see the exquisite writing on Mircea Eliade about his stay in an ashram in Rishikesh in 1931. His thoughts on what his stay inspired themselves provide grounds

for meditation. "What I had attempted, in my desire to tear myself loose from my Western roots, the better to mingle in an exotic spiritual universe, essentially meant that I had to give up my creativity first. To create, it is necessary to live in a world one belongs to" (*Memoires I, Les Promesses de l'Equinox*, Gallimard, 1980, p. 281).

If you want to understand the English gentry at the time of the British raj, go to Goa, an old Portuguese trading post in Southwest India, a strange and casual throwback to the British Empire. You will find the most diverse samples of *Homo Europeanus* from the last 20 years—meditators and activists, punks and intellectuals, old bums and beardless striplings, hermits and speechifiers, preachers and fools, middle-class people dressed like fakirs, ruffians, and gurus, not to mention the regular contingent of wrecks, failures, discards, and ruined lives that is always around in these climes. Here, the white man enjoys his diversity to the fullest, with his boundless capacity for disguising himself and putting on different costumes. It is like being in a nonstop spectacle: the beauty of clothing in shimmering colors, the splendor of embroidery and silks, the display of some dressed up as pirates, as beggars, as Arab sheikhs, fearfully rolling their eyes or wielding cane or sword in hand. The Westerner dressed up as a comic opera Asian shows off his extravagance to his fellows, before an audience of astonished Indians.

Of course, the grandsons of the former imperialists have changed their habits. They do not play golf, they play backgammon. They have abandoned shorts and helmets and now wear dhotis, string bikinis, or tongas. They cover themselves with jewels, practice astrology like the locals, smoke ganja and opium, sniff cocaine, and take acid instead of alcohol; and their love lives are more like polygamy than the straitlaced conjugal lives of the Victorians. Above all, they go swimming naked, joyfully displaying their bodily freedom. Every uncovered organ proudly declares their membership in a master race. You see how free I am, I, the white man. The Indian who, particularly on Sunday, comes to photograph and sniff at these scantily clad specimens from the Northern hemisphere, stares in perplexity at these tanned breasts and sunburned crotches and buttocks, with a look that is a mixture of envy and disapproval. He himself is stuffed into tight and uncomfortable pants and a cramped shirt, and even highheeled boots. It is an incredible reversal of the past. In 1852, the Portuguese government of Panjim forbade Goans dressed in their native costume to enter the towns of the territory, which were open only to people wearing skirts and pants. At the same time, the English colonizers were commanding the Indians to conceal their offensive nakedness. Today, it is the native of Madras, Bombay, and Delhi who has become the best repository of European values, whereas Frenchmen, Italians, and Germans are rediscovering the qualities of comfort and ease that used to belong to the original inhabitants of the subcontinent. Hence, the stupefaction of the natives: The whites are not what they used to be!

And, now, thousands of hippies have become the new natives of this old trading post: Goa, where colonialism is a snapshot, a picture postcard without its economic or political consequences, a flea on the back of the Indian elephant, now serves to amuse without corrupting. It is a show-case of Europe in foreign territory, and permits the citizenry to come and see for themselves the latest customs of this little-known species, the Westerner. In the dreamy tropics, it is a white man's carnival, where the West parades on display before the East.

28. Mircea Eliade, Alexandra David-Neal, Arnaud Desjardins, Lanza del Vasto, Father Monchanin, Father Le Saux, and Guy Deleury all tried, with varying degrees of success, this voyage beyond the pale. The German Jesuit Hans Waldenfels wrote a beautiful retrospective on nine years in Japan, entitled *La Meditation en Orient et en Occident* (Paris: Seuil, 1981).

29. Harvey Cox wrote, very astutely, "But curiously, it is precisely America's receptivity, its eagerness to hear, explore, and experience, which creates the most difficult barrier to our actually learning from Eastern spirituality. The very insatiable hunger for novelty, for intimacy, even for a kind of spirituality, which motivates so many Americans to turn toward the East also virtually guarantees that the turn will ulti-mately fail. It is the story of the Trojan horse, only in reverse" *Turning East* (New York: Simon & Schuster, 1977), 135–136.

30. Is Western culture superior? Lévi-Strauss makes two arguments.

1. He says that every culture is the fruit of a coalition, which ex-plains why the great inventions of the human race developed at more or less the same time. The West's claim to credit for the Industrial Revo-lution must therefore be denied, because it would have occurred sooner or later anyway somewhere else on the globe (*Anthropologie structurale II*, Plon, 1973, p. 410). "Here we can put our finger on the absurdity of declaring that one culture is superior to another, because, to the extent that a culture can be considered by itself, it could never be considered 'superior'. . . . It is always present in coalition with other cultures, and that is what allows it to accumulate a series of accomplishments" (ibid., p. 413). True, but this does not explain why, if all societies are the fruit of a coalition, only the West achieved its fullest potential. It does not explain why Europe and Europe alone managed to put together this complex of inventions that distinguished it from other cultures with which it communicated and traded. If all societies, at the beginning, were of the same pattern, how to explain how only ours was able to take off and to succeed as it has done?

2. Ethnocentrism "is an attitude in whose name 'savages' (or all those whom one chooses to consider as such) are rejected. It is precisely the most striking and distinctive attitude of these 'savages' themselves" (ibid., p. 383). "To refuse to consider as human those who appear to be the most 'savage' or 'barbaric' is simply to borrow from them one of their typical attitudes. The barbarian is above all the man who believes in barbarism" (ibid., p. 384). This is a strange argument; to refute Western racism, it begins by justifying it by assuring us that the hated natives are in fact barbarians! So the only thing that should make us avoid ethnocentrism is a heartfelt repugnance for being like these "savages"! It is a strange way to fight evil and bestow upon far-off peoples the dignity that some would deny them! It is true that the thought of Lévi-Strauss is so rich that it seems almost impossible to argue with it because it revels in its own contradictions. Yet we have put our finger on what could be called two forms of well-meaning sophistry. In his semi-paternalist desire to prove to other cultures that Europe is nothing, absolutely nothing—always in the name of regret for the past—Claude Lévi-Strauss, almost in spite of himself, shows exactly the opposite. Some intellectual lapses are welcome. . . .

31. This anecdote was cited in Raoul Girardet's excellent *L'Idée coloniale en France,* LGF collection "Pluriel."

32. *L'Islam au défi* (Paris: Gallimard, 1980), 90.

33. "Primitive life is so simple, while our societies are like complex machines. The Tahitian is from the beginning of the world, while the European is from its old age," wrote Diderot in the *Supplement au voyage de Bougainville* (Paris: Garnier-Flammarion), 146. And Condillac said, "We who believe ourselves to be learned, must needs go to the most ignorant of peoples to learn from them the beginnings of our own discoveries; for we need this beginning above all else; we know nothing about it because, for a long time, we have not been willing to learn from nature" ("La langue des calculs," 1760, cited in Gérard Leclerc, *Anthropologie et colonialisme,* Fayard, 1973, p. 223).

34. He suggested a distinction between "authentic" and "spurious" cultures. The former are "harmonious, balanced, and perfectly self-sufficient," while the latter "reduce the individual to a cog in a machine, engendering frustration and alienation" (quoted by Gerard Leclerc, op. cit. p. 155).

35. "What was not seen before now was that it is a civilization built upon the negative, what can be called an absence of principle. That is precisely what gives the modern world its abnormal character, making it a sort of monstrosity" (*La crise du monde moderne,* [1927], Gallimard, collection "Idées" 1974, p. 90–91).

36. "The visitor who sleeps out in the forest with these Indians feels anguish and pity for people who are so deprived. . . . But this pov-

erty is full of tender talk and laughter. Couples embrace as if they were seeking to recapture some lost oneness, and their caresses continue even when a stranger walks by. A tremendous gentleness can be discerned in everyone, a deep carefreeness, a naive and charming animal satisfaction," wrote Lévi-Strauss in *Tristes Tropiques*, op. cit. pp. 335–336. And Pierre Clastres himself wrote of primitive man before the "fall," meaning before the beginning of the "state": "What is described here is in fact the historical moment when History was born, a fateful break that should never have happened, an irrational event which we modern people call, in similar fashion, the birth of the State. La Boétie saw in this fall of society into the voluntary submission of almost everyone to one other person, the repulsive signs of a failure that may be irreversible. . . . Ethnology takes as its perspective the division that was perceived by La Boétie . . . these primitive societies are certainly well-named as such, because they are primary societies that blossomed unaware of social divisions, the first to exist before that fateful mistake" (Liberté, malencontre innomable, in *Discours de la servitude volontaire* by Etienne de la Boétie, Payot, 1972, pp. 231–233).

37. In speaking of African colonization and the respective benefits invaders and natives derived from it, Guy de Bosschère wrote, "The whites, on the other hand, cannot pretend to have given anything to black culture, except the contribution of the debilitating values of their utilitarian and materialist civilizations with their congenital despair" (*Autopsie de la colonisation*, Albin Michel, 1967, p. 180). And Robert Jaulin wrote, "The serenity, discretion, and self-control of the Indian contrast with Western self-dramatization" (*La paix blanche*, Seuil, collection "Combats" 1970, p. 15).

38. For example, let us read this passage from a text from 1555 about the inhabitants of the New World: "It is a fact that, for them, the land belongs to everyone, like sunlight or water. They know nothing about "yours" or "mine," which is the root of all evil. . . . It is the rule of the Golden Age. They have neither ditches nor walls nor hedges to enclose their domains. They live in gardens that are open to all. Without laws, statutes, or judges, they behave with a natural equality" (Pierre Martyr Anghiera, quoted by Richard Marienstras, *Le proche et le lointain*, Minuit, 1981, p. 242.

Compare these lines to the writings of the modern ethnologists who exalt the erotic freedom of the primitive, his hatred of the "state," his refusal of private property, his natural sense of justice, and it becomes clear that the same myth has persisted since the Renaissance. It is a myth that neither field studies nor "scientific" research have weakened in the slightest, but have instead given a sheen of respectability that reinforces it all the more. In the chapter above on militant solidarity it was demonstrated that the observation of facts on the scene can lead to mistakes and can certify the most simple-minded myopia.

39. Jacques Berque, *L'Islam au défi* (Paris: Gallimard, 1980), 275.

40. The essence of the ethnological line has flowered in the ideology of tourism today. For example, in this pamphlet's commentary on the Berber villages of the Southern Desert of Tunisia: "Together they weave the daily activities of a life that has survived like an island of wise simplicity in our world beset by turbulence and disquiet. The voyage now takes on the aspect of a return to our origins." This is perplexing: How can a Berber village constitute a return to his origins for a European?

41. "I am persuaded that primitive societies are complex and sophisticated, and that they are the societies of the future, perhaps our own second chance, because they are fundamentally different from ours, and because there is no hope for mankind except in the diversity of his destiny" (Interview of Jean Malaurie by *Le Nouvel observateur*, March 1981). And said Jaulin, "To link our future with the wisdom of the Indian world seems best on the face of it" (*La paix blanche*, op. cit., p. 259).

42. In *De l'ethnocide*, UGF, 1972, p. 35.

43. Remo Guideri, "Les societies primitives d'aujourd'hui," in *Philosopher*, Fayard, 1980, p. 62.

44. In the conclusion of the remarkable study that he wrote on Lévi-Strauss, Jacques Derrida wrote, "The criticism of ethnocentrism, a theme so dear to the author of *Tristes Tropiques*, most often functions simply to set up the "other" as a model of original and natural goodness, to accuse and humiliate oneself, to exhibit one's own unacceptability in a counter-ethnocentric mirror" (*De la grammatologie*, Minuit, 1967, pp. 167–168).

45. There is no question that the islands in the Indian Ocean, the Caribbean, and the South Pacific look like paradise to us. There is no denying that the long strands of the Seychelles, the coasts of Ceylon, and the Maldives, the rice paddies of Bali and the Philippines, and the beaches of the Antilles are incomparably more enchanting than the suburbs of Liverpool, the great smokestacks of the Ruhr, or the mines of Roubaix. Granting that, the Westerner must remember that he is only getting a fragmentary glimpse of these heavenly climes, usually in the most luxurious and comfortable conditions. And tropical splendor, the sweetness of human contact, the beauty of the flora and fauna should not allow us to forget the extreme precariousness, the difficulty of primitive life, even along the most enchanting seasides. All the same, for us inhabitants of countries with cold and changing seasons, the lands of sunshine will always hold an incomparable fascination.

46. Roger Garaudy, *Pour un dialogue des civilisations*, op. cit., p. 154.

47. Of course, Pierre Clastres never explicitly set up the Guayaqui or the Yanomamo as a model society. His knowledge of the territory allowed him, however, to set up a theoretical model that was functional in certain respects, in order to analyze domination and power in our societies. Nonetheless, his interpretation, whether he was aware of it or not, cannot fail to make us dream about antitheses to our dehumanizing metropolises presented by the Amazon tribes, and thereby activate the myth of the "noble savage."

48. Sodomy is "a marginal sexual activity but it does not lead to a feeling of guilt, which, like remorse, is a feeling that is justly banished from Indian morality," wrote J. Lizot in *Le cercle des feux* (Paris: Seuil, 1970), 44. The April 1, 1976, issue of the magazine *Libération* provides excerpts from the precocious experiences of "Hebewe, the little Indian."

49. In a collection published under the title *Sauvage à la mode,* (Sycomore, 1979), Jean-Loup Amselle, Marc Augé, Jean Copans, Jean-Claude Godin, Christian Deverre, Jean Bazin, and Ugo Fabietti perform a searing and healthy demystification that would be welcome if it were not spoiled by a hidebound Marxist dogmatism. They denounce one form of stupidity while falling into a worse one themselves.

50. Certain forms of ethnology have no credibility when they mix up primitive societies in our theoretical arguments. This is proven, for example, in the refutation of Deleuze-Guattari and Pierre Clastres by Marc Augé, an anthropologist specializing in black Africa, who holds that all societies are repressive, even the most primitive, because they impose social and individual conformity. "The logic of power is always the same, not so much because of the scope of its effects, but because of the rigorous effectiveness of its forms" (*Génie du paganisme,* Gallimard, 1982). How can we laymen make our way amid this avalanche of contradictory thought, since we cannot find out for ourselves in the field?

51. Claude Lévi-Strauss, *Anthropologie structurale, II,* op. cit., p. 322.

52. "What we call the Western enterprise is the application of the intellect to scientific investigation of a demystified nature, which must be violated so that its laws can be known and submitted to the will of mankind. . . . It has led us to a situation that can be called 'anti-demiurgic,' in that it is the negation of the creative act, because it puts the human race in the position of destroying, of annihilating its own habitat, the Earth" (Henri Corbin, *Philosophie iranienne et philosophie comparée,* Teheran, 1977, p. 47).

53. In 1927, René Guénon was already spouting, "These Orientals who have 'Westernized' themselves, who have abandoned their traditions and adopted all the aberrations of the modern spirit, and these depraved elements, thanks to their learning at American and European universities, have become a cause of trouble and agitation in their own

countries" (op. cit., p. 153). The theme of "local bourgeoisies who sold out to European imperialism," which arose from the same order of ideas, became widespread, too, along with the usage that was made of it by certain Orientalists to lambaste President Sadat, renegade of Islam and the Arab cause. Elsewhere, some Indians were cursed by Robert Jaulin because they betrayed their "Indianness" by Westernizing. "Contact, peace, and life with the white man—all this made them into beggars, parasites, people infinitely less aware and more dirty than they had been" (*La Décivilisation*, Editions Complexe, 1974). And Jaulin soon presented himself as the only authentic Indian in the whole Amazon Basin, winner by a knockout in the puristic sweepstakes, since he took over a foreign culture himself! And it was Jaulin who exalted the theme of the white Indian, the romance of the outlaw, the outcast, the gangster, the delinquent, in whom burns a pure savagery, which he hoped would save the West by its capacity for revolt and disorder. But it is in India where the outer limits of the absolutely ridiculous can be found because, in contrast to people who talk of Aryan racial purity, there is a sect just as bizarre that believes in Dravidian purity. The people in South India are proclaimed exempt from any corrupting contact with the West. As a splendid example of this rigidity, the eminent Alain Daniélou dismisses not only Gandhi and Nehru with a stroke of the pen, but also Tagore, Vivekananda and Aurobino, because they are all guilty of having collaborated with English culture (*Les Chemins du labyrinthe*, Laffont, 1981, pp. 146–147). He is the true Hindu, and the others can only try!

What is the militant's complaint against the ethnologist? That he has not discovered class conflict among Andaman and Nicobar Island natives; that he has forgotten the universal law of exploitation from the Orinoco Basin or the foothills of Kilimajaro. In his eyes, everything is clear, and the ethnologist is an "individualist aristocrat" who favors "Buddhism that quiets the masses" (a reproach aimed at Claude Lévi-Strauss in *Le Sauvage à la mode*, op. cit., p. 45), the myth of the "noble savage," and fundamentalist Islam, so as to turn peoples away from their revolutionary duty; in short, he is an agent of Western imperialism. For him, "Marxist, communist and totalitarian ideology is a historical ruse aimed at speeding up the Westernization of peoples who had not been touched by it up to the present time" (Claude Lévi-Strauss, in an interview in *Le Monde*, January 21–22, 1979), a form of colonialism like the others. The conditioned responses of the dialogue between communists and ethnologists about the West are remarkably orchestrated, like two actors who ritually attack each other. And the poor West is sandwiched in between systems of thought that violently reject it and attack it head on, even though they are its offspring. It is a sad time when a whole civilization is made into an epithet synonymous with barbarity and fascism.

54. "A Statement on Human Rights," *American Anthropologist* (1947), quoted by Gérard Leclerc, op. cit., pp. 161–163.

55. In his book, *L'Europe et l'Islam* (Seuil, 1978, pp. 184–185), Hichem Djait objects discreetly to "the concert of new voices . . . raised in the West to implore the Muslims to remain themselves [and that] represents, above all, the naive, guilty consciences of the West which, faced with the alienation from which it suffers, sees in a mythical or real Islam the opposite of its suffering: a sense of happiness, spirituality, and community values."

56. *Le Monde et l'Occident* (Paris: Gonthier, 1965), 72.

57. *Anthropologie Structurale, II*, op. cit., p. 417.

58. Melville Herskovits, an American anthropologist and founder of cultural relativism, defined ethnocentrism as "the position of those who think that their way of life is preferable to all others" (quoted by Gérard Leclerc, op. cit., p. 157).

59. For example, after Father Michel Lelong, Vatican delegate for relations with outside religions, decided that the Koran was a call to justice, adoration, and action, like the Bible, wrote, "The spiritual universe of Islam is the very same as that of Judaeo-Christian tradition" (*Deux fidélités, une espérance,* Cerf, 1979).

60. What is revealing in this regard is the change undergone by French missionaries. In the good old days of colonialism, the three Ms—merchant, military, and missionary—supposedly walked hand in hand, even though this vision is oversimplified. After that came the doubts and uncertainty of a certain left-leaning Christianity, which refused even to spread the Gospel. After independence was achieved and native religions reestablished in their own right, many young missionaries underwent a spectacular about-face, as Antoine-Marcel Henry's work, *L'Asie nous interpelle* (Cerf, 1979) shows in its stricken comprehensiveness, "It must be understood that we make no conversions. . . . Today we recoil from directly transmitting Christ's message. . . . Each person has his religion, each his conscience. That is the slogan of today" (pp. 150–151). After that, missions were less concerned with conversion than with being with and plunging into the human soup (p. 178). They became more attached to charitable missions, such as the Little Sisters of Father de Fouca in Beirut, Teheran, or Kabul, and the Missionaries of Charity of Mother Theresa in India. They dressed in local clothing, the better to melt into the local populace, with nuns wearing saris in India and Bangladesh, the national tunic in Vietnam, and kimonos in Japan. In sum, they fell back on service to others, and preferred to prove their faith, rather than impose it by means of rational arguments. And the author concludes, "Missionaries are not the bearers of a civilization and a culture, but the witnesses of Christ through the medium of their own culture . . . they should first of all be themselves and believers, and then those who witness them

will 'see' what must be accepted" (pp. 186–187). This idea presents a painful dilemma. How can we detach Christianity from its Western context without denying the universal scope of the Gospel's revelation?

61. *L'Islam au défi,* op. cit., p. 298.

62. Tolerance cannot be shown in the same way with regard to small societies, for whom the slightest admixture would be fatal—which Robert Jaulin explained very well in *La Paix Blanche*—and larger scale, solid and structured social formations that allow themselves cultural egalitarianism so as to suspend all judgment regarding the inhuman acts they perpetrate.

63. This is the accusation hurled at Europe by Mohammed Bedjaoui, the Ambassador of Algeria to the United Nations, in his preface to the book by Roger Garaudy, *Promesses de l'Islam,* op. cit., pp. 12–13.

64. Statements by the Revolutionary Guards, as reported by Marc Kravetz in his book on Iran, *Irano Nox* (Grasset, 1982).

65. The American anthropologist Melville Herskovits wondered if it was possible to make value judgments about one culture or another, because "judgments are based on experience, and everyone interprets experience in the framework of his acculturation; thus, it is an illusion for European and American culture to try to make judgments about other cultures, because these judgments could then serve as a basis for colonialist practices" (quoted by Gérard Leclerc, op. cit., pp. 156–157).

66. This is precisely the conclusion of the book *Orientalism,* (Paris: Seuil, 1980) by Edward Said. If we are to believe Said, the West, blinded by its imperial prejudices, has always been mistaken in its vision of the Orient. In fact, the latter is so mysterious that only its admirers and unconditional supporters can hear its innermost harmony. In other words, as Said argues, support the policy of the PLO and the ineffable secret of Islam will be revealed to you in a great flash!

67. Roger Caillois made a humorous and intelligent response to Lévi-Strauss when the latter was admitted to the Académie Française. He sketched a portrait of the ethnologist that has troubling elements of truth. "They [the natives] did not resign themselves to being objects of studies and museum pieces, or inhabitants of reservations where measures were taken to protect them from progress. When they became students, scholarship holders, and overseas workers, their faith in the eloquence of the explorers was not increased, because those who abandoned their own civilization for this "savage" state, which they praised effusively, knew little about it. They were aware that these intellectuals came to study them with sympathy, understanding, and admiration, that they shared their way of life. But they resented the idea that these passing guests were there primarily to write a thesis or get a diploma, because they went back to teach their students what strange and "primitive" customs they had observed, and that they had also discovered

automobiles, telephones, central heating, and refrigerators there—the thousands of commodities that technology brings. After that, it is understandable that they should be irritated to listen to these good apostles boast about the conditions of rustic happiness, stability, and simple wisdom that perpetuated illiteracy. Once they awakened to these new ambitions, the generations that studied—who used to be objects of study—listened with sarcasm to flattering speeches in which they thought they could hear the tender tones of the wealthy explaining to the poor that money does not bring happiness. And neither do the resources of industrial civilization. For others, of course" (Le Monde, June 28, 1974).

68. "I have flown over all the summits of the world. . . . I have bathed in all its oceans. . . . I have entered all its gates. . . . I have meditated in all the high places where man has left the traces of his works . . . " Roger Garaudy, Pour un dialogue des civilisations, op. cit., p. 9.

69. "It is time to search amid the wisdom of the three worlds, to try to conceive of and live by other forms of existence. It may be too late, and if so we are condemned to lives bereft of meaning and direction, and to death" (Roger Garaudy, Promesses de l'Islam, op. cit., p. 58).

70. "There is only one religion, and it is the same in pre-Columbian America, in China, and India, the same in Greece and in medieval Europe. There is always a God above other gods, heroes, saints, and demons, always the mystery of the creation of the world, always an immortal soul" (Drieu la Rochelle, "Journal d'un delicat," in Histoires deplaisants, Gallimard, 1963, p. 78).

71. Ahmen Baba Miske, in Lettre ouverte aux élites du tiers monde, was right when he said, "No European can boast (or complain) of having invested the time, study, and effort in understanding a 'traditional' society . . . that thousands of intellectuals of the Third World have in learning what Europe has to say."

72. For example, Arnold Toynbee, in La Civilisation à l'épreuve, Gallimard, 1951, pp. 101–102, wrote, "Our descendants will not be, like us, simply Westerners. They will be the heirs of Confucius and Lao Tse as well as of Socrates, Plato, and Plotinus, heirs of Gautama Buddha as well as Isaiah and Christ, heirs of Zarathustra and Mohammed as well as Elijah and Elysium . . . of Lenin, Gandhi, and Sun Yat-Sen as well as Cromwell, George Washington, and Mazzini.

73. In a remarkable refutation of cultural universalism, Kolakowski wrote, "To imagine that our grandchildren will combine all contradictory traditions in a harmonious whole, that they will at the same time be pantheists, deists, and atheists; liberals and totalitarians; lovers and enemies of violence, is to imagine that they will live in a world that not only surpasses our imagination and our capacity to see the future, but one in which there is no longer any viable tradition, which means that they will

be barbarians in the strongest sense of the term" (*Commentaire*, Juillard, Autumn 1980, p. 369).

74. *Pour un dialogue des civilisations*, op. cit., p. 94. See also *Appel aux vivants* and *Promesses de l'Islam*, in which the author himself seems to have embraced the intransigent Islam of the Iranian regime.

75. In a lecture given in Hawaii in December 1981, entitled "La Xenitheia, ou la voie del'expatriation," the former Jesuit Guy Deleury correctly emphasized the absurdity of talking of God in Hinduism or Buddhism, because our idea of God is understandable only in the context of Western religious tradition.

76. For a critique of Roger Garaudy, see the excellent study by Michel Crépu in *Esprit* magazine, July 1980, as well as the acerbic article by Pierre Chaunu in *Le Figaro*, January 23, 1982, entitled "Un sottisier plein à ras bords."

77. "The human race has adopted a single culture. It has taken to the mass production of civilization like that of sugar beets. Its regular diet will include nothing but this one dish" (Claude Lévi-Strauss, *Tristes Tropiques*, op. cit., p. 39).

78. It may be, as was shown in the Austro-Hungarian Empire, that there is no real cosmopolitanism except within the physical confines of Europe. And European culture, in spite of its Latin, Anglo-Saxon, Celtic, Nordic, Jewish, Oriental, and Slavic versions, drinks from the common wellspring of Judaism and Christianity, the Renaissance and the Enlightenment. And, of course, cosmopolitanism is a reality in the artistic domain where influence, borrowing, and plagiarism are the very substance of creative fruitfulness. But what is possible in the literary, artistic, or musical fields is not possible in everyday life. It is not possible to profit from the style of life of another civilization without renouncing one's own. Unless what we call cosmopolitanism means eating couscous, tacos, and stir-fried rice, wearing Chinese silk, listening to Oriental music, and dying our hair with henna. The deserved discredit heaped on regional chauvinism should not lead to this amiable sort of dilettantism.

Chapter 4

1. *Un peuple de fauves* (Stock, 1973, p. 27) is the account Turnbull wrote of his years with the Ik.

2. Turnbull has written two books about hunting peoples, one about the Mbuti Pygmies, *Le Peuple de la forêt* (Stock, 1963) and *l'Africain désemparé* (Seuil, 1965).

3. Original from Turnbull: "Fortunately the Ik are not numerous; there are about two thousand of them, and the last two years have substantially reduced their number. . . . I am only sorry that so many in-

dividuals must die slowly and painfully before the end comes for all" (op. cit., p. 274).

4. There are two reviews of Colin Turnbull's work in French: Maurice Godelier, "Heures et Malheurs de l'ethnologue," *Les Temps modernes*, March 1975; and Jean-Loup Amselle, "Le sauvage mechant," *Le Sauvage à la mode*, Sycomore, 1979.

5. Roger Garaudy, *Les Promesses de l'Islam*, (Paris: Seuil, 1980), 20.

6. Jaspers would say that this is a confusion of conception by genus with conception by type (cf. *La Culpabilité allemande*, Minuit, 1946, pp. 76–77). The mechanism of group stereotyping, as Albert Memmi points out in his famous essay, recalls the picture of the colonized that was always held by the colonizer. It is a great irony of history that Westerners are now applying to themselves the same cartoon-like caricature that in the past they imposed on subject peoples.

7. Quoted by Vladimir Jankélévitch, *La Mauvaise conscience* (Aubier, 1970).

8. This is exactly like a certain kind of affection for the Jews. They were adored as long as they were persecuted, wandering, and uprooted, but were detested as soon as they obtained a land, a State, and an army. In sum, in the Israelite, what was loved was not a memory, a culture, or a particular relationship to the Scriptures and to faith; what was loved was a depersonalized, suffering victim, a pure projection of Christian fantasy.

9. Perhaps nothing illustrates the sheer silliness of Third-Worldism as much as the view expressed in Cuba in June 1982 by Minister of Culture Jack Lang, when he blessed the regime of Fidel Castro by denouncing American imperialism. For a man who is neither an idiot nor a totalitarian, such muddled talk can only have been the result of carelessness. The Cuban people and the thousands of victims of Castro's dictatorship may not have caught his attention, but this is because finding blame or praise for a banana republic are nothing but mundane formalities. In conversations or banquets, praising a tropical dictator was appropriate for public speaking.

10. The colonial system was to have been abolished as soon as the task of civilizing had born fruit and the gap between the mother country and the colony had been reduced. These were the justifications used by the occupiers to put off independence into the indefinite future. In 1919, the League of Nations recognized in its statutes, for example, that the countries of the Levant were not yet ready to govern themselves "in the particularly difficult conditions of the modern world," and decided to entrust them as mandates to the countries that were occupying them. In another area, the newspaper *L'Humanité* waited until 1954 to drop the slogan of Maurice Thorez that defined Algeria as a "nation in for-

mation." All ideologies of development and backwardness clearly follow from this metaphor of childhood and maturity.

11. J. B. Pontalis, *Nouvelle revue de psychanalyse,* special issue on childhood, 1979.

12. This is the only theoretical basis of the thought of Frantz Fanon. As a counter-example, the psychoanalyst Gérard Mendel gave one of his works the title, *Pour décoloniser l'enfant* (Payot, 1971).

13. *Le Tiers Monde et la Gauche,* a collection edited by *Le Nouvel observateur,* Seuil, 1979, p. 132.

14. *Promesses de l'Islam,* op. cit., pp. 164–165.

15. Ibid., p. 166.

16. "Neo-colonial dependence does not explain all of the political territory we live in," wrote Hélé Beji regarding Tunisia in *Le Désenchantement national* (Maspéro, 1982), an excellent analysis of the disorder and distress that seized the countries of North Africa on the morrow of decolonization. The author smashes the simplistic and caricatured vision that systematically blames all setbacks and oppressions of former colonies on outside forces. He uncovers the workings of a new state nationalism that evokes its own relations of domination within the society after the departure of the colonizers, around the charismatic figure of the chief and supreme commander.

17. Samir Amin, in *Classe et nation* (Minuit, 1979) pushed the analysis of the "comprador bourgeoisie" to its limits. But the theme has run throughout Third-Worldist writing from the very beginning. Here are two quotes from among many. "The non-representativeness of those who demand the right to speak for the subordinate people before the imperialist rulers . . . is the heart of the problem of international relations . . . " (Jean Ziegler, *Main basse sur l'Afrique,* op. cit., p. 266). "The peripheral elites define themselves from birth as an appendage of the ruling classes in the northern countries. They constantly go outside their own society in search of almost all their values and social norms, their scientific, philosophical, and political thought, and even a large part of their literary inspiration" (Yves Eudes, *La Conquête des esprits,* Maspéro, 1982, p. 13).

18. In the November 1981 *Le Monde diplomatique,* Jean Bayart, the editor in chief of *Politique africaine,* demonstrates that the appearance of an African bourgeoisie is not a by-product of imperialism but rather an expression of the historical domination of traditional elites, and urges that the transformation of countries of the Southern hemisphere not be explained from the perspective of Western history (pp. 17, 18). In *India, a Wounded Civilization,* V. S. Naipaul explains that borrowing from the British way of life by the Indian middle class constituted an additional social distinction in the caste system rather than an alteration of their cultural heritage.

19. Ahmed Baba Miske does this with vigor, when he invites the elite of Africa and Asia to undertake their own redeeming renaissance without waiting for the West (*Lettre ouverte aux élites du tiers monde*, Sycomore, 1981).

20. Hélé Beji (op. cit.), and, of course, all the fiction and essays of V. S. Naipaul, an immense body of thought on the wreckage and chaos of newly decolonized nations.

21. In an issue of *Esprit* from January 1980, the Lebanese philosopher Georges Corm argues that unequal exchange theories and imperialism are of no help at all in the domestic understanding of underdevelopment because they only assign it external causes. "It is always more reassuring to think that the sickness is due to a germ from the outside, and that by uniting in revolutionary brotherhood to fight it . . . the sick societies of the Third World will be restored to health" (p. 113).

22. On the theme that "they couldn't have done such horrible things," it is interesting to read the exchange between Régis Debray and Noam Chomsky, published under the title, "Narration et pouvoir" by *Change* magazine (volume 38, October 1979). The French philosopher and the American linguist agree to minimize the genocide in Cambodia—according to them scarcely 100,000 people were killed, victims of "local peasants' revenge" (p. 106)—and with equal spirit denounce the real bad guy, the only true criminal, the big bad wolf—the West. In their eyes, the "genocide" was an invention of the media, a brainwashing organized by the Western press to discredit revolutionary states and to cover up their own real responsibilities.

23. Here we are using the title of an excellent article by Manuel Pietri that appeared in *Le Matin* on April 25, 1982.

24. "Ici et la-bas, d'abord bien se nourrir," a brochure published by Frères des Hommes and Terre des Hommes.

25. The global village is finished. A page of history is being turned today. The worldwide system that collapsed at the end of the 1970s also ceased to control our view of the world. The world never seemed as compartmentalized as today, and a worldwide order no longer looks like a possibility on the horizon for the human race. There is no longer an ultimate meaning above or beyond the nations of the world for ordering them into a happy harmony. Under these conditions any attempt to re-create international unity, even in the context of a confrontation between the two superpowers, can only be contrived and artificial. Unless one single way of thinking is set up as the one worldwide truth, work must stop on the task of building another universal system on the ruins of a previous one.

In particular, all the remedies proposed during the last three decades for pulling the Southern hemisphere out of its rut have failed. The revolutionary way, as well as policies of integration or cooperation, have shown themselves to be inapplicable or catastrophic in the countries where they were applied. The old systems are falling apart, but no new ones have appeared. In light of this gap, the only possible course is to try tentative hypotheses, as in the sciences, and to increase both the moderation and the factual basis of our approach. With regard to the Third World, we no longer have anything but negative certainties; we know what we should not do. This means that we must temporarily suspend judgment and develop patterns of thought that are appropriate to the challenges before our planet. History has become improvisation again.

In sum, we have gone back to the eighteenth century, without the illusions of the Enlightenment but with rapid communications. Far from being a single, powerful community, a global village "in which all people are equidistant" (Lester Brown) that does away with cultural, ideological, or natural misunderstandings, the world has once again become a swarming of tribes that are hostile and mistrustful. At a moment when hegemonies are crumbling, when Uncle Sam and Uncle Ivan are watching their empires come apart at the seams, a generalized Balkanization is splitting the human race into opposing ethnic, religious, and racial groups. And the risk is always there that the world will collapse into an anthill of sealed-off compartments, dissolving from its own differentness. The fact that it has become possible to think about other societies does not mean that they have become understandable to us; on the contrary, they have increased our incomprehension and obscurity. Everywhere, speed and light, the results of science and technology, have made things cumbersome and shadowy. The extent of what we do not know far surpasses what we know. It is not our knowledge that is growing, but our ignorance, which is becoming more refined and complex. How is it possible to distinguish between good and bad causes, to dissect the conflicts that afflict our terrestrial sphere? The globe may be small and finite, but it has never before been so dark.

26. For example, René Dumont proposes the concept of "maldevelopment" to explain the imbalances of newly industrialized countries such as Mexico, Colombia, and Brazil that are living on the profits of exported raw materials but not developing an adequate agricultural sector. Alden Clausen, the director of the World Bank, holds that there are eight economic zones: Four zones are composed of industrialized regions (Northern Europe, Western America, Japan, and Eastern Europe); the fifth comprises countries of the Near East that export oil for excess profits; the sixth is composed of 20 industrializing countries (South Africa, Argentina, Brazil, South Korea, Columbia, the Philippines, Hong Kong, Israel, etc.); the seventh includes the highly populated countries of Asia (China, India, Indonesia, Bangladesh, and Pakistan); and the eighth is made up of the very poor countries of sub-Saharan Africa.

27. For example, how can anyone believe the statements made by the director general of UNESCO, Amadou Mahtar M'Bow, who declared in *Third World Quarterly* magazine (London, 1982): "The countries of the Third World are the bearers of hope in the world. In spite of their internal weakness and their inadequate natural resources, they are natural crusaders for justice and freedom."

28. This is true of the violence in Argentina, which is known to have become a national sport practiced by the Left and the Right. For example, every book by an Ernesto Sabato or a Borges is a reflection on this mystery, this atypical country that is the broken land between America and Europe. The men who founded it were intellectuals inspired by the French Enlightenment, and carried *The Social Contract* and *Emile* in their pockets; but they were also the heirs of the greatest genocide in history, that of the Indians. In a more general sense, it is strange to see how much the South American Left—with the exception of the Brazilian socialists—makes American imperialism into an all-too-easy scapegoat for the evils that have afflicted Latin countries for the last two centuries. Even a book as admirable on the literary plane as Eduardo Galeano's *Les Veines ouvertes de l'Amerique Latine* has no other purpose than to absolve Latin Americans of all responsibility and to place all the blame on outside invaders—the Spanish, English, Portuguese, Americans, etc. What they are doing is continuing down a dead-end street, and giving themselves a clear conscience on the cheap, by putting on the cloak of the eternal victim. Not to mention the openly Stalinist position of great South American intellectuals such as Gabriela Marquez, whose unconditional support for the USSR and the regimes of Castro and the Sandinistas, is astonishing.

29. In this sense, the state of Israel, which often has recourse to this sort of argument, tries to combine the advantages of being a nation of the Southern hemisphere with that of being a Western people. In the name of the immense wrong inflicted on the Jewish people, the Israeli government perceives all criticism as a direct threat to its existence, and all enemies as potential mass murderers. Conversely, the Palestinians present themselves as archetypically dispossessed, and claim for themselves all the old wrongs that the Jews once claimed—diaspora, persecution, genocide, etc. This leads to a competition in victimization between Jews and Arabs that could be summed up as follows: We are the most unfortunate; therefore, we have all right on our side, and our enemies have none. It is a stupefying argument. Whereas European anti-Semitism has been adopted wholesale by Arab countries, Israel has begun to speak the Third World language of absolute innocence. "The Jews will bow to no one but God," declared Begin, for example, during the summer of 1982. On the other hand, the Palestinians present themselves as the wretched folk of history, driven out by the "Zionist Nazis." Both

want to monopolize the highest rank of deprivation, and hold up their adversaries as criminals.

Once there was simply one land for two peoples, but now the argument is over which represents absolute evil. In this struggle of the purest, rhetorical overkill paralyzes both sides and leads both to the worst excesses. This leads the peace party in Israel and among the Palestinians to escape this double bind and to prevent both peoples from living as the "other"—untouchable, intact, and free of all responsibility.

Israel is hated because it is a Western country that presents itself in a Third World guise and camouflages its power beneath a cloak of timeless injustice. It has taken over the rhetoric of previously colonized peoples, and has used it as a weapon against them. In this, the Arab-Israeli conflict is both typical and unique. It is unique in that it shows up the North-South problem in its purest form. It is typical in that the hatred of the West now takes the form of hatred of the Jews, who have become its emblematic community after having been its scapegoat for 2,000 years. It is well-known, for example, that, in France as well as in Germany, the more one moves leftward on the political spectrum, the more virulent are the attacks against Israel. This is because the Left has fastened its anti-Western principles onto the Hebrew state. The old reproach of the anti-Semitic far right was that of cosmopolitanism; the leftist version of this is that of illegitimacy—Israel incarnates all the obscenity of the West, the more so because it is located in a land of the East! Its affiliation with the invisible empire of the North, according to some, has made it into a reincarnation of the Third Reich. In short, it is a monster more formidable than the Soviet Empire or any Near Eastern dictatorship!

There is no question that Israel has ceased to be the moral creditor of the West. The war in Lebanon and the policy of colonization practiced in the occupied territories have exhausted the stock of sympathy that it enjoyed in the public eye, and has speeded up the process of its becoming normal. Emmanuel Lévinas said this as early as 1963, when he wrote, "Israel has not become worse than the world around her, no matter what the anti-Semites say. But it has ceased to be the best" (*Difficile liberté*, Albin Michel, 1963, p. 16).

One might suggest that Israel became a country like all the others after the bombing of Beirut. A democratic country like France, Italy, or England, yes, but not a despotic state such as Iraq, Syria, or Egypt. This distinction is fundamental, because it prevents us from ever criminalizing the Jewish state, just as it was useless to portray France as diabolical during the Algerian conflict or the USA the same way during the war in Vietnam.

30. The Friday sermon in the mosques of Cairo says, "The nonbelievers do not have the right to come and see how we live, how we

treat our women, how we govern our Islamic country" (quoted by J. Peroncel-Hugoz, *Le Monde*, October 24, 1980).

31. Noam Chomsky is renowned as the all-time champion of self-flagellation. He has become the world ace at this nonsense, which consists of blackening one part of the human race—Yankees, of course—and whitening the other, the Third World. For this lover of poor countries, the planet is a magical land clearly delimited into the temperate countries' evil zone, and the extraordinary lands of the Southern hemisphere.

32. *Le Tiers-monde et la Gauche*, edited by *le Nouvel Observateur*, Seuil, 1979, p. 125.

33. Jean-Marie Domenach sums this up in a notable contribution to the book *Philosopher* (Fayard, 1980).

34. Régis Debray, in *le Tiers monde et la Gauche*, op. cit., 92–93.

35. This is the argument of René Dumont: bread first, civil liberties later. The result is liberty stifled and still no bread.

36. Remember that, contrary to popular European wisdom, it is often social groups themselves that form the greatest reservoir of despotism and cruelty in the countries of the Southern hemisphere. See, for example, the horrible violence engendered by the caste system in India, the warfare between religious factions in Lebanon, or the falling back on mores of the past in Muslim societies that is so brilliantly illustrated in the film "Yol" by Yilmaz Guney. Very often, the state plays the role of conciliator and even moderator between rival groups in a society wounded by the shock of modernity. In nations with weak states, individuals find themselves with no authority or institutions to guarantee their basic rights. See my article on this subject, "L'Inde ou les malheurs d'une société sans Etat," in *Le Débat* (January 1982).

37. It would be interesting to find out what Régis Debray, who has gained considerable political importance since May 10, 1981, thinks about the election that carried his side to power. Would he agree that it is nothing but a masquerade between two cliques in a rich country that is struggling for worldwide supremacy? Would not such a judgment invalidate the socialist victory, and consequently his functions as counsellor to the president?

38. The Chinese dissident Wei Jingsheng was entirely right when he asserted that, "The fifth modernization is democracy," in a text published in 1978 during the liberalization in Peking. For him, China's program of modernization undertaken by the regime's strongman Deng Xiaoping, could not take place without the democratization of the system. In October 1979, Wei was sentenced to 20 years in prison.

39. In this sense, the best possible evaluation of a democracy lies in its treatment of women. If, as Charles Fourier said, "The extension of women's privileges is the general principle of all human progress," the fate of the second sex is the means whereby to measure the degree

of openness of a society. Jankélévitch says, that woman is the "vehicle of otherness," and she is also the angle at which otherness impinges on the comfortable fabric of identity. Hence, the vigilance of traditional societies regarding the question of morality, the only real barrier for them, and their difficulty in allowing wives, mothers, and virgins to escape from the minority status allotted them by almost all religions. In these countries, as in France on the eve of the Revolution, everything that we call "women's liberation," they call "immorality," and is perceived as widespread in the ruling classes. Every woman of the elite is supposedly a harlot, and power is synonymous with moral turpitude. When a woman is involved in public affairs, she can only be seen as having affairs in public. See, for example, the criticisms aimed at Indira Gandhi in India and at Mme. Bandarinaike in Ceylon. The taboo of traditional culture often serves to justify the worst treatment of women and to perpetuate barbarian traditions. It is notable that, in addition to the grievances traditionally addressed to rich countries since the 1960s, debauchery has been added. Women's emancipation is seen as a supreme threat that not only emasculates men but breaks down all social boundaries. At the same time, it is well-known how difficult it is for a woman to travel alone in certain parts of the world, particularly in Moslem countries. In this sense, mysogyny is the main pillar of Third-Worldist ideology.

40. Every year the terrible report of Amnesty International is published, a systematic survey of human-rights abuses, a monstrous list of violence inflicted by states on their citizens. This kind of book presumes that evil can be calculated, as did the heretics of the Middle Ages, who believed there was a fixed number of sins and committed all of them in hopes of speeding up the return of the Messiah. In the form of a telephone book, with unquestionable integrity, impartiality without double standards or different benchmarks, the report points the finger to wherever people suffer from arbitrary power: Syria, Pakistan, the USSR, and South Africa. Every country is impartially assessed according to the strict yardstick of human rights.

Can we find reason to despair in this systematic display to the human race of its own dregs? Perhaps. However, it is only in our era that the worth of this reckoning appeared. A century ago, an account crammed full of information on prison camps around the world would certainly have resulted in a hundred more pages. Thus, this summation of mass murder, of executions without trial, paradoxically demonstrates immense progress. This interminable list of abuses and atrocities proves not only that it is harder and harder to conceal repression, but that our intolerance with regard to evil is still growing. What used to be admitted has become shameful, and the scope of violations makes them commensurately unacceptable. Our moral conscience is being developed, and the fact that regimes, even if they do continue to torture and imprison people, must hide behind humanist phrase-making to explain why they have recourse to these measures, proves that the idea of *habeas corpus* is becoming rooted in public life. The abstract and moralistic agenda of human rights is, therefore, beginning to be acted on. It is certainly not complete, but it would be foolish to underestimate it on the pretext that it is only partial and does not respond to the greatest need. The unbearable monotony of the report may therefore lead to qualified optimism. It is shameful to appear in the report of Amnesty International. This British organization, even if it does not overthrow dictatorship, throws them into a state of crisis.

41. President Mobutu, in a press conference during François Mitterand's trip to Kinshasa on October 7, 1982.

42. It is in this sense that Mexican writer Carlos Fuentes (*Le Débat*, November 1981), calls on the USA to cease all interference in Central America, in the name of the values defended by the young American nation when it was struggling against British imperialism. Washington's policy in Latin America presents "an extraordinary mixture of innocence and villany, of arrogance and ignorance," and in the name of fundamental American values this policy might be condemned, and the United States remain faithful to itself as a community that was born from a revolution.

43. *La civilisation quotidienne en Côte-d'Ivoire* (Paris: Karthala, 1982).

44. Darius Shayegan, in an interview in *Le Matin*, November 23, 1979. Darius Shayegan, a Persian philosopher and disciple of Corbin, gives a masterly analysis of this perversion in his excellent book, *Qu'est-ce qu'une révolution réligieuse?* (Presses d'Aujourd'hui, 1981), a first and exemplary study of Moslem fundamentalism.

45. This slogan has a lot in common with the "neither left nor right" of the prewar fascists and the "neither Gulag nor hamburger" of the New Right in France today. It also reminds us that an anti-Western spirit was the focal point of the pan-Slavist and pan-Germanic movements in pre-Revolutionary Russia and pre-Hitler Germany and Austria. Both exalted the deep, rich irrationality of the Russian soul or the German *volk*, in contrast to the superficiality and corruption of the West. See the analysis of these currents of thought in Hannah Arendt's masterly *L'Impérialisme* (Fayard, 1982), 209.

46. First Nietzsche, and then Husserl, Valéry, Malraux, Raymond Aron, and today Leszek Kolakowski and Milan Kundera have all made illuminating contributions to the notion that the West's mission is to reveal to other societies that there is no solution to the problem of human existence. A Swiss academic, Andre Reszila, has devoted a whole book to European self-criticism, entitled *L'Intellectuel contre l'Europe*, (PUF 1976).

47. Thus, the birth of a secular Europe emerged from its own divisions. When Francis I concluded an alliance with Sultan Suleiman the Magnificent against Charles V, it marked the end of religious solidarities based on Christianity. See J. B. Duroselle, *L'Idee de l'Europe dans l'Histoire*, Denoel, p. 72, and B. Voyenne, *Histoire de l'idée europeenne*, Payot, 1980, p. 70.

48. It is not well-known that anticolonialism appeared on the eve of the French Revolution, and that it did not reappear afterward. See Marcel Merle, *L'Anticolonialisme européen de las Cases à Karl Marx* (Armand Colin, 1969), 22.

49. Simone de Beauvoir apparently did not understand this when she wrote, "The West has always provided such striking cases of barbarity that it is indecent to use such a term to characterize practices [the sexual mutilation of young girls in Africa] that, even though cruel and ridiculous, have no relation to the Nazi camps, the hell of Latin America, or the Gulag" (*Les Nouvelles littéraires*, October 29, 1981). And yet, when the Vietcong accused the USA of atrocities or the PLO (wrongly) squawked of genocide during the Israeli bombing of Beirut, they used ideas formed in the West to defend themselves against Western nations.

50. The strength of Europe is that it is a paradox pushed to its limits. It invented everything—oppression as well as democracy, barbarism as well as sainthood. The dissolution of the feudal state gave way to the rationalistic state. Absolute monarchy engendered democracy, medieval absolutism gave birth to the relativistic world of the Renaissance, oppression by the Church to freedom of thought, and national antagonism to the idea of international community. The damage suffered by colonized peoples was traumatic, an incalculable harm, but it was also a challenge, a call to the genius of the subjugated peoples themselves. If colonialism was nothing but sordid and stupid oppression by adventurers thirsty for gold and blood, why did the colonized nations, on the morrow of indepedence, all freely adopt political systems and values inherited from the former mother country? The words "Europe" and "Occident," now out of vogue because of the polemical use made of them by a few dictatorships and groups on the extreme right, have come to be repellent, outlaw terms whose use is so questionable that they have to be put in quotation marks. It is time for a reevaluation, for the Left to reclaim Europe and no longer let it be monopolized by worm-eaten reactionaries or sick despots who pervert its meaning.

51. America's imperialism is wrong but under control, whereas in the Soviet Union there is no significant opposition that can rein in or even set limits on the decisions taken by the party. This difference is enormously important, because it means that the USSR is the only really imperialist nation in the world. It reigns over Eastern Europe, it is occupying Afghanistan by force of arms, and it intervenes in Africa, Asia,

and South America by means of Cuban and Vietnamese proxies. Foolishly asserting equivalence between American and Soviet imperialism, the West German writer Günther Grass wrote a sadly memorable article (*Die Zeit*, Autumn 1982, reprinted in *Le Nouvel observateur*, January 1-7, 1983), in which he dared to compare the Polish solidarity movement with the present-day Nicaraguan government, both of which were supposedly in the grip of their region's supreme power. At a time when the Sandinista regime was cracking down in Managua, persecuting opponents, filling up its prisons, and deporting the Miskito Indians, Grass wrote the following lines (which one could hardly believe possible in 1983, coming from the pen of an intellectual): "The French, American, and Russian revolutions saw the guillotine, reprisals, bullets in the back of the head, and mass executions. Until today, all revolutions have drowned their idealistic will to make mankind happy in a sea of blood. For the first time, the Sandinista revolution provides a different course. In a sparsely populated little country worn out by exploitation, the words of Christ have finally been taken seriously." I cannot imagine a worse case of gullibility, falsehood, and simple ignorance.

52. "A phantom is hovering over Europe and its past, the guilty awareness of a stunning success that contradicts the very principles that made it possible. The affirmation of liberty has transformed itself into a desire for domination, the search for equality has engendered servitude, the proclamation of fraternity has led to so many bloody struggles and hopeless hostilities. . . . Our future is burdened with our own suspicion of ourselves that brings about the death-struggles of our youth" (Monsignor Lustiger, in a speech at the meeting of the churches of Germany, October 8, 1981). "It was in Europe that two world wars broke out a few years apart, which led to infinite suffering among so many people and plunged the entire human race into fear and terror. It was from Europe that ideologies spread to the whole world, in such a way as to have the overwhelming influence of a communicable disease. This shared guilt signifies for Europe a particular responsibility, that of helping to find a definitive contribution to solving the present world crisis" (Pope John Paul II in a speech at a meeting of the Cultural Institute of Rome, November 12, 1981).

Conclusion

1. This is why Francis Jeanson, during the war in Algeria, agreed to support the FLN, to ensure the possibility of Franco-Algerian friendship after the war. Treason against French power was committed so that France might be saved. See Hervé Hamon and Patrick Rotman, *Les Por-*

teurs de valises, Albin Michel, 1979 (reissued in the collection "Points Histoire" by Seuil) p. 91.

2. This may be why Israel fascinates—or irritates—Europeans. As a pioneer state condemned to death at birth by its enemies, it serves both as a model and a foil for a Europe that long ago was overtaken by uncertainty and softness. These "Hebrew-speaking Cossacks" (the word is Begin's and was applied to Sharon) are free of any guilty conscience, reviving the myth of the founder and soldier, rightly reminding us that a society is only strong at the beginning, when it has the will to fight and assert itself. Whether you approve or not, Israel must be recognized as our own past and a still-living call to resistance.

3. Today, it has become absurd to think of the spiritual Orient as opposed to the materialist Occident. It is no longer possible to argue, as Elie Faure did in 1932, that "The Oriental has lived inside himself to the point where he has forgotten the world outside," and that "The Occidental has attached himself to the outside world, to the point where he has forgotten his inner self" ("D'autres terres en vue," *Nouvelle Revue critique*). But the contrast of East and West is still relevant, not in the sense that these two terms fit into each other like the two matching halves of an egg, but because each one is the excess of the other, and they are like the two poles of a magnet. The content ascribed to each is less important than the juxtaposition itself, which is rich in meaning. It is a semantic device that triggers something and leads to rewarding insights. The old categories are mixed up, because it is now possible to talk of Asian business sense and European mysticism; the East may be operating in an experiential mode and the West in a revelational mode. What is essential is that each keep in mind the other's point of view. See, for example, the admirable study by Roland Barthes that contrasted a refined and civilized Japan with the ideology of the natural and the spiritual that flourished in Europe and America at the end of the 1960s (*L'Empire des signes,* Skira, 1971). Only in this way is it possible to continue to use the Orient as a place of utopian criticism, a joyous antidote to our descent into narrow-minded custom.

4. No matter how perfectly I may master a foreign language, even if I know its obscurities and subtleties, there are always aspects that escape me. My mother tongue, my home, my refuge, puts me in a position of dependence that I cannot escape. I am so deeply rooted in it that nothing could tear me loose. The basic framework that opens up the world to me closes some of its expressions off from me. This medium of communication is the main obstacle to communication; common ground is also a barrier. The manifold requirements of syntax and meaning, whose imprint on me take the form of culture, demonstrate that the universe is not entirely encompassed by the words I utter. My life is

constructed around the silence of languages I do not understand. My entry into another language is both an opening of and a limitation to understanding others.

Translation is also the essential experience of the differentness of human beings. The genius of every language is expressed in a unique dimension, and there are some things that cannot be transferred, which I will never grasp. At the common wellspring of this unfolding of words that speak and are silent in turn, there is first and foremost a separateness. Language may be the "abode of being" that Heidegger talked of, but what makes conversation possible from one abode to the other is also what makes it impossible to visit all of them. I may speak two or many languages, but I will always lack the grasp of tones and breathing that are the everyday experience of foreign peoples. Hence, the joy and suffering of learning a foreign language. In my heart of hearts, I come up against the barrier of a way of speaking that is irreducibly foreign. No matter how well I know English, German, Chinese, or Arabic, I will never be more than the pretended owner of this noise of vowels and consonants. I am still unable to command my mother tongue, and so my language learning does not mean that I have gained power. Or rather, my power is built out of impotence; it is a sovereignty without a kingdom. All significant communication between nations takes place amid this weakness, always recurring but always overcome.

5. "For me, exile is always something compulsory, something forced, a monstrous moment in the struggle between men. It means that someone is uprooted by brute force: The choice is between being killed, imprisoned, and silenced and continuing to express oneself in a land of asylum. It is from this starting point that all exiles owe themselves to begin thinking and reacting against the specific mechanisms of exile" (Julio Cortazar, *Le Monde*, April 15–16, 1981).

6. Instead of colonialism's classical education or the topsy-turvy teaching of Third-Worldism, we must set up a dialogue in which the two hemispheres face each other as teacher and student, student and teacher. As the Brazilian Paolo Freire says, "Nobody educates another person, and nobody educates himself alone. Only people educate one another through the medium of the world" (*Pédagogie des opprimés*, Maspéro, 1974).

7. It is obvious that the relations between the states of Europe, including Eastern and Western Europe, replicate the relations between Europe and the rest of the world. This entails, first, a desire to reconquer the part of Europe colonized by the Soviet Empire, and secondly, the greatest possible accessibility of every nation to its neighbors, which means the renunciation of aggressive nationalism once and for all. The establisment of a real community goes well beyond events in the development of agricultural policy or conflicts over exports. Only today, for

example, must every European of standing be trilingual, so that no citizen of the continent feels an outsider anywhere in its confines.

8. For example, it is well-known that many travelers, soldiers, and researchers returned to a belief in Europe and the Christian faith, as a result of their sojourn in the lands of Islam. Psichari, Lyautey, and Massignon are the best known of many.

9. For us French-speakers, the two masterly figures of Leopold Senghor and Aime Cesaire are those that should inspire us more than any others. They are not just great poets of Africa and Martinique, they are the spokesmen for the anxieties and hopes of the whole of mankind, the carrier waves for countless masses who find such great resonance in them—because of their refusal to deny any part of their heritage, their position as men at the crossroads of Africa, the Caribbean, and France; because of the courage with which they resisted all fanaticism and were in the forefront of the traditions that met in them; because of the admirable examples that gave of refusing to cave in to Paris at the time of its imperial expansion, and then, once independence was achieved, their insistence on maintaining a dialogue with France. The irony of history is that, nowadays, we have more to learn from these former "subjects" of the Empire than we do from our own countrymen.

10. And so, the last canvas Gauguin painted in Tahiti before he died in 1903 was "Breton village after Snowfall." The painting was purchased by Victor Segalen several months after the artist's death.

11. The first genius of the British Empire was to transmit its every manner and ritual to the farthest reaches of the world. Today, there is a second one that consists of the mode of association between former lands of the Crown, called the Commonwealth, which opens up previously subject people to one another. It goes beyond their legitimate rancor and resentment and expiates the old sin of its rapacity by learning from them. Whereas France has kept only commercial or technical contacts with Algeria, Vietnam, and black Africa, and pulled itself back inside its original borders, England has successively experienced the influence of India, Malaysia, the United States, the Caribbean, and southern Africa. The backwash of the colonies into the island may be a source of racism and conflict between hostile communities on the soil of Great Britain itself, but it also points up the mutual fascination of cultures that 30 years ago did not have any relationship at all except subjugation. The frugal austerity of Anglicanism was capable of understanding and absorbing the baroque richness of many other religions and rituals.

England, of course, died from her own immensity, but she died victorious, because everyone speaks English. The soldiers of Her Majesty left a treasure trove in the countries from which they pillaged gold and riches: their language. It is an extraordinarily plastic language, common to master and slave; a language of domination and revolution, of order and rebellion, of power and freedom; a language of the crossroads and the fruit of many nations, the water of an ocean that links all islands together and makes us feel at home even in the most far-off climes. At the same time, English has exploded into a vast array of different idioms: Jamaican, Nigerian, American, Anglo-Indian, and Australian, so many mixtures sprang from the old refined language of Oxford. Threatened, weakened, divided, Great Britain, whatever reservations one might have about her, has succeeded better than any other in the constant fertilization of the colonizer by those he colonizes, the final destiny of all empires. Her victory is that she can no longer recognize herself except by beholding her former subjects, and that, in order to continue to exist, she must listen to and love them. This wonderful stepmother, from whom the modern world has sprung, is really the motherland of us all. Today, every European is a bit of an Englishman.

12. How can the hedging and hesitation of the Left toward Poland be explained? They are incapable of thinking of Europe as a colony. Because the West is imperialist by nature, how could it be colonized in turn by another empire? As long as the struggle of the Poles, Czechs, and Hungarians against the USSR is not also seen as a fight for national sovereignty and the reunification of a divided Europe, they will offer them nothing but condescending expressions of sympathy, shameful Third-Worldism, and a vague 'intellectual alliance." Lamartine reacted to the Polish patriots the same way in 1848, when they asked him for arms and he sent them fine speeches and generous proclamations.

13. In this sense, perhaps it is a good thing that purely spectacular and emotional forms of solidarity—marches, meetings, demonstrations, petitions, etc.—are on the wane, giving way to actions and efforts that are more discreet but often more effective. Remember, for example, the ships outfitted by "Médecins du monde" to pick up Vietnamese boat people off the coast of Thailand. In big demonstrations, there is so much exhibitionist fervor that they are suspect, and lead quickly to disaffection.

14. See the fairly comprehensive collection put together on this subject by *Le Monde diplomatique,* August 1980.

15. Jean-Yves Carfantin and Charles Condamines, *Qui a peur du tiers monde?* (Paris: Seuil, 1980), pp. 240–242.

16. 303. See René Pomeau, *L'Europe des Lumières,* (Geneva: Slatkine, 1981), pp. 85–87.

17. One kind of exoticism is on the wane today, one that lends prestige to lands that are particularly isolated. This is a loss of enthusiasm on the level of images, not people. The world can seem uniform only from the point of view of an impoverished vision, that of a small terrestrial globe. The idea of a homogeneous place, which was endorsed by Lévi-Strauss himself, takes up a theme begun by the Romantics. It foresees

the disappearance of differences, and limits its perceptions to the most visible, the most superficial aspects of a country or a culture. It requires a singular lack of human awareness to ignore the immense difference between two countries as close as Switzerland and France, not to mention between two continents such as Europe and Africa. From the fact that many countries of the Southern hemisphere now have highways, skyscrapers, and cars just like us, some conclude that they must inevitably converge and resemble each other. But an African who wears a necktie and jacket is a very different man from a Spaniard or an Italian who wears the same outfit. Differentness is not a single quantity that declines because of the uniformization of the world; it is a permanent creation of human beings who grow in their numbers as in their differences.

Index

235